Software Quality

Springer
Berlin
Heidelberg
New York
Barcelona
Hong Kong
London
Milan
Paris
Singapore
Tokyo

Martin Wieczorek
Dirk Meyerhoff (Eds.)

Software Quality

State of the Art
in Management, Testing, and Tools

With Contributions of

R. Baltus, G. Bazzana, A. Birk, H. Bons, M. Bromnick,
W. Dzida, J. F. Perpiñán, A. Fitzke, R. Freitag, R. Göldner,
D. Huberty, G. Jahnke, J. Johansen, A.M.Jonassen Hass,
P. Keese, T. Lovrić, W. Mellis, D. Meyerhoff, C. Nagel,
J. Pries-Heje, C. Radu, B. Roberts, D. Rombach, F. Sazama,
M. Timpe, H. Uebel, R. van Megen, D. Vohwinkel, J. Warlitz,
M. J. Wieczorek

Springer

Martin Wieczorek
Dirk Meyerhoff
SQS Software Quality Systems AG
Stollwerkstr. 11
51149 Köln, Germany
{martin.wieczorek; dirk.meyerhoff}@sqs.de

With 99 Figures and 14 Tables

ISBN 3-540-41441-X Springer-Verlag Berlin Heidelberg New York

Library of Congress Cataloging-in-Publication Data applied for

Die Deutsche Bibliothek - CIP-Einheitsaufnahme
Software quality: state of the art in management, testing, and tools/Martin Wieczorek;
Dirk Meyerhoff (ed). With contributions of R. Baltus ... - Berlin; Heidelberg; New York;
Barcelona; Hong Kong; London; Milan; Paris; Singapore; Tokyo: Springer, 2001
ISBN 3-540-41441-X

Springer-Verlag Berlin Heidelberg New York
a member of BertelsmannSpringer Science+Business Media GmbH

© Springer-Verlag Berlin Heidelberg 2001
Printed in Germany

Cover design: Künkel + Lopka, Heidelberg
Typesetting: perform, Heidelberg from author´s data
Printing and binding: Beltz, Hemsbach
Printed on acid-free paper   SPIN 10870211   33/3111   5 4 3 2 1

List of Contributors

ROB BALTUS
Head of Department Software Quality
Management, Comma Soft AG
Pützchens Chaussee 202-204a,
53229 Bonn, Germany
Email: rob.baltus@comma-soft.com
Web: www.comma-soft.com
Telephone: + 49 228 9770 0
Fax: + 49 228 9770 200

GUALTIERO BAZZANA, DR.
Partner and Managing Director
Onion SpA
Brescia 25131, via L. Gusalli n 9, Italy
Email: gb@onion.it
Web: www.onion.it
Telephone: + 39 030 3581510
Fax: + 39 030 3581525

ANDREAS BIRK
Researcher
Fraunhofer Institute for Experimental
Software Engineering
Sauerwiesen 6, 67661 Kaiserslautern,
Germany
Email: birk@iese.fhg.de
Web: www.iese.fhg.de
Telephone: + 49 6301 707 256
Fax: + 49 6301 707 200

HEINZ BONS
Member of the Board
SQS Software Quality Systems AG
Stollwerckstraße 11, 51149 Köln, Germany

Email: heinz.bons@sqs.de
Web: www.sqs.de
Telephone: + 49 2203 9154 0
Fax: + 49 2203 9154 15

MIRIAM BROMNICK
Consultant
Ovum Ltd
Cardinal Tower, 12 Farringdon Road,
London EC1M 3HS, United Kingdom
Email: MBK@ovum.com
Web: www.ovum.com
Telephone: + 44 20 7551 9169
Fax: + 44 20 7551 9090

WOLFGANG DZIDA, DR.
Senior Scientist
GMD, Institute for Autonomous
Intelligent Systems
Schloß Birlinghoven, 53754 Sankt Augustin,
Germany
Email: dzida@gmd.de
Web: www.gmd.de
Telephone: +49 2241 14 2275
Fax: +49 2241 14 2324

JAVIER FERNÁNDEZ PERPIÑÁN
Consultant
DTK GmbH
Palmaille 82, 22767 Hamburg, Germany
Email: fernandez@dtkhh.de
Web: www.dtkhh.de
Telephone: + 49 40 389970 0
Fax: +49 40 389970 20

ANDRÉ FITZKE
Safety Manager
Alcatel SEL AG
Lorenzstr. 10, 70435 Stuttgart, Germany
Email: a.fitzke@alcatel.de
Web: www.alcatel.de
Telephone: + 49 711 821 46518
Fax: +49 711 821 44317

REGINE FREITAG
Researcher
GMD, Institute for Autonomous Intelligent
Systems
Schloß Birlinghoven, 53754 Sankt Augustin,
Germany
Email: regine.freitag@gmd.de
Web: www.gmd.de
Telephone: +49 2241 14 2047
Fax: +49 2241 14 2324

RUDOLF GÖLDNER
Head of Department Application
Development
RZF NRW – IT Centre of Northrine West-
phalia's Finance Department
Ross-Straße 131, 40476 Düsseldorf,
Germany
Email:
Rudolf.Goeldner@RZF.FinVerwNRW.de
Web: www.rzf-nrw.de
Telephone: + 49 211 4572 432
Fax: +49 211 4783 3003

DIRK HUBERTY
Senior Consultant
SQS Software Quality Systems AG
Stollwerckstraße 11, 51149 Köln, Germany
Email: dirk.huberty@sqs.de
Web: www.sqs.de
Telephone: + 49 2203 9154 0
Fax: + 49 2203 9154 15

GREGOR JAHNKE
Head of Department Quality Assurance
ARGE IS KV GmbH
Bismarckstr. 36, 45128 Essen, Germany
Email: jahnke@iskv.de
Web: www.iskv.de
Telephone: +49 201 1094 139
Fax: +49 201 1094 130

JØRN JOHANSEN
Department Manager
DELTA Danish Electronics, Light &
Acoustics, Department Software Technology
Venlighedsvej 4, DK-2970 Hørsholm,
Denmark
Email: joj@delta.dk
Web: www.delta.dk
Telephone: +45 45 86 77 22
Fax: +45 45 86 58 96

ANNE METTE JONASSEN HASS
Senior Software Consultant
DELTA Danish Electronics, Light &
Acoustics, Department Software Technology
Venlighedsvej 4, DK-2970 Hørsholm,
Denmark
Email: amj@delta.dk
Web: www.delta.dk
Telephone: +45 45 86 77 22
Fax: +45 45 86 58 96

PAUL KEESE
Senior Consultant
SQS Software Quality Systems AG
Stollwerckstraße 11, 51149 Köln, Germany
Email: paul.keese@sqs.de
Web: www.sqs.de
Telephone: + 49 2203 9154 0
Fax: + 49 2203 9154 15

TOMISLAV LOVRIĆ, DR.
Head of Department Software-Based Safe
Computer Architecture
TÜV InterTraffic GmbH, ISEB
Am Grauen Stein, 51105 Köln, Germany
Email: bahn-tuev@iseb.com
Web: www.iseb.com
Telephone: + 49 221 806 18 05
Fax: + 49 221 806 2581

WERNER MELLIS, PROF. DR.
Head of Information Systems Department
University of Cologne
Pohligstr. 1, 50969 Köln, Germany
Email: werner.mellis@uni-koeln.de
Web: www.uni-koeln.de
Telephone: + 49 221 470 5368
Fax: + 49 221 470 5386

DIRK MEYERHOFF, DR.
Head of Departments Consultancy
Products / Performance Testing
SQS Software Quality Systems AG
Stollwerckstraße 11, 51149 Köln, Germany
Email: dirk.meyerhoff@sqs.de
Web: www.sqs.de
Telephone: + 49 2203 9154 0
Fax: + 49 2203 9154 15

CHRISTOF NAGEL, DR.
Team Software Engineering
T-Nova Deutsche Telekom Innovationsge-
sellschaft mbH
Neugrabenweg 4, 66123 Saarbrücken, Ger-
many
Email: christof.nagel@telekom.de
Web: www.telekom.de
Telephone: + 49 681 909 3216
Fax: + 49 7161 9255 5757

JAN PRIES-HEJE, PH.D.
Member of Department of Computer
Information Systems
J. Mack Robinson College of Business
P.O.Box 4015, Atlanta, GA 30302-4015, USA
Email: jpries@cis.gsu.edu
Web: www.cis.gsu.edu
Telephone: +1 404 651 3880

CRISTIAN RADU, DR.
Senior Consultant
Integri nv
Leuvensesteenweg 325, 1932 Zaventem,
Belgium
Email: cradu@integri.be
Web: www.integri.be
Telephone: + 32 2 712 0750
Fax: + 32 2 712 0767

BARBARA ROBERTS
DSDM Consultant
F.I. Group plc
Campus 300, Maylands Avenue, Hemel
Hempstead, HP2 7TQ, United Kingdom
Email: Barbara_Roberts@figroup.co.uk
Web: www.figroup.co.uk
Telephone: + 44 1476 861855
Fax: + 44 1476 861855

DIETER ROMBACH, PROF. DR.
Executive Director
Fraunhofer Institute for Experimental
Software Engineering
Sauerwiesen 6, 67661 Kaiserslautern,
Germany
Email: rombach@iese.fhg.de
Web: www.iese.fhg.de
Telephone: + 49 6301 707 100
Fax: + 49 6301 707 200

FRANK SAZAMA
Researcher
DaimlerChrysler AG, Research and
Technology / SW Engineering
P.O. Box 2660, 89013 Ulm, Germany
(with Q-Labs since October 1, 2000)
Email: frank.sazama@q-labs.de
Web: www.daimlerchrysler.com
Telephone: + 49 711 8060 81 31
Fax: + 49 711 8060 81 99

MICHAEL TIMPE
Head of Software Development Department
MED medicine online AG
Friedrich-Ebert-Straße, Haus 51,
51429 Bergisch Gladbach, Germany
Email: michael.timpe@medicineonline.de
Web: www.medicineonline.de
Telephone: + 49 02204 843730
Fax: + 49 02204 843731

HELMUT UEBEL
Marketing Director
Alcatel SEL AG
Lorenzstr. 10, 70435 Stuttgart, Germany
Email: h.uebel@alcatel.de
Web: www.alcatel.de
Telephone: + 49 711 821 44492
Fax: +49 711 821 46813

RUDOLF VAN MEGEN
Member of the Board
SQS Software Quality Systems AG
Stollwerckstraße 11, 51149 Köln, Germany
Email: rudolf.van_megen@sqs.de
Web: www.sqs.de
Telephone: + 49 2203 9154 0
Fax: + 49 2203 9154 15

DETLEF VOHWINKEL
Senior Consultant
SQS Software Quality Systems AG
Stollwerckstraße 11, 51149 Köln, Germany
Email: detlef.vohwinkel@sqs.de
Web: www.sqs.de
Telephone: + 49 2203 9154 0
Fax: + 49 2203 9154 15

JOACHIM WARLITZ, DR.
Head of Assessment Department
Alcatel SEL AG
Lorenzstr. 10, 70435 Stuttgart, Germany
Email: j.warlitz@alcatel.de
Web: www.alcatel.de
Telephone: + 49 711 821 46176
Fax: +49 711 821 46902

MARTIN J. WIECZOREK, DR.
Head of Departments Telecommunication /
Public and Care
SQS Software Quality Systems AG
Stollwerckstraße 11, 51149 Köln, Germany
Email: martin.wieczorek@sqs.de
Web: www.sqs.de
Telephone: + 49 2203 9154 0
Fax: + 49 2203 9154 15

Preface to the Series software.quality@xpert.press

Quality management and software testing are among the most important topics in software development and IT management, responsible for about 40 per cent of the costs of software projects. During the development phase over a third of all money is spent on the retrieval, prevention and removal of errors. Unless the significance of quality management and testing is recognised, IT projects can easily fail, as application and implementation errors can cause considerable follow-up costs and very high upgrade expenses.

In the early 90s, the completion of the new Denver International Airport (Colorado, USA), for instance, was delayed by 16 months (*Harvard Business Manager 6/2000*). Originally, this major airport was to start operating in autumn 1993, but the opening had to be postponed until February 1995. The delay was due to inadequate testing of the programs controlling the computerised baggage routing system. The project had to be discontinued, and the original idea was abandoned. By then the delay in commissioning had caused additional expenses of nearly US$ 2 billion.

Another example is the launch of an IT system for the billing of share transactions at the London Stock Exchange. The project, called "Taurus", started in May 1986 and was stopped seven years later, after the Stock Exchange had invested over £89 million and brokerage firms had spent another £400 million on developing Taurus-compatible systems. The development of an electronic transfer system had failed, and the bull – "Taurus" – had hit a brick wall.

These are two among many failures of IT projects which could have been avoided through systematic software quality management. But IT projects can proceed quite differently – without straining the budget and without loss of time. This is borne out by numerous successful projects from a variety of industries, where the main focus was on software quality management and software testing from the very beginning. The quality of the software was prioritised as a key factor for the success and economic viability of IT projects.

In the age of Internet and e-commerce, the reliability of IT systems is becoming increasingly important. Whereas software errors could still be removed "manually" in the days of host computers, the Internet mercilessly reveals every single IT error to a company's customers. Moreover, once a potential customer has tried to place an online order and has failed, he is unlikely to return. In a global economy where worldwide competitors are virtually on the customer's doorstep, no enterprise can afford such a loss, whatever its size.

But we are also being faced with software quality in our daily lives. Nowadays we are literally surrounded by machinery that carries out small, but vital jobs. A modern vehicle, for instance, has about 60 chips that guarantee a safe ride through the traffic – from the airbag to the most important engine functions.

The increasing importance of high-quality computing systems in our information society is to be the focus of the new series called "software.quality@xpert.press " which is launched by SQS. Issues of this series are to be published by Springer from time to time, highlighting and discussing the state of the art and developments in software quality management and software testing. The focus will be not so much on the scientific background, but on sharing hands-on experience with those involved in day-to-day work.

HEINZ BONS   RUDOLF VAN MEGEN
SQS AG Member of the Board   *SQS AG Member of the Board*

Preface to the Volume Software Quality – State of the Art in Management, Testing and Tools

Many companies, administrative bodies and organisations are facing the same questions: How can we improve the quality of our IT while at the same time reducing our costs? Unlike in traditional production, which brought forth economic trend concepts such as "lean production", the idea of "quality and IT" is still rather nebulous for many. Yet software quality management has long been part of everyday life and, on many markets, a decisive competitive factor. In particular, this includes areas such as e-business, financial services and telecommunication, as no company can afford rejected orders, failed monetary transfers or faulty phone bills.

With this first volume of Springer's new series "software.quality@xpert.press" we are providing a collection of articles on topical issues of software quality management and software testing, written by authors of national and international reputation. The articles are largely the result of two conferences held in 2000: SQM® "Software Quality Management" and the ICSTEST® "International Conference on Software Testing". Both are organised and conducted on an annual basis by SQS Software Quality Systems AG.

The articles bridge the gap between strategic quality planning and everyday operations in corporate IT departments. They largely reflect current practices and experience. Everything that is said is the result of successful projects from a variety of sectors, countries and types of companies, offering new and sometimes unusual approaches to topics that are thought to be rather well-known.

This first volume is divided into three parts. The first part discusses topics from software quality management: the latest approaches to software development and their effects on current methods and procedures in quality assurance, practical experience in the application of process improvement programs as well as the effects of knowledge management on quality management. One important issue that can foster the significance and acceptance of software tests is the question of financial profitability. Are software tests worthwhile? This question is answered in practical cost/benefit models.

The second part is about the certification and testing of software and of systems that integrate software as an important component. The focus is particularly on the Internet and electronic commerce, as these are areas where software testing has been significant and obvious to all users. Here, even the slightest errors would be detected by customers immediately, so that web applications – particularly banking modules – need to stand up to any test. Another example is safety-critical software: for instance, because of their commitment towards public licensing authorities, railway suppliers have been pioneers in the testing and certification of software. Their experience can provide important stimuli to all other sectors.

Finally, part three of this volume presents the state of the art in testing tools and discusses new trends and perspectives in this area.

This volume is aimed at IT decision makers and executives as well as IT specialists from the various corporate divisions that are concerned with questions of software quality management, software quality assurance and software testing.

We would like to thank all the authors for their great interest in this book project and for their outstanding support in its realisation. Without them, it would have been impossible to compile this high-quality collection of highly practical examples from software development and software quality management projects. We hope that all everyday examples from everyday life, compiled for the first time in this book, will serve as signposts – and perhaps also as instructions – towards better IT quality and economic viability.

MARTIN WIECZOREK   DIRK MEYERHOFF
SQS AG   *SQS AG*

Table of Contents

Part I

Software Quality Management

Process and Product Orientation in Software Development and their Effect on Software Quality Management

WERNER MELLIS

University of Cologne, Department of Information Systems (Germany)

Abstract: During the last decade process oriented software quality management was considered the successful paradigm of developing quality software. But the constant pace of change in the IT world brought up new challenges demanding for a different model of software development. In this paper product orientation is described as an alternative to process orientation, which is specifically adapted to some of those new challenges. Both development models are adapted to different environments or development tasks. And they are based on different concepts of product quality and quality management.

Keywords: Engineering Management, Quality Concepts, Quality Management, Development, Organization, Rapid Development

1 Challenges for the Management of Software Development

Asking managers in software development for their toughest challenges you will probably conclude, that a significant portion of software production is confronted with at least one of the three following challenges:

1. User centered applicationsIncreasing user orientation lead to unclear, individually different, changing requirements. Managers striving to satisfy their users are confronted with endless lists of requirements, which are nice-to-have but not really necessary. Unlimited effort for satisfaction of nice-to-have requirements results in exploding costs and development time.
2. Reduction of delivery timeThe accelerated dynamics of many markets demand for rapid delivery. Delivering a software at the end of several years of development time in many cases will lead to an obsolete or outdated product. Some years ago

when a system development project was started the system was defined, the requirements were identified and the IT-department was asked how long it would take to build it. Today systems development starts by defining the system, the budget and the delivery time. Identifying requirements is only the second step. And the list of requirements to be satisfied is cut according to the available resources. I.e. some years ago requirements determined resources, nowadays resources determine requirements.

3. Technology and market dynamicsSoftware production is often operating in a turbulent environment, i.e. an environment where the relevant parameters, customer demand, number and type of competitors and technological possibilities, are changing fast and simultaneously. This leads to extreme uncertainty about the technological opportunities and the competitive situation of the projected products. Under such circumstances many managers urge for fast innovation and the ability to adapt the software to the ever changing technology and market until close to delivery.

But despite of the growing sensitivity to costs and despite of the environmental turbulence and the extreme uncertainty and instability it creates for development and despite of the growing quest for speed and flexibility the celebrated paradigm of software production (Fox, Frakes 1997a and 1997b) is what we call process oriented software quality management (PSQM). It aims at a stable and reliable software process, promised as the result of a yearlong effort in software process improvement based on rigorous project management and statistical process control, following standards like ISO 9000 (ISO 1994a, ISO 1994b), Capability Maturity Model (CMM) (Paulk et al. 1995), Bootstrap (Kuvaja, Bicego 1994) or ISO 15504 SPICE (Emam et al. 1998, ISO/IEC 1997).

The idea of a stable, reliable software process sharply contrasts the instability and uncertainty of the environment, which seem to give the fast and flexible a cutting edge over the reliable but slow. This leads to a sharp criticism of the Capability Maturity Model (CMM) and other representatives of PSQM as being a serious risk to a company's competitive potential (Bach 1994, p. 14).

This recently led to a vivid but also confusing discussion of alternative models of software development. To name just a few of these alternatives to PSQM:

Extreme Programming (Beck 1999), Synch-and-Stabilize-Approach (Cusumano, Selby 1995), Adaptive Development (Highsmith 1998), Rapid Application Development (Martin 1992), Dynamic Systems Development Method (Stapleton 1997).

Proponents of the various models argue, that their proposal offers a reduction of cost or development time or an improved ability to embrace change in technology or market. Opponents see at least some of those proposals as a step back to older hacking traditions, leading to the well known problems of immature software processes and doubt their ability to deliver software quality.

But however good the case of PSQM is defended, the question is up: What is wrong with PSQM? Do we need to replace PSQM by a different model of software development? What is the right model? What will be the consequences for Software quality management?

In order to answer these questions, we will first briefly examine the evidence for and against PSQM. This will lead to statement about the future stand of PSQM. We will than outline how software development models may be constructed systematically and will use this idea to contrast process and product orientation as two opposing models of software development. Finally we will draw some conclusions about software quality management in process and product oriented development.

2 What is Wrong with Process Oriented Software Quality Management?

Until recently nothing seemed to be wrong with PSQM. When Fox and Frakes in the Communications of the ACM titled "The Quality Approach: Is it Delivering?" they as well as most experts regard this a purely rhetorical question. They close the editorial referring to empirical investigation stating: "Evidence from early adopters of the quality paradigm support the claim that it can significantly improve return on investment, customer satisfaction, productivity, and other important measures of software development success." (Fox, Frakes 1997b, p. 29)

Relevant empirical studies report impressive results of applying PQSM. Decreasing error densities in delivered software products, shrinking time to market and reduced total effort as well as high returns on investment on the capital invested in software process improvement are reported by companies applying the CMM (Goldenson, Herbsleb 1995; Hayes, Zubrow 1995; Herbsleb et al. 1994). But also the gain of applying the ISO 9000 standard for software process improvement is judged positively (Loken, Skramstad 1995; Stelzer, Mellis, Herzwurm 1996).

However, the considerable evidence in favour of PSQM is balanced by evidence against it. Therefore some critics vehemently advice against PSQM (Bach 1994; Bollinger, McGowan 1991; Gilb 1996, p. 6; Ould 1996; Coallier 1994; Haynes, Meyn 1994; Matsubara 1994; DeMarco 1996; Beirne, Panteli, Ramsay 1997).

The essential hint to a critical discussion of PSQM comes from the fact, that the world's most successful software companies obviously do not follow process improvement according to ISO 9000 or CMM.

Software companies producing shrink-wrap software (or "commercial of the shelf software") like for example Borland, Claris, Apple, Symantec, Microsoft and Lotus obviously do not organize their software processes according to the CMM or the ISO 9000 (Bach 1994, p. 14). They rarely manage for example their requirements documents as formal (Bach 1994, p. 14; Cusumano, Selby 1995, pp. 207 ff.) as is recommended in the key process area "Requirements Management" of the CMM's second maturity level

(Paulk et al. 1995) or in the quality elements 4.4 or 4.5 of the ISO 9001 standard (ISO 9001 1994).

For those companies the recommendation, to give highest priority to software process improvement according to the ideas of PSQM seems not to be appropriate. And even though most advocates of PSQM are not ready to accept these facts as counter arguments against the fundamental assumptions of PSQM, some seem to accept, that PSQM is not a universal model of software development management. E.g. Herbsleb et al. states: "We need to learn how, when, why, and for whom process improvement pays off." (Herbsleb et al. 1994, p. 9)

Bach characterize the companies for which the CMM may not be appropriate: "For these reasons, the CMM is unpopular among many of the highly competitive and innovative companies producing commercial shrink-wrap software." He points out what he considers the CMM's essential deficiencies: "Here in the Valley [Silicon Valley], innovation reigns supreme, and it is from the vantage point of the innovator that the CMM seems most lost." (Bach 1994, p. 16).

Mellis and Stelzer (Mellis, Stelzer 1999) examine the evidence for and against PSQM in more detail and reconstruct some of Bach's arguments about the significance of flexibility using the sound theoretical distinction between two types of markets, markets with increasing and markets with decreasing returns (Arthur 1996). They argue that PSQM is a management concept adapted to a stable, placid environment, while in a turbulent environment a different style of management is appropriate, which is described in more detail in (Mellis 2000a). In (Mellis 2000b) the effect of task clarity is analysed on the basis of well established hypotheses in organizational theory, demonstrating that innovation, typically resulting in unclear development tasks, demand a different design of software development than PSQM.

Looking on the long list of substantially differing alternative designs of software development mentioned above, we conclude, that PSQM is not a universal design of software development and that different situational conditions demand for different development designs. Therefore in the next chapter we will discuss, how to systematically tailor a development design to the situational conditions under which a software production operates.

3 Constructing Development Models Systematically

Organizational theory offers a well established body of hypotheses, which can be used to tie situational factors to various organizational dimensions. Based on these hypotheses a software development design can be tailored to a software production's situational conditions. An example of how this can be done in detail will be given elsewhere. Here we concentrate on the basic idea of the situational approach and use it to contrast the fundamental difference of process and product orientation and its effect on quality management.

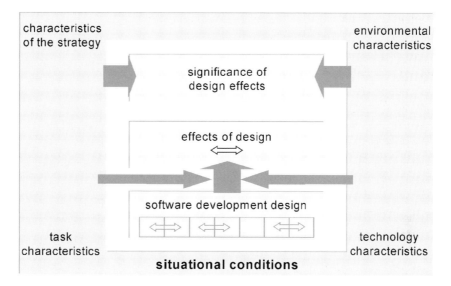

Figure 1: Contingency approach

As already mentioned above, different situational factors need to be considered. Beside environmental characteristics like environmental dynamics, task characteristics like task clarity need to be considered as has been described in (Mellis 2000b and Mellis et al. 2000). Further relevant factors are the strategic goals set by management and different technologies like object orientation or pattern oriented design.

To describe the various designs of software development a set of design dimensions are used. Those dimensions belong to two classes, dimensions of the organizational design and dimensions of the technical and methodological design. The dimensions of the first class are rooted in the fact, that software except in trivial cases is the result of the organized cooperation of many individuals. But even if we abstract from the division of labour and consider software development the work of one individual or entity, there is a complicated technical and methodological structure. This is described by the dimensions of the second class.

Some of the dimensions are indicated in figure 2 and explained in (Mellis 2000b or Mellis et al. 2000). In the following we only use the two fundamental organizational dimensions, the kind of the horizontal division of labour and the process organisation. The kind of horizontal division of labour is used to describe how the task of software development is divided among the organizational units (positions and departments). We distinguish only two different kinds of division of labour, process oriented and product oriented division of labour. The division of labour is called process oriented, if different organizational units specialize on different activities or work processes like analysis, design, coding or testing. The division of labour is called product oriented, if different organizational units specialize on different components of the software.

dimensions of software development design
organizational design
division of labor
coordination
process design
formalization
motivation and leadership
...
engineering design
requirements engineering
quality assurance
architectural design
design methods
...

Figure 2: Dimensions of software development design

We distinguish two types of process organization, activity oriented and progress oriented process organization. In an activity oriented process organization work is broken down into phases according to activities like analysis, design, coding and test. These phases are acted out one after the other without any overlap in time. In a progress oriented process organization the work is broken down into phases according to stages of completion of the product. The different phases are separated by gates called for example vision defined (when a rough specification of the product is reached), first build (when the first operational system is reached), concept freeze (after which only minor changes to the functionality and architecture of the product are accepted), product stabilized (after which only minor changes to the products internal structure are accepted), ready to delivery. In this process organization the activities analysis, design, coding and test are not separated in phases, but are carried out all the time from the gate vision defined until the gate ready to delivery.

Different software development designs described by the various dimensions effect for example development time or costs or the ability to conform to planned time, budget, functionality and quality. The effects may be moderated by situational conditions. E.g. a development design like PSQM may lead to low development costs in a placid environment, but to high costs in a turbulent environment, if requirements and technology change rapidly and the development process need to be stopped and set back frequently. The different effects are not always equally relevant. In case a novel product is to be developed it may be of primary importance to deliver it to the market first. For a safety critical product on the other hand development time may be of no relevance at all.

4 Process and Product Orientation

Process orientation is the conception, that software development is to be understood as a process. I.e. every action of a member of the software development organization is seen as part of a repeatable process. Designing, planning, leading and controlling software development is understood as designing, planning, leading and controlling the process.

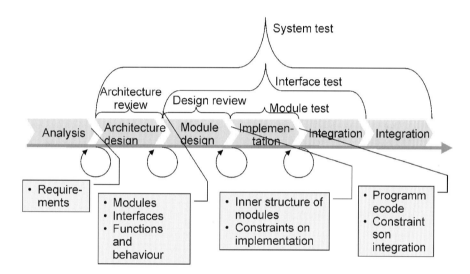

Figure 3: Process orientation

Usually process orientation is accompanied with the assumption, that the intended use of the software is to automate a well defined part of an existing interactive system, i.e. the relevant part of the system can be determined exactly and completely and be described in a model (see e.g. McMenamin, Palmer 1984). Therefore an activity oriented process organization is possible, where the activities analysis, design, coding and testing are performed one after the other without any overlap in time.

An important advantage of this process organization is that it has clear cut phases, each producing a well defined document as its result. This improves the visibility of the process and allows to control the activities by checking the quality of the document it produces. Further it suggests that a correct and complete phase result guarantees that the phase is definitely finished, provides sufficient information for the next phase and does not need to be revisited. Thus it yields an efficient and predictable process.

The kind of division of labour is not very important in process orientation. If under the given situational conditions it cannot be expected that one person has command of both the application related know how and the technological know how, then it is reasonable to consider a process oriented division of labour with application specialists for analysis on one hand and technology specialist for design and coding on the other hand. Testing may be another specialization. Otherwise a product oriented or even combined division of labour may be used.

An entirely different organizational design results from product orientation. Product orientation is the conception, that software development in the large is to be understood as a set of coordinated software development tasks in the small. I.e. it is assumed that a complex software can be decomposed independently from development activities (i.e. in the beginning of a development project) into a set of loosely coupled simple subsystems or modules, with defined narrow interfaces and little interaction. The tasks to develop these simple subsystems are almost independent. In case the subsystems are small enough, they can be understood as development in the small.

Usually product orientation is accompanied by the idea to assign the tasks to develop the subsystems to different organizational units, i.e. the idea of a product oriented division of labour. In this case there is a congruence of product or problem structure and the organizational structure. Loose coupling of the subsystems or modules map onto little need for coordination between the organizational units.

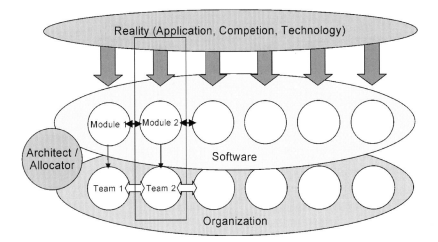

Figure 4: Product orientation

As a consequence of the reduction of software development in the large to software development in the small, process organization for the work of the individual organizational units is of minor importance. It is neither needed to make progress visible, not is it needed as a means of leading and controlling as in process orientation. A process organization is needed to control the risk, that different individual development projects are synchronized. This is done by a progress oriented process organization.

In order to give a concise comparison of process and product orientation we state, that process orientation maps the structure of the activities onto the process organization, while product orientation maps the structure of the problem, which is congruent to the structure of the product, onto the static structure of organization.

We will now flesh out the fundamental organizational designs of process and product orientation by two different organizational structures. These styles are closely related to the concept of mechanistic and organic organizations introduced by Burns and Stalker (Burns, Stalker 1961). They claim that mechanistic organizations develop in a stable environment, while organic organizations are adapted to a dynamic environment.

In a mechanistic structure individual tasks are considered limited technical problems which can be defined separately from the overall organizational goal. Therefore mechanistic structures are characterized by detailed task descriptions for any organizational unit. The tasks are precisely cut and stable over time. Extensive rules and regulations standardize work processes. Mechanistic structures are control oriented and use extensive and detailed planning. For individuals on the lowest level of the hierarchy deep knowledge of their locally limited problems is more important than an understanding of the organization's goals and the cooperation of its various units. Mechanistic structures stress hierarchical relations and tend to concentrate information at the top of the hierarchy. Therefore communication is mainly vertical and reporting in style.

The rapid changes in a dynamic environment do not allow detailed and fixed task descriptions and extensive standardization of work processes by detailed rules and regulations. Therefore changing tasks and adaptations of work processes are characteristics of organic structures. Organic structures are less control oriented. Planning is limited. Individuals need a good understanding of the organization's goals and the cooperation of its various units. Information and decision power is decentralized, communication is independent of the hierarchical relations. The style of communication is more often consulting and informing than reporting.

The combination of process orientation and mechanistic structure we call transformational development, to stress that it transforms a model of a given interactive system in several steps into software. Transformational development is a reconstruction of PSQM in terms of the organizational dimensions introduced above. The combination of product orientation with organic structure we call adaptive development, to stress that the software is not a transformation of a model of a given interactive system to be automated but is gradually adapted to the real world to create a new interactive system. According to the construction of the two models of development they offer different advantages. Transformational development is especially suited to the automation of given systems in a placid environment, where predictability of the development is an advantage. Adaptive development is especially suited for developing novel products in a dynamic environment, where the ability to adapt the product to the ever changing environment until close to delivery is an important advantage.

In the next chapter we will contrast transformational and adaptive development in respect to quality management.

5 Two Different Approaches to Quality Management

Before we discus how quality is managed in the two different development models transformational and adaptive development, we have to understand, that the two models are associated with different concepts of quality.

In transformational development the automation of a given system is intended. The system must not exist in reality before the end of the development project, it might also be given as a blueprint, defining the system in any detail. Therefore the software is of good quality if it behaves like the corresponding part of the given system. As transformational development starts with building a model of the system that is considered a specification of the software, (product) quality in transformational development is conformance to given requirements or conformance to a specification. Since the overwhelming part of requirements in a typical development project consists of functional requirements, this concept of conformance to given requirements is usually reduced to low defect density.

In contrast to transformational development in adaptive development there is no given system to be automated. The reason may be that no such system exists in reality. But there may also be other reasons for not conceiving the development as the automation of a given system. One reason could be that there are many similar systems, without being known, which of them is relevant or the best. Think for example of the situation in which text processing software was invented. Almost everybody was doing text processing by hand or typewriter. But there were many different styles. The software to be developed should suit as many people as possible for any type of text.

Since adaptive development does not start with a given specification of the software, conformance to a given specification it not an appropriate quality concept. Therefore the quality concept is adequacy for use in some application context.

The different quality concepts demand for different approaches to quality assurance. Product quality in transformational development depends on the quality of the specification and the conformance of the software to the specification. The later is the consequence of careful execution of carefully prescribed process steps. In adaptive development quality is the result of an intensive confrontation and adaptation of the product to the application conditions without the intermediate instrument of explicitly stated requirements.

I.e. in transformational development the task of quality assurance is to control transformational risk. Related to the individual project this is achieved by the verification of each step's output against the output of the preceding step. Independently from individual projects it is done by formalizing, standardizing and improving the procedures of development. This is the essence of PSQM.

On the other hand in adaptive development the goal of quality assurance is to control adaptation risk by an intensive confrontation of the product to the application conditions. Related to the individual project this is achieved for example by providing extensive feedback from the application environment by validating intermediate product versions in usability tests and by making the contribution of individual developers to the product's success as visible as possible. Independently from individual projects it is done for example by improving the understanding of architectures. The architecture is a cue to adaptive development. Modularity of the architecture leads to reduced coordination need (Sanchez, Mahoney 1997) in a product oriented division of labour. Pattern orientation (Gamma et al. 1995) helps to build well reasoned architectures, which limit the need to adapt the architecture while the software's functionality gradually develops and changes during adaptive development. A better understanding of refactoring helps to maintain quality of the architecture (Fowler 1999).

6 References

Arthur 1996 Arthur, W. B. (1996) Increasing Returns and the New World of Business. In: Harvard Business Review 74, 4, pp. 100–109.

Bach 1994 Bach J. (1994) The Immaturity of the CMM, in *American Programmer,* Vol. 7, No. 9, pp. 13–18.

Beck 1999 Beck K (1999) Extreme Programming Explained: Embrace Change. Addison-Wesley, Reading, Mass.

Beirne et al. 1997 Beirne M., Panteli A., Ramsay H. (1997) Going soft on quality?: Process management in the Scottish software industry. In: Software Quality Journal 6, 3, pp. 195-209.

Bollinger/McGowan 1991 Bollinger T. B., McGowan C. (1991) A Critical Look at Software Capability Evaluations. In: IEEE Software. No. 4, 1991, pp. 25–48.

Burns/Stalker 1961 Burns T, Stalker G. M. (1961) The Management of Innovation. London.

Coallier 1994 Coallier F. (1994) How ISO 9001 fits into the software world. In: IEEE Software 11, 1, pp. 98–100.

Cusumano/Selby 1995 Cusumano M. A., Selby R. 1995 Microsoft Secrets. Free Press, New York.

DeMarco 1996 DeMarco T. (1996) The Role of Software Development Methodologies: Past, Present, and Future. In: 18th International Conference on Software Engineering. March 25-29, 1996 Berlin. Proceedings. IEEE Computer Society Press, Los Alamitos, CA 1996, pp. 2–4.

El Emam et al. 1998 El Emam K., Drouin J. N., Melo W. (1998) SPICE The Theory and Practice of Software Process Improvement and Capability Determination. IEEE Computer Society Press, Los Alamitos, CA.

Fowler 1999 Fowler M. (1999) Refactoring: Improving the Design of Existing Code. Addison-Wesley, Reading Mass.

Fox/Frakes 1997a Fox C., Frakes W. (1997) Elements of the Quality Paradigm, in Communications of the ACM, 40, 6, p. 26.

Fox/Frakes 1997b Fox C., Frakes W. (1997) The Quality Approach: Is It Delivering? in Communications of the ACM, 40, 6, pp. 25–29.

Gamma et al. 1995 Gamma E., Helm R., Johnson R., Vlissides J. (1995) Design Patterns: Elements of Reusable Object-Oriented Software. Addison-Wesley, Reading, Mass.

Gilb 1996 Gilb T. (1996) Level 6: Why we can't get there from here. In: IEEE Software 13, 1, pp. 97–103.

Goldenson/Herbsleb 1995 Goldenson D. R., Herbsleb J. D. (1995) After the Appraisal: A Systematic Survey of Process Improvement, its Benefits, and Factors that Influence Success. Technical report CMU/SEI-95-TR-009. Pittsburgh.

Haynes/Meyn 1994 Haynes P., Meyn S. (1994) Is ISO 9000 going to put you out of business? In: American Programmer 7, 2, pp. 25–29.

Hayes/Zubrow 1995 Hayes W., Zubrow D. (1995) Moving on up: Data and Experience doing CMM-Based Process Improvement. Technical Report. CMU/SEI-95-TR-008. ESC-TR-95-008. Carnegie Mellon University, Pittsburgh, PA.

Herbsleb et al. 1994 Herbsleb J. D., Zubrow D., Siegel J., Rozum J., Carleton A. (1994) Software Process Improvement: State of the payoff. In: American Programmer. No. 9, 1994, pp. 2–12.

Highsmith 1998 Highsmith J. 1998 Adaptive Software Development. A Collaborative Approach to Managing Complex Systems. Dorset House, New York.

ISO (Eds.) (1994a) ISO (Eds.) (1994) Normen zum Qualitätsmanagement und zur Qualitätssicherung / QM-Darlegung. Teil 1: Leitfaden zur Auswahl und Anwendung. DIN EN ISO 9000-1: 1994-08. Beuth, Berlin.

ISO (Eds.) (1994b) ISO (Eds.) (1994) Qualitätsmanagementsysteme. Modell zur Qualitätssicherung/QM-Darlegung in Design/ Entwicklung, Produktion, Montage und Wartung. DIN EN ISO 9001: 1994-08. Beuth, Berlin.

ISO/IEC (Eds.) (1997) ISO/IEC (Eds.) (1997) ISO/IEC PDTR 15504. Software Process Assessment - Part 1: Concepts and Introductory Guide (SPICE V2.0). International Organization for Standardization, Genf.

Kuvaja/Bicego 1994 Kuvaja, P., Bicego, A. (1994) BOOTSTRAP – a European assessment methodology. In: Software Quality Journal 3, 3, pp. 117–128.

Loken/Skramstad 1995 Loken C. B., Skramstad T. (1995) ISO 9000 Certification - Experiences from Europe. In: American Society for Quality Control (ASQC) et al. (Eds.): Proceedings of the First World Congress for Software Quality, June 20-22, 1995, ASQC, San Francisco, CA, Session Y, pp. 1–11.

Martin 1992 Martin J. 1992 Rapid Application Development. Prentice Hall, Upper Saddle River, N.Y.

Matsubara 1994 Matsubara T. (1994) Does ISO 9000 really help improve Software Quality? In: American Programmer 7, 2, pp. 38–45.

McMenamin/Palmer 1984 McMenamin S. M., Palmer J. F. (1984) Essential Systems Analysis: Tools and Techniques. Yourdon Press, Englewood Cliffs.

Mellis W. (2000a) Mellis W. (2000) Software Quality Management in Turbulent Times - Are there Alternatives to Process oriented Software Quality Management? Accepted for publication in Software Quality Journal.

Mellis W. (2000b) Mellis W. (2000) A Systematic Analysis of the Effect of Task Clarity on Software Development Design. European Conference on Information Systems ECIS 2000, Wien

Mellis/Stelzer 1999 Mellis W., Stelzer D. (1999) Das Rätsel des prozeßorientierten Softwarequalitätsmanagement. Wirtschaftsinformatik.

Mellis et al. 2000 Mellis W., Herzwurm G., Müller U., Schlang H., Schockert S., Trittmann, R. (2000) Adaptive Software Development. Shaker, Aachen to appear.

Ould 1996 Ould M. A. (1996) CMM and ISO 9001. In: Software Process – Improvement and Practice 2, 4, pp. 281–289.

Paulk et al. 1995 Paulk, M. C., Weber C. V., Curtis B., Chrissis M. B. (1995) The Capability Maturity Model: Guidelines for Improving the Software Process. Addison-Wesley, Reading, MA.

Sanchez/Mahoney 1997 Sanchez R., Mahoney J. T. (1997) Modularity, Flexibility and Knowledge Management in Product and Organization Design. In: IEEE Engineering Management Review 25, 4, pp. 50–61.

Stapleton 1997 Stapleton J. 1997 Dynamic Systems Development Method. Addison-Wesley, Reading, Mass.

Stelzer et al. 1996 Stelzer D., Mellis W., Herzwurm G. (1996) Software Process Improvement via ISO 9000? Results of Two Surveys Among European Software Houses. In: Software Process - Improvement and Practice 2, 3, pp. 197–210.

Dynamic Systems Development Method, The Standard for Rapid Application Development

BARBARA ROBERTS
F.I. Group (United Kingdom)

Abstract: This chapter presents Dynamic Systems Development Method (DSDM), the de facto standard for Rapid Application Development. DSDM is a formalised framework to allow rapid delivery of systems within a controlled and manageable environment, thus giving organisations the confidence to meet deal with one of the major problems facing the IT departments of the 21st century – how to reduce their time to market whilst being still responsive to business change. It explains how the DSDM Consortium membership have built the method based on industry best practice. The 9 DSDM Principles are explained, together with the core techniques. The DSDM lifecycle is explained, and the chapter shows how the combination of all these elements delivers quality systems which meet the business purpose. Finally the chapter explains how to find additional background material about DSDM, and the type of accredited training currently available, which can be used to lead on to personal accreditation as a DSDM Practitioner.

Keywords: principles, techniques, lifecycle, speed, control

Figure 1: DSDM Consortium

1 Background

1.1 The Pressure on Information Technology (IT)

"In today's environment, the ability to react quickly to change by reducing the development life cycle in order to be first to market will give a company an important competitive edge." – James Martin

The market conditions of the 21st century put business under continual pressure. The most successful companies are those who are able to reduce their time to market, to launch initiatives before their competitors, to respond very rapidly to opportunities in the marketplace or to change direction in response to a move by the competition or a change in circumstances. All of these business initiatives rely on support from Information Technology (IT). For a business to launch a new product in three months time, the supporting IT processes must be available and working in that three month time frame. In this fast moving environment, late IT delivery is not acceptable and may pose a major risk to the business.

The marketplace of 21st century business measures timescales in months, whereas in the past, timescales of two to three years were more typical. Internet related and e-business projects frequently require even tighter timescales, measured in days rather than months. This need for speed puts tremendous pressure on IT departments.

Pressure does not just come from the need for speed. There is also an ever-increasing rate of change within business. Even in shorter timescale projects, the probability of changes to requirements is very high. Business cannot afford to stand still, even for the short life of the project. So, in the modern business environment, the pressure is on the IT department to deliver rapid solutions and at the same time to cope with frequent change.

1.2 Why Rapid Application Development (RAD)?

Until recently, the process used by IT to support development was designed for a very different environment, one where IT planned for longer projects, where change was the exception and where the constraints of technology meant IT needed to understand the full requirement up-front. The traditional (or waterfall) process moves through a series of stages, completing and signing off each stage before moving on to the next. This is a comfortable and familiar environment for those responsible for Quality within an organisation.

The need for rapid delivery of solutions, coupled with the advent of more modern technology in the late 1980s and 1990s has forced a major move away from the controlled quality process of the traditional project towards a Rapid Application Development (RAD) approach. The availability of prototyping toolsets, together with the ease of use and freedom of the PC environment meant that developers could produce solutions very quickly and bypass all the traditional controls. In the short-term, this appeared to be an effective solution to an immediate problem – a working system delivered quickly and driven by the business needs. But for an organisation where quality is important, RAD's focus on "Code and Deliver" introduces some major risks.

1.3 The Risks of RAD

From a customer perspective, a RAD approach may appear an attractive option on the surface, giving speedy delivery of a working system and a feeling of being in control of the IT department. However, although RAD has some major benefits – it ensures fast delivery of a working system and actively involves the users – it also has pitfalls. There is generally no defined structure or process to a RAD project, and the traditional focus on control and quality has been abandoned. The focus remains on code and delivery, frequently with little or no effort put into the early stages (requirements capture, analysis and design) or the later stages (testing, documentation and support). The end result is often a quick-fix system, which works on day one, but may be badly designed and impossible to maintain or enhance in the future. So what appears to be a cheap option at the beginning may turn out to be very expensive in the longer term, as systems need to be re-written instead of enhanced, or as maintenance costs spiral out of control.

1.4 RAD and Quality

From a quality and audit perspective, RAD projects can be a nightmare. The team often comprises an enthusiastic developer working with an equally enthusiastic user on a technology platform that allows very rapid prototyping and change. What should an auditor look for? Where are the defined measures of completion or success? Typically these do not exist. To make matters worse, RAD does not have a defined process, so it is impossible to track the project through defined stages. This presents a major risk to any organisation where quality standards are important, but also presents the organisation with a dilemma:

How to deliver systems rapidly to the customer and to balance the need for speed against the need for quality?

2 Dynamic Systems Development Method

2.1 Best Practice – Right and Rapid (RAD²)

It is against this background that Dynamic Systems Development Method (DSDM) came into existence. In 1994 a number of major companies in the UK got together to discuss the problems of delivering quality systems in short timescales. They compared their successful RAD projects with the less successful ones to see what made the difference. Using these successful projects as a base, they pooled their knowledge and experiences to draw up a best practice for RAD, which focused on delivering quality software to tight timescales. The result was the Dynamic Systems Development Method (DSDM).

DSDM Consortium members recognised that the less successful RAD projects only focused on one driver – speed – but there are actually two sides to a RAD project – speed and quality. What is needed is a process to balance the two sides, a process that encourages rapid delivery, but with sufficient controls to ensure the right level of quality is built in from the start. The initial version of DSDM, based firmly on industry best practice and a background of successful delivery, was launched in Spring 1995 to ensure "Right and Rapid" RAD projects,

2.2 The DSDM Consortium

The Dynamic Systems Development Method Consortium was formed, with a membership which includes a wide range of organisations, large and small, who were both vendors and users of IT. DSDM (Version 1) was launched in the UK in spring 1995 as a non-proprietary method, available to Consortium members. Over the first few months, initial projects following the DSDM approach, called the Early Adopters, were assessed. At the same time the DSDM membership gave feedback on the method. In the light of the Early Adopters and the membership feedback, DSDM was updated and version 2 launched in Autumn 1995. Version 3 (the current version) was launched in Autumn 1997, to address the needs of an audience with very differing levels of DSDM expertise. Since version 3, the rate of feedback and improvement has slowed, since the method is now tried, tested and very stable – it works! DSDM is accepted as the de facto RAD standard in the UK, and is spreading throughout the world, with DSDM Consortia in the UK, France, Benelux, Sweden, and Denmark, and members and interest groups in North America, Africa, India and Europe.

2.3 What is DSDM?

DSDM is a formalised RAD method, embodying industry best practice, providing a framework of controls for rapid and responsive delivery of software systems. DSDM is based around a number of concepts. On a DSDM project, it is recognised that user involvement should be on-going throughout the project. This is to ensure that the right business solution is delivered and that the project always tracks the business. DSDM accepts that, even on a short project, it is highly likely that requirements will evolve. In the early stages the timescale is fixed, and an on-time final delivery is guaranteed. However, DSDM recognises that early partial deliveries may also be very cost-effective provided they are business focused. The business may be able to start using the system and may be able to get some early pay-back. DSDM accepts that to build a 100% complete and tested system takes a long time. However typically 80% of the functionality can be built with 20% of the effort, and it is often possible to deliver a system rapidly by focusing on the 80% – the major business benefits – and to leave the 20% – the bells and whistles – to a later stage. You only need to think of the functionality in a word processor for an illustration of this. DSDM also accepts that it is extremely unlikely to deliver the perfect solution first time round. Hence, cycles of feedback and review are built into the DSDM process.

3 The 9 Principles of DSDM

The concepts of DSDM are built into the nine principles.

3.1 Active user involvement is imperative

On a DSDM project, users become actively involved and remain involved at all stages. There will be at least one user representative as part of the development team, ensuring knowledgeable, accurate and timely information about the business needs. Wider user involvement is ensured by identifying user roles at different levels within the organisation and planning in where and when these roles feed in their knowledge. If there is a shift within the business, this information is immediately available to the project team. This ensures that the project can track the business much more closely than on a traditional project where the team may be working to goals and objectives that are no longer valid. The careful selection of respected and knowledgeable users to fulfil the various DSDM user roles ensures that the right business knowledge is always available when necessary. Representation will be at all levels, from the end-user to the middle manager to the business visionary to the business sponsor. In this way DSDM projects can take in the bigger picture and have a wider perspective than may have been possible on a traditional project.

3.2 DSDM teams must be empowered to make decisions

On DSDM projects, speed is always one of the two major drivers (the other being quality). In order to ensure rapid development and delivery, it is vital to speed up the decision-making process. Therefore on a DSDM project, the team members are empowered to make decisions on a day-to-day basis about the project. Since the team comprises both business and IT representatives, who all have an excellent understanding of the problems and issues, the team members are the best placed to make the appropriate decision. Empowerment does not give the team a completely free hand, however, since empowerment generally works within certain constraints at a project level. Examples of typical constraints would be that the team is not empowered to change the scope of the project, or that the technical architecture, once agreed, cannot be changed by the team. These sorts of decisions are very major ones and potentially far-reaching, so would always need to be referred up to an executive level. However, within the given constraints, the majority of day-to-day decisions can be very effectively and rapidly agreed by a knowledgeable team, who have the full story on the current problems and issues. This combination of business and technical expertise within an empowered team is a powerful one, which ensures a high quality decisions about project issues.

3.3 Focus is on frequent delivery of products

DSDM takes a product based approach to developing a solution. The aim is to make the progress and assessment of quality much more visible to the business. On a traditional project, there may be long periods where, from a business perspective, there is nothing to be seen. After the sign off of the functional specification, the next user delivery is a system for user acceptance testing. In between, progress is measured via the progress report. DSDM recognises that by focusing on making visible deliveries of products back to the business, it becomes easier to assess and understand what is actually happening. Thus progress from stage to stage is measured against the products delivered, and the planning reflects how the products will be produced. This product based approach also allows more flexibility, making it possible to move forwards on completion of a product.

3.4 Fitness for business purpose is the essential criterion for acceptance of deliverables

DSDM accepts the importance of delivering a solution that works and meets the business needs. Acceptance should be measured in terms of "Does it work? Can I do my job?" rather than "Does it satisfy the contents of the requirements document?" Many technically perfect solutions fail to meet the business purpose, although they deliver what was originally specified.

DSDM is about delivering the right solution for the business at the right time. This may mean re-engineering the solution at a later stage, if this is an acceptable approach and is the only way to deliver on time. Or it may mean delivering a partial solution in the short term, with additional functionality planned for later delivery. For this approach to succeed it is important to understand clearly the business purpose and to work together as a team to achieve this.

3.5 An iterative and incremental development is required to converge on a accurate business solution

DSDM recognises that it is difficult, if not impossible, to define a requirement and then deliver the exact solution first-time around. What is needed is a process of review and feedback, so that there are regular checks to confirm progress is always moving in the right direction. This iterative process of development – prototyping – has been around for many years. DSDM recognised the benefits of the approach, but also saw the risks of prototyping if used without some elements of control. On a DSDM project, prototyping is used as a way of evolving a requirement through a number of planned stages, taking feedback to ensure the requirement will actually work i.e. meet the business requirement, and allowing adjustments where necessary. Each iteration is built on an understanding and acceptance of what has gone before. In this way DSDM encourages a culture of "No nasty surprises". But importantly, DSDM builds in control of the prototypes, so than prototyping becomes a planned approach, not an ad-hoc unplanned and wandering development. As the prototype moves through the various stages, it gets nearer and nearer to what the business needs and also gets better and better from a technical perspective, until a production quality system, or component, is ready to move to the live environment.

3.6 All changes during development are reversible

On a DSDM project, the system will be developed rapidly, using a prototype and review approach. This means numerous and rapid changes. In order to keep control of this environment, good configuration management and version control are critical. It should always be possible to roll back to the last baseline – the last agreed point. Therefore it is not just the programs that need to be treated as configuration items. For this roll-back to work, other elements must also be controlled. In addition to the code, typical configuration items could be models, test scripts, database creation scripts, interfaces, user documentation. Without this ability to reverse out changes, or where backtracking is difficult, there will always be a temptation to try to sign off and close off at each iteration. The problem with this is that taking a wrong turn may sometimes be part of the learning process. It must be possible to explore an idea, realise it is incorrect and go backwards, use what has been learnt and move on in the right direction.

3.7 Requirements are baselined at a high level

Using DSDM, the detail of the requirement is added throughout the project. This is very different from a traditional project where the low level detail is identified and fixed in the very early stages. In the early stages of a DSDM project, the problem, scope and objectives of the project will be defined, and these become the bounds of the project. As an example, at the DSDM Feasibility Study stage, the project may be defined using a Level 0 Data Flow Diagram or Context Diagram. This becomes the project baseline, and ensures the overall scope of the project is not allowed to grow. Gradually as the project moves through the DSDM process, the detail within the scope is added. At the next DSDM stage, the Business Study, additional detail is added, to identify the requirements and the priorities. This provides the DSDM team with a great deal of information about the requirement. Once again this is then baselined, before moving on. Then in the later DSDM prototyping stages, Functional Model Iteration and Design and Build Iteration, the low level detail is added, and at regular points within this cycle, a new baseline is drawn. At each stage, enough information must be available in order to move on.

This approach allows flexibility, but at the same time ensures control.

3.8 Testing is integrated throughout the lifecycle

Integrated testing is key to the success and the quality of DSDM projects. Traditionally the bulk of testing is carried out towards the end of a project, with user acceptance testing as the final task before implementation. This approach presents a big risk, since any mistakes or misunderstandings which are picked up at the end of a project may have a major impact if all the previous stages have been completed and signed off. In order to address this risk, DSDM carries out testing on the evolving system all the way through development, with business and IT testing being carried out in tandem. As the system evolves, both developers and users test it to ensure that to meets not only the IT requirements, but also the business needs. In the very early stages, the business is able to carry out basic tests to ensure the system being developed is going to deliver what they expect. Any errors or misunderstandings picked up at such an early stage can frequently be corrected with minimal effort. An additional benefit of integrated testing is a continuous process of building confidence in the system under development. At each stage, the business is aware of what the system will do, and how it will work. This is very different from a traditional approach where the users may have no view of the system after the production of the functional specification until immediately before implementation.

3.9 A collaborative, co-operative approach is required between all stakeholders

DSDM projects are all about shared responsibility. This means business and IT sharing their knowledge and expertise in order to solve a problem. But the collaboration and co-operation extend beyond those directly involved in the project. For this approach to work, it is important that all sides understand the approach being taken, and understand that it may be necessary to make compromises. DSDM is about give and take from all parties. It is also important to remember that DSDM impacts beyond those directly involved from the business and IT areas. Its impact extends to others, such as quality groups, maintenance teams, production testing and integration teams. The best way to get a collaborative and co-operative approach is to ensure that all parties have the same understanding of what DSDM means, and can apply this to make sure any effects on their areas are addressed. This can be done in a variety of ways. Organising some basic DSDM training is very effective, especially where an organisation or IT department or business area are new to DSDM. Alternatively running an introductory DSDM session at the start of each project can be effective where there is already a background of DSDM within IT and the business needs to be brought up to speed.

4 Core Techniques

DSDM has brought together a number of basic techniques which underpin the approach.

4.1 Facilitated Workshops

Facilitated workshops are an excellent team based information gathering and decision making technique. They are designed to speed up business planning and development.

They involve experienced and empowered personnel working in one or more sessions run by an independent facilitator to reach high quality decisions in a short timescale.

Facilitated workshops offer a way of allowing a wider participation on the project in a managed environment. Workshops are used throughout the DSDM lifecycle, from project initiation to post project review. The aim of a workshop is to reach decisions that are mutually acceptable, to achieve consensus. Use of facilitated workshops during the DSDM lifecycle offers many benefits:

- **Speed** – Because all the stakeholders are gathered together and hear the same information, it is usually possible to greatly speed up the decision making process.
- **Ownership** – The group decision making process ensures participants take ownership of the problems and issues as well as the decisions.
- **Productivity** – Participants are able to build on one another's ideas and knowledge, and misunderstandings can be clarified quickly.
- **Consensus** – Open discussions on problems and issues make it easier for the group to reach consensus.
- Quality of decision making – Because of the active participation of the stakeholders, the quality of the decisions and the confidence in what has been agreed is generally very high.
- **Overall perspective** – One of the major advantages of this approach is that participants understand the importance not just of their own business area, but of all business areas within the overall perspective of the project.

4.2 Timeboxing

DSDM takes the overall timescale for the project, which has a fixed end date, and divides it into lower-level timeboxes, to provide a series of fixed deadlines by which interim or final products will be produced. Timeboxing is about setting deadlines to meet objectives. So each timebox has an agreed scope and clear objectives, with the overall aim of making something. Timeboxing is a product-based approach, it is not about activities. Each timebox aims to produce something visible, so that progress and quality can be assessed. Timeboxes are kept short, typically between two and six weeks, as a way of maintaining focus and keeping productivity at an optimum. Developers and users agree the objectives of the timebox and then agree what can realistically be achieved by the deadline. If during the timebox, it appears that the deadline will be missed, then the timebox must be de-scoped, so that it can still deliver something useful on time. Any de-scoping is done in discussion between the developers and the users, and it is the lowest priority requirements that are pushed out of the timebox.

4.3 Controlled Prototyping

Prototypes allow users to ensure the details and operation of a requirement are correct. Within DSDM prototypes have two uses. A prototype is a communication medium, allowing users to ensure the details and operation of a requirement are correct and are what they expect. But also with DSDM's incremental prototyping approach, a prototype is the latest version of the evolving system, which becomes the final, production system.

Prototyping is one of the foundations of a RAD approach, but it is also recognised that prototyping must be very carefully controlled if it is to be effective. DSDM uses three prototyping cycles to Investigate, Refine and Consolidate which manages the progression of a prototype and prevents over-engineering. DSDM has also put in place a number of other measures to ensure controlled prototyping. These are:

- **Timeboxing** – strict adherence to timeboxes means that prototyping must maintain focus on delivery of the agreed priorities.
- **Quality assurance of products** – within each timebox the quality of the products is assessed.
- **Change control** – procedures must allow change to be introduced effectively and quickly. Change control must not be bureaucratic or slow.
- **Configuration management** – This is needed to allow backtracking and reversion to a previous prototype.
- **User involvement** – This ensures the prototypes continue to move in the right direction, and address the business needs, according to the agreed priorities. To keep the prototyping moving forward rapidly, it is important that user availability is agreed and the level of availability is maintained.
- **Learning from earlier iterations** – DSDM keeps the same team throughout development, which ensures that team members learn from previous prototyping activity. In this way the quality of the products and the productivity of the team can be improved.

4.4 Prioritisation

DSDM uses MoSCoW prioritisation, to ensure that effort is always focused on the highest priorities first. The priorities are :

| **M** MUST HAVE | For requirements that are fundamental to the system. The MUST HAVEs define a minimum usable subset, and a DSDM project guarantees to satisfy all the MUST HAVEs |

S	SHOULD HAVE	Important requirements for which there is a work around in the short term. These would be mandatory if time were not so short. But the system will still be usable without these.
C	COULD HAVE	For requirements that can more easily be left out of the increment under development
W	WANT TO HAVE, but WON'T HAVE this time round	Valuable requirements that can wait until later development takes place.

The MoSCoW list of Prioritised Requirements provides the basis for decisions about the project – where effort should be focused, what can be left out, what must be included from day one. The priorities are discussed and agreed in the early stages of the project (during Business Study) but continue to be reviewed throughout the project and in the light of any changes to ensure they are still valid.

5 The DSDM Lifecycle

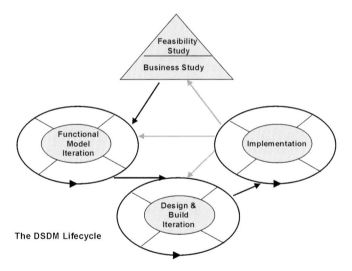

Figure 2: The DSDM Life Cycle

5.1 Feasibility Study

The objectives of the Feasibility Study on a DSDM project are to establish whether the proposed requirement can meet the business requirements. This is the first point where the project's suitability for DSDM can be assessed. The earlier DSDM issues can be addressed, the more value DSDM may be able to offer. Part of the Feasibility Study may be to outline possible or alternative technical solutions. At the end of the Feasibility Study stage, first-cut estimates of timescales, resources and money will be produced. Although not accurate at this stage, these first-cut estimates form the basis for the decision on if or how the project will move forward. The final stage of the Feasibility Study is to produce an Outline Plan, showing, in detail, how the Business Study will be achieved, and in outline the plans for the later project stages.

5.2 Business Study

Much information gathering, early investigation and planning is carried out during the Business Study stage. This is where all the foundations for the later prototyping stages are laid down. The objectives of the Business Study on a DSDM project are to scope the business processes to be supported. The future development, in terms of prototyping deliverables and prototyping controls are outlined here. For each of the prototyping activities, user classes and their representatives are identified so that their involvement can be planned in. Once the requirements have been clarified, these then need to be prioritised (using MoSCoW) as this prioritised list forms the basis for planning the timeboxes during the iterative stages (Functional Model Iteration, Design and Build Iteration, Implementation). Once the detailed investigation of requirements has been carried out, the team need to agree on the technical platform for development and production, and to scope (and prioritise) any key non-functional requirements. It is important to assess the likely impact of key non-functional requirements on the project. Examples of key non-functional requirements could be performance, security or availability. At this point DSDM suitability is re-assessed to ensure it is still the best approach, and that it is not introducing unacceptable risks. The final stage of the Business Study is to produce an Outline Prototyping Plan, which is a plan for the iterative, prototyping stages.

Once Business Study is complete, the project moves into the later lifecycle stages, which are carried out iteratively.

5.3 Functional Model Iteration

The objectives of the Functional Model Iteration are to demonstrate the required functionality, using a functional model, which may comprise both working prototypes and static models. At the same time, non-functional requirements, which may not be visible within the prototype, are recorded. Examples of these would be security, performance, throughput, recovery from failure etc. In summary, the aim here is to make sure both the business representatives and IT developers have the same understanding of how the business see the system, ensuring they are building the "right" system.

5.4 Design and Build Iteration

The objective of the Design and Build Iteration is to refine the Functional Prototypes to meet the non-functional requirements. This involves engineering the application so that it demonstrably satisfies the user requirements. In summary, the aim is to build the system "right".

5.5 Implementation

The objective of the Implementation Stage is to place the tested system safely in the users' working environment. Before going live, user training should also be completed, as well as any training of operators and support staff. Finally there should be a review to decide any future development requirements. Depending on the requirements and the production environment, a DSDM project could have a single or multiple implementation stages.

5.6 How to use the DSDM Lifecycle

Functional Model Iteration, Design and Build Iteration and Implementation are stages that are managed within timeboxes. Use of some types of technology means that Functional Model Iteration and Design and Build Iteration are phases which must be performed completely separately from each other. With other technology Functional Model Iteration and Design and Build Iteration are very closely linked – for example where modelling the functionality leads automatically on to code generation, so that a prototype moves seamlessly from Functional Modelling through to Design and Build. The DSDM lifecyle is not prescriptive, but offers a framework which can be effectively adapted to meet specific technical or business issues.

6 DSDM Products

At each lifecycle stage, DSDM defines a core set of products which should be produced. The products from each stage contain the information needed to move forward to the next stage. Associated with each product are quality criteria and a list of the suggested acceptors. In DSDM, products are accepted rather signed off. This is because a product may be revisited later. Acceptance implies the product in its current state meets the defined quality criteria to allow it to move forward. The format of the products is varied. Some products would typically be electronic prototypes, in other words the growing system. Other products might be documents, review records or test records.

From an auditor's point of view, the products offer an excellent way of reviewing a project and assessing whether the pre-requisites have been met, before moving on to a subsequent stage.

7 DSDM and Quality

Quality is an integral part of the DSDM approach. DSDM is about delivering Fit For Purpose systems; systems that work and that meet the business needs. This is ensured by maintaining appropriate user involvement throughout the lifecycle. User involvement is not just at the beginning and the end. In the early stages, facilitated workshops ensure wider user involvement so that the business requirements can be properly thought through, from all aspects. Continuous user involvement and on-going reviews ensures that the development tracks the business and the system meets the business needs from day one. With the emphasis on continued focus on business requirements, there is a constant emphasis on validation against those requirements.

The fact that testing is integrated throughout the lifecycle and that business and IT testing is carried out in parallel ensures a very high quality of testing. Confidence in the evolving system continues to grow, and each iteration is built from the previous one, so there should never be any nasty surprises or unexpected change of direction.

The longer-term quality of the project is addressed by formal assessment of the maintainability objectives at an early stage in the project lifecycle. This ensures that issues such as scaleability and enhancement have been considered and where necessary allowed for in the longer-term plans.

From an quality auditor's point of view, DSDM provides a clearly defined process against which projects can be audited. Mapping onto the lifecycle process, there are defined products with associated quality criteria which should form part of the audit process. DSDM also defines the roles and responsibilities, which should be assigned to all team members. This ensures everyone understands their part in the project team, and it also ensures all responsibilities have been addressed and assigned. The DSDM Manual offers the following guidance – questions to consider when auditing a DSDM project:

- Is the user involvement there?
- Are the users empowered?
- Is the life-cycle being followed?
- Are comments from prototype reviews being incorporated?
- Is backtracking allowed when necessary?
- Are priorities being adhered to?
- Are timeboxes being respected?

DSDM is all about providing a controlled framework for rapid delivery of solutions, and it is this framework that ensures the right level of quality – "Right and Rapid".

8 DSDM Accreditation

There is a formal accreditation process for DSDM, at two levels – accredited training courses and personal accreditation.

8.1 DSDM Training

There are three accredited DSDM training courses.

- **DSDM Aware** – this single day overview of DSDM is designed to provide a good grounding in the basics of DSDM – the principles, the process, the people and the products. It is aimed at those needing a high level of understanding, such as IT strategy decision-makers, quality managers and auditors, business people, production and support staff. Attendance on the Aware course is generally chosen by project managers and team leaders to provide the pre-requisite DSDM knowledge for attending the Managing DSDM Projects course .
- **DSDM Practitioner** – this highly practical 3-day course is designed to give DSDM team members knowledge and practical experience to enable them to take an active role as part of a DSDM team. There are no pre-requisites for this course.
- **Managing DSDM Projects** – Designed for Project Managers and Team Leaders, this highly practical 2-day course focuses on the differences between managing a traditional project and planning and managing a DSDM project. Knowledge of project management and an awareness of DSDM are pre-requisites for this course.

All accredited DSDM courses are delivered by accredited DSDM trainers, who must have in-depth practical experience as a DSDM Practitioner, as well as the skills of a trainer.

8.2 Personal DSDM Accreditation

DSDM offers personal accreditation in DSDM.

DSDM Practitioner

- to become an accredited DSDM Practitioner, applicants require:-

- a minimum of 2 years system development experience, to include a minimum of 6 months DSDM/RAD experience
- proof of attendance on DSDM Practitioner course or proof of attendance on DSDM Aware + Managing DSDM Projects courses – (total of 3 days accredited training)

Applicants write a project synopsis (minimum 2000 words) to demonstrate a thorough understanding of DSDM, and relate the theoretical knowledge back to practical project experience. If the project synopsis reaches the required standard, the candidate is invited for an oral examination. On successful completion of the oral examination, the DSDM Practitioner accreditation is awarded to the candidate.

For holders of the DSDM Practitioner certificate, further personal accreditation is available.

DSDM Project Manager – demonstrating detailed knowledge, understanding and practical application of DSDM from a project manager's perspective. (An alternative route is available for very experienced project managers who do not already hold the DSDM Practitioner certificate).

DSDM Trainer – Building on the knowledge already demonstrated at DSDM Practitioner level, a DSDM Trainer must demonstrate a very detailed knowledge and practical application of DSDM, together with the ability to put the method across in a training environment and to clarify misunderstandings and misconceptions.

DSDM Consultant – This is the highest level of DSDM accreditation. Applicants must have 5 years in-depth consultancy experience, with at least 2 years DSDM consultancy, and must demonstrate very detailed knowledge of all aspects of DSDM, both the method and the White Papers.

9 Conclusion

In this short article, I have tried to give readers an outline understanding of DSDM and to show how DSDM is setting the standard for RAD developments. For many organisations, DSDM offers the only choice to ensure quality systems can be delivered in the rapid timescales of 21st century business. I hope that readers have found enough of interest in the article to generate an enthusiasm to find out more about DSDM and to look for answers to the more in-depth questions relating to your own organisations. We have built up much information, knowledge and practical experience on DSDM in the last six years, and all the time the knowledge and experience base is growing.

10   Further Information on DSDM

For further information about DSDM, or to request an information pack, contact The Dynamic Systems Development Method Consortium at :-

Invicta Business Centre
Monument Way
Orbital Park
Ashford
Kent
TN24 0HB
United Kingdom
Telephone: +44 (0)1233 501300
e mail: secretariat@dsdm.org

Web address: www.dsdm.org

Further information is available in DSDM – The Method in Practice. This guide offers practical guidelines, examples, anecdotes and case studies for DSDM.

DSDM & TickIt offers guidance for customers, suppliers and auditors to assist users of DSDM to meet the quality requirements of ISO 9001.

If you would like to know more about business technology services company, F.I.GROUP, contact their website at www.figroup.co.uk

To contact F.I Group regarding DSDM or talk to one of FI's DSDM Consultants, please e-mail dsdmpractice@figroup.co.uk

11   References

Stapleton DSDM – The Method in Practice by Jennifer Stapleton Published by Addison-Wesley, ISBN 0-201-17889-3

BSI The Dynamic System Development Method & TickIt Published by BSI, ISBN 0-580-27081-5

A Practical Approach to Continuous Improvement in Software Engineering

Andreas Birk and Dieter Rombach
Fraunhofer Institute for Experimental Software Engineering IESE (Germany)

Abstract: The software industry is undergoing dramatic changes that require the continuous evolution and improvement of the applied software engineering practices. Improvement initiatives must be driven by explicitly stated goals. They require specific management functions and an appropriate support infrastructure. Improvement processes must be tailored to the specific goals and characteristics of the given software organization. They should include methods for the stabilization of work practices, for gaining intellectual control over software development, and for sharing and reusing relevant knowledge and experience. Software organizations must also learn continuously about their improvement practices in order to further develop their improvement capabilities. This paper presents the principles and building blocks that are needed to establish continuous improvement in software organizations. The presented improvement approach is based on extensive experience from many industrial improvement programs.

Keywords: Software process improvement, software quality, improvement management, knowledge management, learning software organization.

1 Introduction

The software industry is highly dynamic: The degree of software based functionality in today's products is growing dramatically, and existing solutions must be integrated into more and more complex systems. An increasing number of businesses operate under very high cost pressure, and product cycle times become shorter and shorter. In addition, technology is progressing very fast, requiring a constant development of the technical staffs' competence and qualification.

In order to manage these requirements, the software industry must continuously evolve and improve its software development practices. This is a particularly challenging task, because unlike other engineering disciplines software engineering has not yet established an accepted body of standard development practices. For this reason, every individual software organization must develop its own practices of continuous self-improvement and establish an appropriate improvement infra-structure.

This article describes the principles and building blocks of continuous improvement in software engineering. The presented approach is based on extensive experience from industrial improvement programs.

2 Principles of Continuous Improvement

Improvement programs do typically deploy only one or few of the many available improvement methods (e.g., process assessment, measurement, or introduction of quality management system). They often lack explicitly stated goals that are communicated clearly throughout the organization. In addition, the personnel responsible for improvement is sometimes not integrated well with the project organization and is not very visible for the management.

Effective improvement programs that eventually become established as a continuous improvement initiative should learn from these issues. They should implement a set of important principles, which is listed in the following. They are derived from the experience of many improvement programs at industrial software companies, which the authors could participate or were able to observe:

- Improvement must be goal-oriented.
- Improvement requires specialized management functions.
- Improvement must be guided by systematic processes.
- Improvement processes must be built of three key practices:
    - Stabilization of work practices
    - Intellectual control over development practices
    - Sharing and reuse of knowledge and experience
- Improvement processes must be tailored to the specific goals and characteristics of a software organization.
- Organizational infrastructures for continuous improvement must be established.
- Each company as well as the software engineering community must accumulate and share its knowledge about improvement strategies.

The following sections describe how these principles can be implemented with the help of established software engineering techniques.

3 Goal-Oriented Improvement

The most important concepts of improvement programs are the improvement goals. They trigger the improvement program, guide its planning and execution, and determine whether the improvement program has been successful or not. A well-balanced system of long-term and short-term goals keeps continuous improvement focused and maintains its momentum.

Improvement goals can refer to aspects of the developed software products (e.g., reliability or maintainability), the software process (e.g., time to market or flexibility), or the software engineering workforce (e.g., qualification or motivation). They should be defined clearly and communicated throughout the relevant parts of the organization. It should be possible to derive measurable or observable indicators in order to assess and control goal attainment.

It is important that not too many improvement goals are addressed at one point in time in order to keep the improvement program focused. It should also be possible to attain the goals within about one year. If an important improvement goal requires more time to be attained, it should be broken down into a set of goals that can be addressed in subsequent iteration cycles of a continuous improvement initiative.

4 Improvement Management

The continuous maintenance of improvement initiatives in a software organization requires that a specialized management function for improvement is established. It must be supported by an improvement team that performs the technical tasks of the improvement programs. Improvement management and team need not to be full-time positions. But they must be clearly visible organizational instances. In smaller improvement programs, both kinds of tasks can be performed by the same person.

Figure 1 depicts the structure of a systematic improvement program that distinguishes improvement management from the technical tasks. Improvement management consists of three phases: (1) Improvement planning, (2) improvement program execution and control, and (3) Improvement evaluation. The technical improvement activities are part of an improvement process, which is tailored to the specific goals and needs of the software organization. Each phase is described further below.

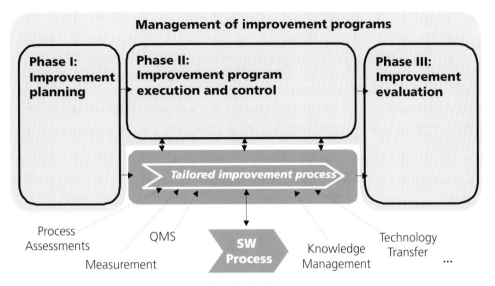

Figure 1: The relations between managerial and technical tasks in improvement programs.

The tailored improvement process applies a set of improvement methods for attaining the goals of the improvement program. Well-known examples of improvement methods are process assessments, measurement, and technology transfer. The following section will address the technical aspects of improvement programs in more detail.

4.1 Improvement Planning

Improvement planning is the first and possibly most important step of an improvement program. It identifies improvement actions based on three types of input information: (1) Explicitly defined improvement goals, (2) an analysis of the given situation (i.e., characteristics of the software project, the software organization, and their environment), as well as (3) experience and technological knowledge about what improvement actions are suited best to attain the improvement goals in the given situation. In order to gain the required input information for improvement planning, appropriate improvement methods (e.g., process assessments, measurement, knowledge management etc.) must be selected and integrated into a tailored improvement process.

From the viewpoint of improvement management, another important task of improvement planning is the definition of checkpoints and measurement procedures for the improvement program. They provide the information needed for controlling the improvement program and for evaluating later whether it has successfully attained the improvement goals. An approach for the continuous measurement of improvement programs has been presented in [7].

4.2 Improvement Program Execution and Control

Improvement program execution and control applies the developed improvement process to one or more software projects. It is executed according to the previously planned process. In charge of the improvement program execution is the technical staff of the improvement team or external coaches or consultants. Depending on the selected improvement methods, they can act as process assessors, measurement engineers, technology transfer experts, etc.

The monitoring and control of the improvement program are under the responsibility of the improvement program manager. Monitoring is performed according to the planned measurement and assessment procedures. The measurement and assessment results are compared to the predefined target profile. If the actual data deviates from the target, the improvement program manager, together with the team, decide about possibly required corrective actions. If needed, the improvement process must be redefined. Possibly, new commitment must be gained from the sponsor of the improvement program. The measurement and assessment results as well as all major decisions about the execution of the improvement program should be documented and stored for the later evaluation.

4.3 Improvement Evaluation

The improvement evaluation phase evaluates the success of the improvement program and identifies lessons learnt for future improvement programs. This can trigger a new iteration cycle of the improvement program for which new goals are set, or the improvement program is extended to other parts of the organization.

Experience gained from the evaluation should be packaged and disseminated so that the entire organization and future improvement programs can benefit from it.

5 Technical Improvement Activities

For implementing effective improvement processes, a software organization does usually need to establish appropriate improvement methods for three different key tasks (or *base practices*) of systematic improvement:

- Stabilization of work practices (e.g., through defined process models and software development standards)
- Intellectual control of software development
- Sharing and reuse of relevant knowledge and experience

These base practices are the core building blocks of systematic improvement programs. That is, every software organization that wants to establish systematic improvement needs to implement these practices in a manner that meets the specific needs and characteristics of the organization. It can thus move beyond the limits of traditional improvement methodologies, which usually pay little attention to customization and are often grouped around one improvement paradigm only.

For instance, improvement methodologies that are only based on process assessment can easily distract an organization from the timely establishment of a focused measurement program. At the other hand, a fixation on measurement can delay the development of possibly needed quality management practices.

The three base practices proposed in the following are independent of specific improvement approaches. They provide a baseline for guiding improvement planning in a way that is well customized to the specific needs and characteristics of a given software organization.

5.1 Stabilization of work practices

An important prerequisite for the manageability and efficiency of quality software development is that the applied work practices achieve a minimum level of stability. Different actors within a software project should agree upon their common way of how to conduct their software engineering tasks. This implies that they follow virtually the same processes and procedures. They also should agree about the content and form of the involved documents and artifacts.

Congruent and stable (i.e., repeatable) work practices are important for enabling the smooth collaboration and interaction of agents. A common understanding of work practices throughout a project team does also help to change task assignments flexibly. In addition, it accelerates the integration of new team members.

Appropriate means for developing stable work practices are the definition of standard development processes and document standards for important workproducts and artifacts (cf. [11] [19]).

5.2 Intellectual control over software development

While the stabilization of work practices aims at ensuring the proper fulfillment of technical tasks, the managerial aspects of software development and improvement are addressed in the base practice *gain intellectual control over software development*.

This base practice includes four core tasks: Monitoring, control, estimation, and simulation. Monitoring provides the baseline information needed for developing an understanding of the course of a software project. It is a prerequisite for taking the right control actions. Estimation supports the planning of a software project. It also allows for the definition of target values and checkpoints against which the monitoring data can be compared and possible control actions can be triggered. Simulation is a means for developing and verifying estimations as well as for anticipating the effects of planned improvement actions.

An important method for implementing this base practice is goal-oriented measurement. The two most well-known approaches are Goal/Question/Metric (GQM) [3] [8] [14] [20] and Practical Software Measurement (PSM) [12].

5.3 Sharing and reuse of knowledge and experience

Most software development work consists of intellectual tasks that are to be performed by human actors. The base practice *share and reuse knowledge and experience* aims at establishing and maintaining the qualification of the software engineering workforce.

The knowledge to be shared includes the following dimensions:

- Basic knowledge needed for applying the required software engineering technologies (e.g., programming languages, design and test methods, CASE and configuration management tools)
- Knowledge about the business and application domain
- Knowledge about the product to be developed and user requirements
- Knowledge about the goals, risks, and status of the software project
- Experience (or know-how) of how to conduct the various work practices in an effective form (e.g., lessons learnt, experience-based guidelines)

There are various different means for sharing and reusing knowledge and experience. They can be purely human-based, or they can deploy latest communication and archiving technology. Examples of such knowledge instruments are:

- Training and education of the workforce
- Knowledge repositories and lessons learnt databases
- Newsgroups and intranet-based discussion forums
- Yellow pages and competence databases
- Project evaluation and discussion meetings
- Conferences and symposia
- Nomination of information brokers
- Integrated and customized knowledge management tool environments

This collection of knowledge management instruments shows that there is a wide spectrum of possibilities for establishing this base practice. These knowledge management instruments can include the use of specific software tools, but they do not necessarily need so. Although tools can facilitate knowledge management and organizational learning considerably, they never can be effective without appropriate underlying methodological concepts.

5.4 Tailored Improvement Processes

A common improvement strategy is to start an improvement with a process assessment. The resulting process capability profiles, together with the previously defined improvement goals, assist in the identification of improvement actions. A goal-oriented measurement program can then be established to support the implementation and fine-tuning of the improvement actions (e.g., changes to the development process). The next improvement cycle starts by a focused re-assessment, which may uncover new areas for improvement. In parallel, gained experience is accumulated in an experience repository and disseminated throughout the organization. This improvement strategy is defined in the PROFES improvement methodology [18]. Similar approaches are the Quality Improvement Paradigm (QIP) / Experience Factory (EF) [2] and the IDEAL cycle [15].

Another improvement strategy builds on a combination of process modeling with software measurement (cf. [9]). For small or medium-sized organizations, it can be most appropriate to conduct first a short, *light-weight* product or process assessment. The selected process change should then be introduced to the development team in a brief workshop. Its implementation should be supported by training-on-the-job measures.

The systematic improvement planning and management described above takes care that an appropriate and well-tailored improvement process is designed, which fits the specific goals and characteristics of a given software organization.

6 The Infrastructure for Improvement

The successful execution of an improvement program requires an appropriate organizational infrastructure, which ensures that all tasks are conducted in an effective and efficient manner. The typical organizational infrastructure of a systematic improvement program is shown in Figure 2. The improvement program team establishes a bridge between the sponsors of an improvement program (often higher-level management) and the software engineering staff of the projects in which the improvement program is performed. This team consist of a co-ordinator (or *improvement manager*), technical staff for performing the relevant improvement techniques (e.g., process assessors, measurement engineers, trainers, QMS experts), and measurement engineer responsible for (meta-)measurement about the improvement program.

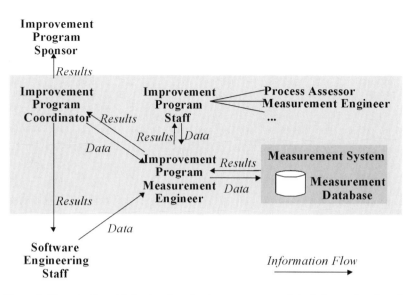

Figure 2: Organizational infrastructure for improvement and the information flow for improvement monitoring and control.

The organizational infrastructure should be complemented with an appropriate tool infrastructure. The core element of the tool infrastructure is the measurement database for data about the improvement process, which can be a database or spreadsheet application. This database is an important tool for monitoring and controlling the improvement program. In addition, tools are needed for data collection (e.g., paper forms or on-line questionnaires), for data analysis (again, database or spreadsheet applications), for data presentation, and for the storage of measurement results (e.g., a document database or a web-based repository).

7 Organizational Learning about Improvement

A software organization must continuously develop its improvement capabilities. In order to facilitate and support this, it should establish appropriate means for organizational learning about improvement methods and management. The two fundamental strategies for implementing organizational learning are communication and documentation. A communication-based technique are project post-mortem reviews or workshops (cf. [10] [1]). The various documentation-based techniques deploy some kind of repository or experience base that stores improvement-related knowledge and experience (cf. [2]). The two strategies should be combined to be most effective.

For fostering the experience exchange on software engineering and improvement topics, the Software Experience Center (SEC™) has been founded in 1999. It is a consortium of, at date, five industrial companies from Europe and the US, which is moderated by Fraunhofer IESE and the Fraunhofer-Center Maryland. The international set-up is expected to create insight into software engineering and improvement issues across different cultural environments. Collection and dissemination of experience will be performed mainly by the means of workshops, reports, and an experience base, so that the SEC members can directly utilize the gained experience in their own organizations.

Two repositories about improvement-related knowledge and experience have been developed by the European applied research and technology transfer project PROFES[1] [18]. The first repository collects information about the effects and application prerequisites of software engineering technology [6] [16]. This information can be used to support the goal-driven selection of improvement actions during improvement planning. The second repository contains effort models of improvement methods (e.g., process assessments and GQM measurement) [17]. Both repositories can be accessed through the internet.

8 Summary

A practical approach for continuous improvement in software engineering has been presented. Its main principles and building blocks are the focus on explicitly defined improvement goals, the establishment of specific management functions for improvement and an associated support infrastructure, as well as tailored improvement processes that fit the goals and characteristics of the given software organization. A software organization should also establish some form of organizational learning about its improvement practices in order to develop further its improvement capabilities.

The effectiveness of the presented approach has been demonstrated in many improvement programs at different industrial software companies. Its basic principles have been developed and applied at the NASA Software Engineering Laboratory [4]. Other examples are the product quality driven improvement programs conducted at Dräger Medical Electronics, Ericsson Finland, and Tokheim in the PROFES project [18], the experiences at Allianz, Alstom Energietechnik, DaimlerChrysler, and Siemens from the SoftQuali project [13], as well as the improvement program at Siemens Health Services [5]. The presented principles have made the companies attain their improvement goals fast and with little overhead effort. They also have increased further the understanding of their software development practices and capitalized on the gained experience.

---

[1] ESPRIT Project No. 23236, PROFES, has been supported by the CEC. The project results can be accessed at the web site www.profes.org.

9 List of References

[1] K.-D. Althoff and W. Müller. Proceedings of the 2nd Workshop on Learning Software Organizations. Fraunhofer IESE, Kaiserslautern, Germany. (http://www.iese.fhg.de/LSOworkshop2000)

[2] V.R. Basili, G. Caldiera, and H.D. Rombach. Experience Factory. In J.J. Marciniak, ed., Encycl. of SE, vol. 1, pp. 469–476. John Wiley & Sons, 1994.

[3] V.R. Basili, G. Caldiera, and H.D. Rombach. Goal Question Metric Paradigm. In J.J. Marciniak, ed., Encycl. of SE, vol. 1, pp. 528–532. John Wiley & Sons, 1994.

[4] V.R. Basili, M. Zelkowitz, F. McGarry, J. Page, S. Waligora, and R. Pajerski. SEL's SW process-improvement program. IEEE SW, 12(6):83–87, Nov. 1995.

[5] H. Biedermann, A. Birk, G. Chrobok-Diening, B. Nothelfer-Kolb, M. Ochs, D. Pfahl. Kontinuierliche Prozessverbesserung (in German). Presentation session at the 5th Congress "Software Quality Management" (SQM'2000), SQS Gesellschaft für Qualitätssicherung mbH, Cologne, 2000.

[6] A. Birk. A knowledge management infrastructure for systematic improvement in software engineering. Doctoral dissertation, University of Kaiserslautern, Kaiserslautern, Germany, 2000. (to appear)

[7] A. Birk, D. Hamann, and S. Hartkopf. A framework for the continuous monitoring and evaluation of improvement programmes. In: F. Bomarius, M. Oivo, Proceedings of the Second International Conference on Product-Focused Software Process Improvement (PROFES2000), Lecture Notes in Computer Science, Springer, Berlin, 2000.

[8] L.C. Briand, Ch. Differding, H.D. Rombach. Practical Guidelines for Measurement-Based Process Improvement. Software Process Improvement and Practice 2 (4), pp. 253–280, 1996.

[9] A. Bröckers, Ch. Differding, and G. Threin. The role of software process modeling in planning industrial measurement programs. In Proc. of the 3rd Int. SW Metrics Symp., Berlin, March 1996. IEEE CS Press.

[10] B. Collier, T. DeMarco, and P. Fearey. A defined process for project postmortem review. IEEE Software, July 1996, pp. 65–72.

[11] B. Curtis, M. Kellner, and J. Over. Process modelling. Communications of the ACM, Vol. 35, No. 9, Sept. 1992.

[12] W.A. Florac, R.E. Park, and A.D. Carleton. Practical software measurement: Measuring for process management and improvement. Technical Report CMU/SEI-97-HB-003, SEI, Carnegie Mellon University, April 1997.

[13] H. Kempter, J. Kuntermann, H. Neumeyer, M. Rheindt, F. Sazama, and D. Surmann. Systematische Qualitätsverbesserung durch Software-Inspektionen und Organisation von Erfahrungswissen (in German). Presentation session at the 4th Congress "Software Quality Management" (SQM'99), SQS Gesellschaft für Qualitätssicherung mbH, Cologne, 1999.

[14] F. van Latum, R. van Solingen, M. Oivo, B. Hoisl, D. Rombach, and G. Ruhe. Adopting GQM-based measurement in an industrial environment. IEEE Software, 15(1):78–86, 1998.

[15] B. McFeeley. IDEAL: A user's guide for software process improvement. Technical Report CMU/SEI-96-HB-001, SEI, Carnegie Mellon University, 1996.

[16] The PROFES Consortium. The PROFES Repository of Product/Process Dependency (PPD). http://www.iese.fhg.de/profes/PPDRepository.

[17] The PROFES Consortium. The PROFES Cost/Benefit Repository. http://www.iese.fhg.de/profes/CBRepository

[18] The PROFES Consortium. PROFES User Manual. Fraunhofer IRB Verlag, Stuttgart, Germany 2000.

[19] D. Rombach, and M. Verlage. Directions in software process research. In M. Zelkowitz (ed.): Advances in Computers, Vol. 41, Academic Press, pp. 1–63, 1995.

[20] R. van Solingen, E. Berghout, The G/Q/M Method. McGraw-Hill. London, 1999.

Taking the Temperature on Danish Software Quality

JAN PRIES-HEJE & ANNE METTE JONASSEN HASS AND JØRN JOHANSEN
Georgia State University, Atlanta (USA) & DELTA, Danish Electronics,
Light & Acoustics, Hørsholm (Denmark)

Abstract: The question is: Can an ISO 9001 certificate lead to software improvement? The answer is: yes – based on 50 BOOTSTRAP maturity assessments carried out in Danish companies.

One conclusions is that there is a clear correlation between the maturity in software development process and the holding of an ISO 9001 certificate. It is not only the quality system and the software quality management that is influenced by an ISO 9001 certification: but other software processes such as e.g. projects management. In other words there is a spin-of effect from an ISO 9001 certification leading to software process improvement in other, not closely related areas.

This paper also concludes, that maturity is correlated with the size of the company. Finally it shows which recommendations are the often given as a result of an BOOTSTRAP assessment – where are the main problems?

Keywords: Software, Process, Improvement, Quality, ISO 9001

1 Introduction

Quality is a term often used – and misused. Everyone is for it, everyone feels they understand it, and everyone feels that all problems are caused by other people (Crosby, 1980). Three different way of looking and talking about quality have appeared over the last 20 years. One school of thought focus on fulfilment of customer expectations, thus quality is the degree of fulfilled expectations. Another way of thinking focus on measurable product attributes. I.e. Crosby (1980) defined quality as conformance to requirements. And the third way of looking at quality believes that a good development process will lead to quality.

Within the world of software development the issue of improving quality took two directions around 1990. In Europe software-developing companies took the ISO 9000 standard and adapted it to be used in a software world. In this adaptation companies could use the ISO 9000-3 on how to use the ISO 9001 standard for software. In USA software-developing companies at the same time took the Capability Maturity Model (CMM) in use. CMM is a model characterising a path for software process improvement with five levels, each describing key practices and a number of goals. I.e. to get from level 1 to level 2 an organisation has to achieve the goals for six software processes, the so-called key process areas: Requirements Management, Software Project Planning, Project Tracking and Oversight, Subcontractor Management, Configuration and Change Management, and Software Quality Assurance. The levels chosen were inspired from a framework developed by Phil Crosby (1980), and the general improvement idea build into the model came from work by Juran and Gryna (1988) and Deming (1982). An organisation has to meet the goals at one level to reach the next.

In Europe a methodology called BOOTSTRAP (Kuvaja et al., 1994) combined the features of both ISO 9000 and the CMM. Furthermore the BOOTSTRAP model was extended and adapted to include guidelines European Space Agency (ESA)'s PSS-05 software development standard. In figure 1 the processes included in the BOOTSTRAP model is shown. Each bullet is a process that can be assessed using the model. If you compare BOOTSTRAP with the original CMM the major differences are found in the boxes called Organisation, Technology and Life-cycle functions.

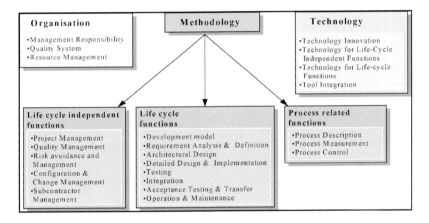

Figure 1: The Bootstrap model version 2.3

The BOOTSTRAP model can be used to assess software-developing companies and projects and recommend improvements. As such BOOTSTRAP has been used in Denmark to assess 50 organisations between April 1996 and October 2000[1]. This chapter reports some of the aggregated results and discuss whether an ISO 9001 certification leads to software process improvement?

The chapter first contains an introduction to capability maturity models and to the details in the BOOTSTRAP model and a short description of how an assessment is carried out. Next findings from the fifty BOOTSTRAP assessments carried out in Denmark until October 2000 is presented.

---

[1] All the assessments reported were based on the use of BOOTSTRAP version 2.3.In the future more and more companies will be using an updated version 3 of BOOTSTRAP that are SPICE (ISO 15504) compatible.

2 The BOOTSTRAP Methodology

When you use the BOOTSTRAP methodology the maturity level for the organisation is determined on a five level scale equal to the scale used by the CMM model. Level one corresponds to the lowest level of maturity and level five to the highest. The BOOTSTRAP scale, however, includes quartiles on each level, made possible by a differentiated answering scheme.

A BOOTSTRAP assessment may be carried out in any software-developing organisation according to the BOOTSTRAP methodology. The assessment week is where the assessment team, consisting of at least 2 licensed assessors, spend 3 – 4 days interviewing in the organisation undergoing the assessment. The actual length of the assessment week depends on the number of projects to be assessed. The typical number is 4 projects, but it may be more or less depending on the nature of the projects the organisation usually undertakes.

The purpose of the pre-meeting is to brief the assessors on the organisation. The purpose of the opening meeting is to give a general introduction to the BOOTSTRAP model and method, in order for all participants in the assessments to have the same starting point.

The actual detailed assessments are based on two questionnaires, one for the SPU (Software Producing Unit – equal with the management of the organisation) as a whole and one for the projects. The questionnaires have two parts, one for general information and one covering the BOOTSTRAP model. The latter part contains about 200 detailed questions. The assessors use the questionnaires as an interview guide for qualitative interviews, and partly as a tool for scoring the results of the assessment.

At the final meeting the preliminary results of the assessment are presented. These results are subsequently further analysed and a final report is produced

The BOOTSTRAP methodology includes an algorithm used for generation of detailed maturity profiles from the completed questionnaires in an objective and valid manner. The maturity profiles show the maturity level for each of the defined development areas in the BOOTSTRAP model individually. From these maturity profiles, absolute strengths and weaknesses for the SPU and for specific projects or all projects as a whole may be derived. From combined maturity profiles it is possible to derive strengths and weaknesses for the SPU relative to a specific project or all projects as a whole.

An analysis of all the maturity profiles and additional information gathered in the organisation during the assessment is performed and areas where improvement actions will be of greater benefit for the organisation are derived. The assessment report contains a top 5 list of improvement areas and a preliminary plan for implementing improvements in these areas in the organisation.

3 BOOTSTRAP Deliverables

At the final meeting the preliminary results of the assessment are presented. These results are subsequently further analysed and a final report is produced by the external assessors. The final report includes:

- maturity profiles in general, for the SPU and for the projects assessed
- analysis of strengths and weaknesses of the organisation in general
- identified key areas for improvement
- suggestions for specific improvement actions

The BOOTSTRAP methodology includes an algorithm used for generation of detailed maturity profiles from the completed questionnaires in an objective and valid manner. A tool is provided to support the calculation of the results, both for the SPU, and for each project or for an average of the findings for all the projects. A detailed explanation of the algorithm used in calculating maturity levels can be found in Kuvaja et al. (1994: 81ff)

The maturity profiles show the maturity level for each of the defined development areas in the BOOTSTRAP model individually. A corresponding profile for the lower level development areas (the three boxes under Methodology in figure 1) is also produced. An example of a maturity profile is shown in figure 2. For the purpose of clarity of this presentation only three projects called P1, P2 and P3 are shown. Normally four or five projects are assessed in an organisation.

If you look at figure 2 you may wonder why there is no results shown for Subcontractor Management. However, that is not the case. In fact what is shown is that in all three projects Subcontractor management was considered "not applicable" – The projects had no subcontractors.

From the maturity profiles, absolute strengths and weaknesses for the SPU and for specific projects or all projects as a whole may be derived. E.g. in figure 2 Development Cycle Model and Acceptance testing and Transfer seems to relative strengths. And (low-level) Testing and Integration (testing) seems to be relative weak.

From the combined maturity profiles it is possible to derive strengths and weaknesses for the SPU relative to a specific project or all projects as a whole. A capability profile may also be presented relative to a mean score profile calculated from relevant data extracted from the BOOTSTRAP Institutes European database. Or said in another way, an organisation can use the European BOOTSTRAP database for benchmarking.

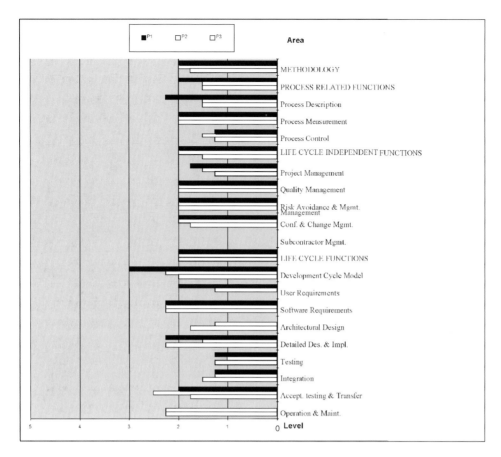

Figure 2: Example of how a maturity profile may look for three projects.

An analysis of all the maturity profiles and additional information gathered about the organisation during the assessment is performed and an analysis matrix produced. This shows selected software development areas sorted according to how well the organisation masters them and how important they are considered to be for the organisation. An example of such an analysis matrix is shown in Table 1.

Table 1: The Analysis Matrix combining measured level with importance for company

Importance for company	Current Status of Point			
	Excellent	Good	Fair	Weak
Crucial	• Development Cycle Model	• User Req. Specification • Configuration & Change Mgmt. • Detailed Design and Impl.	• Architectural Design • Acceptance testing and Transfer	• Project Management • Testing • Integration (testing)
High	• Software Requirements Specification	• Resource Management • Operation and maintenance	• Management Responsibility • Process measurement	• Quality Management • Process description
Medium		• Quality System	• Technology Innovation	• Risk Avoidance and Mgmt.
Low				• Process control

Areas where improvement actions will be of greater benefit for the organisation are derived from the analysis matrix by picking areas from the upper right corner working down towards the lower left corner. The assessment report will contain a top 5 list of improvement areas and a preliminary plan for implementing improvements in these areas in the organisation.

4 Findings from 50 Danish BOOSTRAP Assessments

In the period from April 1996 to October 2000 (4,5 year) DELTA carried out 50 assessments in Denmark. All the results are placed in anonymous form in a database of Danish assessments, and reported to the BOOSTRAP Institute maintaining a European database of assessment results. In this section we report and discuss the findings from the Danish assessments.

In Figure 3 the maturity distribution in the 50 Danish assessments is shown. The average maturity level in Denmark was 2.25 for the SPU and the projects. The highest maturity level found in Denmark was a SPU at 3,25 and a project at 3,75.

Another interesting observation in Figure 3 is that there seems to be a concentration of the population around level 2,00 for projects and 2,25 for the SPU. In short we refer to these two concentrations in the maturity distribution as "the peak". Our hypothesis was that this "peak" could be caused by the difficulty of changing improvement mechanism at level 2. I.e. up to level 2 the organisation focus on improving the individual project, but to get from level 2 to level 3 you need to have some organisational-wide standards in place.

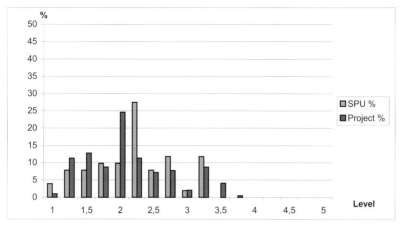

Figure 3: The maturity distribution in 50 Danish assessments

5 Maturity and the Size of the Organisation

In Figure 4 we have taken the maturity level and compared it with the total number of employees (not software developers alone) in the organisation. The line showed in figure 4 is calculated using the least square fit algorithm on the 50 data points from the organisations. The maturity level for an organisation is calculated as the SPU maturity level plus the average project maturity level for that organisation divided by two.

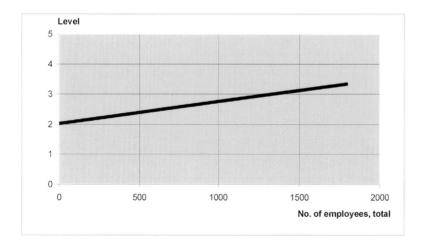

Figure 4: Comparison between maturity levels and number of employees in total

The conclusion that can be drawn from Figure 4 is that there is a positive correlation between size and maturity. We believe the reason could be that when a company grows more bureaucracy, structure, and discipline is needed anyway. Another reason could be that larger companies have more money to use for software process improvement. Finally it has not yet been successfully documented – as far as we know – that very small companies, e.g. companies with less than 10 software developers, can benefit significantly from CMM or BOOTSTRAP based software process improvements.

6 The Influence of an ISO 9001 Certification

One organisational-wide standard that could be used to test this hypothesis is ISO 9000. A number of the companies assessed had gone through an ISO 9000 certification before being assessed. And a number had not. We therefore divided the data into two groups. In Figure 5 the maturity distribution for organisations without an ISO 9001 certification is given. And in Figure 6 the maturity distribution for organisations with an ISO 9001 certification is given.

As can be seen in figure 6 the "peak" has disappeared for organisations without an ISO 9001 certification. More or less the maturity is evenly distributed between level 1 and 2 with a few reaching level 2,25. Overall the average maturity for non-ISO projects is 1,5 and for the non-ISO SPU the average is 1,75.

The opposite observation can be made for companies that had an ISO 9001 certification before they were BOOTSTRAP assessed. The "peak" is preserved with close to 40% of all projects and SPU at either level 2,0 or level 2,25. Very few companies are below level 2, and quite a widespread distribution of projects and SPUs from 2,25 and up to 3,75.

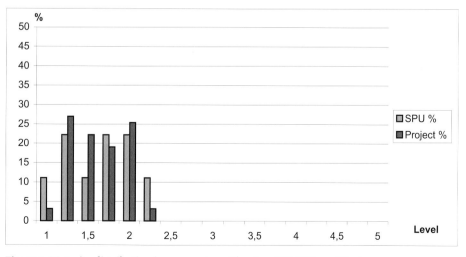

Figure 5: Maturity distribution in companies without an ISO 9001 certificate

Another interesting observation is that in organisations *with* an ISO 9001 certificate the average project is at the same level as the average SPU (2,5), but in organisations *without* an ISO 9001 certification the average SPU level is 0,25 higher (1,75) than the average project maturity level (1,5). An interpretation of this could be that in companies with an ISO 9001 certification management has a better understanding of what the status of software development in fact is.

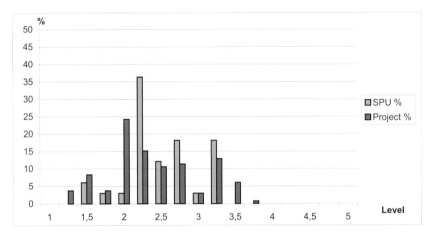

Figure 6: Maturity distribution in companies with an ISO 9001 certificate

One interpretation of the data is that an ISO 9001 certification nearly ensures that you are at level 2, meaning that you have all the basic things in place in the projects, and can begin working with and improving organisation-wide standards for developing software. But nothing in ISO 9001 helps you move beyond level 2[2]. Whether you do that or not depends on other things.

In the section below we carry out a more detailed analysis of ISO versus non-ISO organisations.

7 Looking at the Software Processes in detail

In figure 1 you could see that the BOOTSTRAP model divided software processes into three categories called: Organisation, Methodology, and Technology. In figure 7 we have detailed our maturity level measurements for each individual software process within the two first categories. The white bars represent the SPU measurements; the black bars represent the projects. The bars represent the average of the profiles for the

---

[2] This may change with the updated ISO 9001:2000 standard. However, all the companies analyzed in this context were certified using the "old" ISO 9001: 1994 standard.

companies without an ISO 9001 certificate. The added "Line-bars" represent the average for the ISO certified companies.

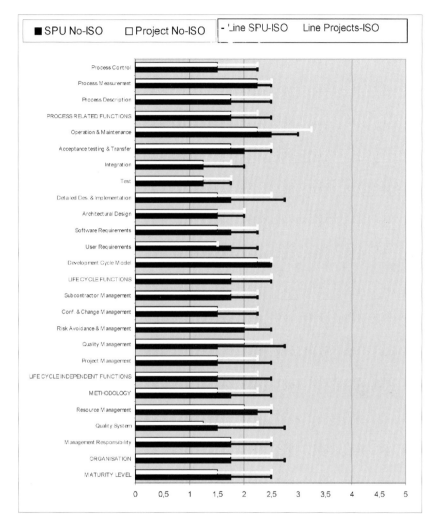

Figure 7: Comparison of detailed assessments of processes for organisations with and without an ISO 9001 certification

When analysing the data shown in Figure 7 we found seven software process areas of the 20 detailed areas with large differences between companies with and without an ISO 9001 certificate, and we found six with a small difference. In Table 2 the differences are one level or more, which seems to be a very significant difference. In Table 3 the differences are ¾ of a level, which is either significant or nearly significant.

Table 2: Process areas with large maturity differences between certified and uncertified companies

++)	Quality System
++)	Quality Management (only SPU)
+)	Project Management (only SPU)
+)	Detailed Design and Implementation
+)	Operations & Maintenance (only projects)

Table 3: Process areas with small maturity differences between certified and uncertified companies

++)	Management Responsibility
++)	Process Description
++)	Process Measurement
++)	Acceptance Testing and Transfer (only projects)
++)	Configuration & Change Management
++)	Integration testing (only SPU)
+)	Software Requirements
+)	Project Management (only projects)

In Table 2 and 3 "+)" indicates a low correlation between the ISO 9001 standard and the requirements in BOOTSTRAP, "++)" indicates a large correlation if not equality.

Since BOOTSTRAP is partly inspired from ISO 9001 it is not surprising that the process areas called Quality System and Quality Management are very different for certified and uncertified companies.

However, for some software process areas there are some surprises. Take for example Project Management. We have found a low correlation between the requirements in BOOTSTRAP for Project Management and the ISO 9001 standard. Nevertheless we find a huge difference between certified and uncertified companies in the Project Management area. We see this as a kind of spin-off effect, that is an effect you get in areas not covered by the ISO 9001 standards when you as an organisation go for an ISO 9001 certification.

The same picture, but with less strength due to the correlation, is seen for Detailed Design Implementation, Operations & Maintenance and Software Requirements.

In this context it is also important to notice that none of the organisations assessed have worked seriously with CMM or BOOTSTRAP or any other maturity model for software before going for an ISO 9001 certification.

As said above it is natural, that Quality System and Quality Management, and to some degree Acceptance Testing & Transfer and Process description are areas with large differences between certified uncertified organisations. By natural we mean that the areas are closely related to and inspired from the core parts of the ISO 9001 standards.

It is more surprising that we found the spin-off effect to Project Management and Management Responsibility. We believe Project Management is improved is because Quality systems are "sold" as a management tool strengthening time estimation and project control. The reason for the large improvement in Management responsibility is because the managers have to involve themselves strongly in order to implement a quality system in a company. And this strong involvement spins off to the area of Management Responsibility in general.

So to conclude we find that for all the five processes in Table 2 and 3 with a measurable difference and no direct correlation between BOOTSTRAP and ISO 9001 – categorised with one "+" – we see the spin off effect in action.

8 Further analysis of the recommended improvement areas

However, this is not the whole story. As said in the introduction we have given each of the 50 companies a top 5 or top 6 list of salient improvement areas. In Table 4 we have summed up all our recommendations – recommendations given to x% of the assessed companies.

It is worth noting that there is a difference between a weak area and a recommended improvement area. For example many organisations were measured to be quite weak in "Process Control" (as can be seen in Figure 7). However, Process Control is not a recommended improvement area in any of the non-certified organisations, and only a recommendation in one third of the ISO 9001 certified companies. The reason for this is that Process Control is a fairly advanced software process. The organisation has to be fairly mature (close to maturity level 3) to implement and achieve the benefits of process control as it is defined in the BOOTSTRAP methodology.

One of the most interesting observations to be made from Table 4 is that surprisingly many companies – 38 out of 50 – could benefit from an improvement of Project Management. It is also interesting, that 28 out of 50 companies need to look closer at Configuration and Change Management. So when we talk about these two weak areas we really mean weak throughout the Danish Software Industry.

Table 4: Recommended improvement areas in % of the assessed companies

Process	Mean %	Non ISO %	ISO %
Project Management	75	78	73
Conf. & Change Management	55	78	42
Test	51	39	58
Quality System	47	78	30
Development Cycle Model	39	67	24
User Requirements	37	33	40
Integration	35	39	33
Quality Management	33	50	24
Process Description	33	39	30
Process Measurement	27	0	42
Architectural Design	25	33	21
Management Responsibility	24	33	18
Software Requirements	24	6	33
Process Control	22	0	33
Detailed Des. & Implementation	22	33	15
Resource Management	10	6	12
Risk Avoidance & Management	8	6	9
Subcontractor Management	8	6	9
Acceptance testing & Transfer	2	5	0
Operation & Maintenance	0	0	0

9 Summary and Conclusion

Measured on a capability maturity scale from 1 (lowest) to 5 (highest) the average maturity level found in Denmark in the 50 assessments performed was 2.25 for the SPU, and 2,125 for the projects. The highest maturity level found in Denmark was an SPU at 3,25 and a project at 3,75.

First of all we found that the size of the company, as a whole, seems to have an effect on the maturity for software development; the bigger the company the higher the maturity level.

Another interesting observation was that there seems to be a "peak" in the concentration of the population between 2,0 and 2,25. We tried out several explanations of this distribution. One possible explanation we tried were whether the assessed organisation had an ISO 9001 certificate before the assessment. To test this hypothesis we divided the 50 assessments into two groups. One group of 32 organisations with an ISO 9001 certificate (also) covering software development. The other group of 18 organisations without an ISO 9001 certificate when the assessment was carried out.

The split into two groups made the "peak" disappear for the non-ISO group. Thus the "peak" around level 2 was found to be solely related to ISO-certified organisations.

Our interpretation of this is that an ISO 9001 certification nearly ensures that you are at level 2, meaning that you have all the basic things in place in the projects, and can begin working with and improving organisation-wide standards for developing software. But nothing in ISO 9001 helps you move beyond level 2. Whether you do that or not depends on other things.

When we looked closer at the data, we found that not only the quality system and software quality management was better in ISO 9001 certified organisations. A number of other software processes not directly addressed by the ISO 9001 standard were affected such as Project management, Detailed Design & Implementation, Operation & Maintenance, and Software Requirements. We concluded that there is a *spin-off effect* from an ISO 9001 certification leading to software process improvement in other not closely related areas.

We believe one reason is that management in company gain maturity when the organisation is preparing for and achieving an ISO 9001 certification. They realised how important and valuable their own commitment and engagement in software processes is thereby creating the ground for the spin-off effect.

Last but not least we summed up the recommended improvement areas from all the assessments, and found that more than 50% of all organisations could benefit from improving Project Management and Configuration & Change Management. Furthermore we found that non-ISO certified companies could benefit from improving their Quality System (78%), their Development Cycle Model (67%) and Quality Management in the projects (50%). Where as ISO-certified organisations could benefit from better low-level Testing (58%), better Process Measurement (42%), and better User Requirements Specification (40%).

10   References

Crosby 1980 Crosby, Philip B. (1980). *"Quality is Free: The art of making quality certain."* New York: Mentor, New American Library. ISBN 0-451-62585-4.

Deming 1982 Deming, Edwards W. (1982). *"Out of the Crisis."* Cambridge, MA: MIT Center for Advanced Engineering Study.

Humphrey 1989 Humphrey, Watts. S. (1989) *"Managing the Software Process"*. Addison-Wesley.

ISO 9001 : 1994 ISO 9001 : 1994. *"Quality Systems - Model for quality assurance in design, development, production, installation and servicing."* International Organization for Standardization.

ISO 9001 : 2000 ISO 9001 : 2000. International Organization for Standardization.

Juran and Gryna 1988 Juran, J.M and Frank M. Gryna (1988). *"Juran´s quality control handbook."* 4th Ed.. New York: McGraw-Hill.

Kuvaja et al. 1994 Kuvaja, Pasi, Jouni Similä, Lech Krzanik, Adriana Bicego, Samuli Saukkonen, Günter Koch (1994). *"Software Process Assessment & Improvement. The BOOTSTRAP Approach."* Blackwell Publishers.

Paulk et al. 1995 Paulk, Mark C., Charles Weber, Bill Curtis, and Mary Beth Chrissis (Principal Contributors and Editors) (1995). *"The Capability Maturity Model: Guidelines for Improving the Software Process."* Carnegie Mellon University, Software Engineering Institute. Addison-Wesley Publ. Company, Reading, Mass.

Test process assessments and improvement

Detlef Vohwinkel
SQS Software Quality Systems AG (Germany)

Abstract: In this paper the needs and benefits for an assessments to measure and improve the test process are discussed. The test process is one of the key process areas to improve the product quality. Therefor the understanding for the actual maturity of the test process and a directed process improvement is of paramount importance for companies. After the need for a specialised assessment is shown a assessment method based on the ISO 15504 compliant BOOTSTRAP method focussed on the test process is presented. The basics of the background model for the test process and the main steps for the improvement of the process will be presented afterwards.

Keywords: assessment, testing, test process improvement, assessment method, test process model

1 Introduction

The need to improve the process maturity to support efficient software engineering and high product quality is no longer neglected in our days. A standard assess the process maturity is defined by the ISO 15504 model, which defines a standard process model and points out the requirements to assess the process quality.

The BOOTSTRAP method as a compliant method to assess the process maturity developed by he BOOTSTRAP institute, which members are actively participating in the SPICE (Software Process Improvement and Capability dEtermination) project.

The process model, includes process which are dealing with the testing activities, but the focus of the model and the method is to assess and to improve the overall maturity of the software development. Therefor quality assurance is only a part of the model. The results of the standard assessments shows a leak in the capability of the test processes and this indicates the need for an focussed test assessment.

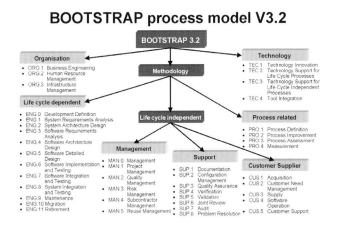

Figure 1: Standard process model in BOOTSTRAP Version 3.2

2 Why focussing on test processes ?

2.1 Goals of process improvement

One of the main goals of process improvement is to establish a efficient software development process. Criteria to measure the efficiency are for example the timeliness of product development, but also the observance of the defined quality goals. A lot of companies has started their process improvement by a certification to ISO 9000 series and by establishing a quality management that proofs their ability to produce software which fulfils the customers requirements, within stated time and resources.

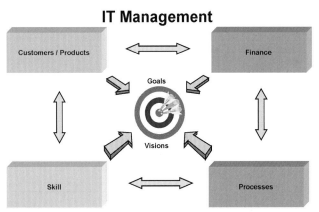

Figure 2: Goals for IT Management

To improve the ability to produce products to meet the quality requirements and the customer needs dealing with the organisation and performing quality relevant processes are of exceptional importance.

2.2 Experience with process deficiencies

When companies are starting with process improvements their focussing on the classic development processes. This means, when leaving level 1 in maturity, and starting with managing processes they are concentrating at the engineering processes and the management processes, especially the project management. One reason for this could be the availability of several documented standard models for software engineering, like the V-model. The project management and in some areas also the configuration management are well documented processes. All mentioned processes are in addition supported by a wide range of tools and besides the knowledge that a tool on its own can not solve the problems of a process their is always the attempt to start and implement process improvements by adopting a tool.

The V+V- model of QA

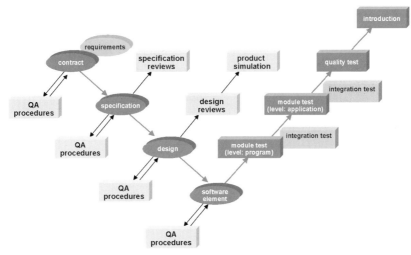

Figure 3: The VV-Model of QA

On the other hand there are the test processes and testing activities.

The processes to fulfil the requirements should be linked and integrated in the software development model:

The need for an detailed test process model and a focussed assessment method to evaluate the needs of the companies in the quality assurance processes is evident. To supply evidence for this need it can be shown as a result of the classic BOOTSTRAP assessments that a lot of companies are struggling with the maturity of their test processes. This is usually the case, when the companies are starting to develop their maturity from level 1.

3 The test process model

3.1 Need for test process model

The standard model for process assessment and improvement includes the main processes for the test processes. But as shown in the paragraphs before the details are insufficient for the definition and improvement. As a starting point for all process improvement activities a more detailed process model is needed.

When looking at the software engineering processes a lot of models are available. They are documented and distributed and their use and tailoring needs are widely known and discussed. The test process itself is often characterised by trial and error implementation from people who are mainly experienced in software engineering and not in the testing area. In addition the models are not well documented and available to the QA responsibles in the companies.

Based on the experiences of the problems known from the BOOTSTRAP assessments in many companies and the experience of more than 15 years in organising and performing test in a wide area of companies a standard test process model was defined by SQS and integrated in the standard assessment method of the BOOTSTRAP institute.

3.2 The test processes model

Like the overall model the process model for testing can be structured in different process clusters. The test cycle dependent (like lifecycle dependent, engineering processes), the organisational processes, the management processes and the support processes.

For each category the processes and the purpose of the processes will be presented in detail.

Test process cluster

Figure 4: The Test process model overview

3.2.1   Organisational processes

Test process definition

The purpose of the test process definition process is to establish the proceedings for a stable and repeatable test process and to document these in a way appropriate for re-use.

Human resource management

The purpose of the human resource management process is to provide the organisation and projects with individuals for testing who possess the skill and knowledge to perform their roles effectively.

Infrastructure management

The purpose of the infrastructure management process is to provide a stable and up-to-date environment with appropriate methods and tools for the software test and prvide the testing staff with an environment for work.

The processes of this cluster are dealing with the framework which allows to perform an efficient test.

3.2.2   Management processes

Test management

The purpose of the test management process is to define the necessary processes for co-ordinating and managing a test project and the appropriate resources for testing a software product.

Quality and test strategy

The purpose of the quality and test strategy process is to identify the appropriate strategy to ensure the quality of the products and services of a project to satisfy the customers needs.

Risk management

The purpose of the risk management process is to continuously identify and mitigate the project risks throughout the life cycle of the project. The process involves establishing a focus on management of risks at both the project and the organisational level.

   The processes of these cluster are dealing with the management of the test project with a focus on the appropriate organisation of the process and a permanent watch on potential risks.

3.2.3   Support processes

Test documentation

The purpose of the test documentation process is to establish a system for the documentation to assure the documentation of the test preparation and test protocols.

Configuration management

The purpose of the configuration management process is to provide a mechanism for identifying, controlling and tracking the versions of all work products of a test project or process (e.g. test documentation, test environment).

Error and Change management

The purpose of the error and change management process is to ensure that all deviations from the requirements are removed and all changes of the requirements are analysed and managed and trends are identified.

Joint reviews

The purpose of the joint reviews process is to maintain a common understanding with the customer of the progress against reaching the customers goals and what should be done to help to ensure the development of a product that satisfies the customer.

   The processes in this cluster are dealing with the supporting processes that provides techniques and infrastructure for an successful test project.

3.2.4   Operative test processes

To implement a well organised test process it is necessary to distinct between test activities in accordance to the test focus of each activity. As shown in figure 3 you can distinguish between the products of each engineering phase and therefor the tests can also be structured in accordance to these products. As a result the standard test process model contains 12 processes in these category:

Test of documentation

The purpose of test of documentation process is to ensure that the documented work products of the project activities (e.g. requirement documents) comply with their defined requirements regarding form an content.

Module test

The purpose of the module test process is to ensure that the modules of the software comply with their defined formal coding requirements and with the requirements of the software design.

Module integration test

The purpose of the module integration test process is to ensure that the integrated software modules complies with its defined requirements.

OO class test

The purpose of the OO class test process is to ensure that the OO classes comply with their defined formal coding requirements and with the requirements of the software design (special test process for OO based development).

OO class integration test

The purpose of the OO class integration test process is to ensure that the integrated OO classes complies with their defined requirements. (special test process for OO based development).

Functional test

The purpose of the functional test process is to ensure that the functions of the application fulfil their functional requirements.

Business workflow test

The purpose of the business workflow test process is to ensure that the business workflow of the functions of the application fulfil its requirements.

Unit interface test

The purpose of user interface test process is to ensure that the user interface of the application fulfil its requirements.

Performance test

The purpose of the performance test process is to ensure that the performance of the application (time and memory) complies with its requirements.

Application interface test

The purpose of the application interface test process is to ensure the interfaces of the application with other systems comply with their requirements.

Installation test

The purpose of the installation test process is to ensure that the deliverable application can be installed in the defined target environments.

Compatibility test

The compatibility test process is to ensure that the application is compatible with other specified application in the target environments.

The processes of this cluster are dealing with distinguished requirements and different work products of the engineering phases.

4 Assessments based on the test process model

Based on the focussed model for testing the standard assessment structure can be used to conduct assessments for test projects.

Assessment structure

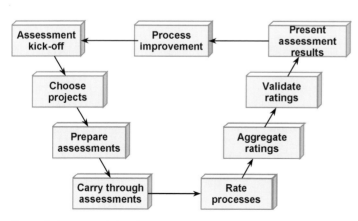

Figure 5: Assessment structure

The rating of the processes is adopted from the BOOTSTRAP method and provides the maturity in the previous shown processes in the capability levels as defined in ISO 15504. In addition it provides the process maturity in quartiles. These detailed information is very helpful to determine the needs for process improvements in the test process. The standard analysis provides also the capability profile which includes the rating for each process attribute. The main contents of the different maturity levels can be seen in the next figure.

One challenge of assessment methods is the usability of the method even for small and medium enterprises as well as for big ones. To fulfil this requirement the assessment can be conducted on three different levels: the self-assessment level, the workshop based assessment and as a full test assessment conducted by two qualified

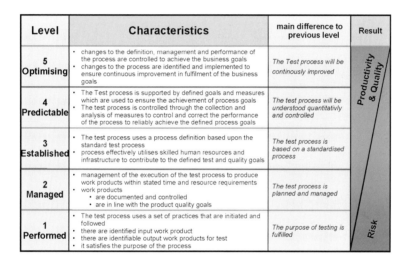

Figure 6: Main contents of the maturity levels

4.1 Self-assessment

The self-assessment for the test process is tool based assessment. Each test project or organisation dealing with tests can do such an self-assessment by its own. The tool TestCHECK ,which is based on the self-assessment tool of BOOTSTRAP, provides the organisation with the process description and the questionnaire to analyse their test processes up to the maturity level 3.

Based on this questionnaire the tool provides the capability profiles of the assessed organisation or project and give a good starting point for the first steps to test process improvement.

4.2 Workshop based assessment

The workshop based assessment gives even small and medium enterprises a chance to use experienced assessor in a short time to assess more than one, typically three or 4 projects in two to three workshop days.

The workshop is based on the use of the self-assessment tool, but instead of just using the tool at least two experienced assessor will provide their assistance in the scoring and rating process. This is done by conducting "light" interviews with the different teams.

The main part of the workshop will start after the assessment. Based on the results the improvement planing will be done.

4.3 Full test assessment

The full assessment is a structured method for an interview based assessment of the test processes conducted by external assessors. During the assessment the findings will be verified by analysing the existing documentation and work products and by inspections at typical working places of the testing staff.

The focus, detail level and number of projects which are assessed are can be defined in the pre-assessment step between the organisation and the assessment team. Typically a full test assessment can be carried out in one to two weeks.

The assessment results are used to define and implement a test process improvement.

5 How to improve the test process

The assessment results consists of two main results:

The capability level of each process
and
The key findings: strength and improvement areas (or weaknesses)

As a starting point to derive an improvement strategy the evaluated goals and business strategies are analysed. To support the defining the goals and their priorities as well as to measure the actual quality of the processes metrics are selected and adopted to the needs of the company.

Based on these metrics and the analysis of the process capabilities, the strength and weaknesses of the test processes the improvement steps are defined. The selection of improvements from the improvement suggestions will be done by the assessed team, a management representative and will be supported by the experienced assessors in an

improvement workshop. The workshop ensures that the improvement areas are defined based on the needs and the experiences of the assessed organisation and the
knowledge of the experts.

The next step is the concrete definition of activities. The activities for the test improvement are planned and controlled like a "normal" Software engineering project.
The predefined metrics are used to define measures that can be used to measure the
success of the improvement.

Typical improvements for projects and organisation who are starting with the test
process improvement, are:

- Guarantee independent quality assurance responsibles
- Implement a structure of testing phases with specified goals and criterias for the
  next phase
- Evaluation and implementation of tool support for testing activities

The following figure shows the basic steps on the way to test process improvement:

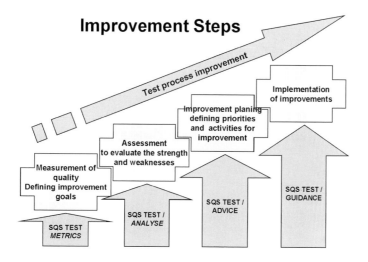

Figure 7: Improvement steps

6 First experiences

At the moment only a small number of such assessments are carried out, but the first
results shows the efficiency and the need for the specialised assessment for the test processes.

The focussed objectives allows companies to focus on the needs of the test processes. The need to focus on test processes are a result of a high percentage of the standard BOOTSTRAP assessments. In opposite to the engineering processes the availability of test process knowledge of standards and process models is poor and the test assessment is a chance to incorporate knowledge from experts and practical approved test models.

The different levels of the test assessment, especially the workshop based assessments allows to start with goal oriented improvements with a well calculated effort and a high impact on the test objectives.

7 Summary

The need for an test assessment is shown by the result of establish standard process assessment and improvement methods. The structure and methodology can be derived from these standard methods. The focussed test assessment has proofed it's suitability in the first practical experiences.

The model, based on the more than 15 years of experience in the test area helps to implement an adequate test process. The metrics supports the objective oriented implementation of improvements and the controlling of the implementation results.

An organizational approach for experience-based process improvement in software engineering: The Software Experience Center

FRANK SAZAMA
DaimlerChrysler AG (Germany)
(with Q-Labs Software Engineering GmbH since October 1, 2000)

Abstract: The constant advancement of processes, methods and tools in software engineering, as well as the steady rise in quality requirements and complexity of products require a systematic improvement approach. This article describes an organizational approach, called Software Experience Center (SEC), for the systematic and experience-based improvement of processes and products. In order to explain the structure and functioning of a SEC more easily the example of a store is used. The six areas of this store are described in more detail: The *Shop Window*, the *Self-Service* department, the *Project Support Counter*, the *Information Network*, the *On-Site Service* area and the *Working Office*. Two general groups with their requirements and functions form the focal point. On the one side is the development organization with their projects. The goal here is product development under given constraints of time, costs and quality. Requirements arise through the use of suitable processes, methods and tools. On the other side there is the SEC support team. This team has to fulfil the requirements coming out of the projects. In addition it has to detect and improve weak points in the whole development organization. Constant observation, reflection and evaluation of the assigned processes, methods and tools is necessary in order to fulfil these requirements. The experiences gained within the projects and the knowledge transfer beyond the project boundaries are the key factors.

Keywords: process improvement, systematic experience transfer, knowledge communities, learning organization, light weight message

1 Motivation

The quality requirements and complexity of the products in software engineering are constantly rising. Systematic improvements of the processes are therefore necessary. To achieve these goals it is necessary to [Romb2000]:

- Understand Process and Product
  We must know our business. The operational sequences themselves and the environment must be understood.

- Define Process and Product qualities
  We must define our business needs and derive goals to achieve them.

- Evaluate Successes and Failures
  We must evaluate every aspect of our business.

- Feed information back for process (e.g., PSP) and project (e.g., TSP) control
  We must have a closed loop process. With a closed feedback loop a better adjustment to the specific requirements is possible.

- Learn from experiences
  Each project should provide information that allows us to do business better (individual to shared).

- Package experiences for reuse under varying project characteristics
  Systematic packaging of experience is the key to building competencies in our areas of business. The reuse of knowledge and experience is the focus of packaging.

- Reuse successful experiences
  We must reuse our competencies and packaged experiences in order to repeat results.

There are different organizational approaches to achieve these goals. In the following discussion two of these approaches with their characteristic features are introduced.

1.1 Experience Factory

The goal of the *Experience Factory* [BCR94] is continuous process improvement within a software organization. This independent unit is concerned with collecting, analyzing, generalizing, formalizing, packaging, storing, searching and reusing common experiences. The project organization can be supported in two different types of way. On the one hand by tips and advice and on the other by direct guidance or collaboration within the improvement activities. In addition, the *Experience Factory* is responsible for introducing new goal-oriented techniques and technologies. It is the competence center for software engineering and has operational responsibility for process improvement. This extensive approach can evolve in a relatively stable environment over years. The experience gained is based mostly on measured investigation and controlled experiment. At this time there is no complete *Experience Factory* in a second environment due to the relatively high expenditure, the stable site conditions necessary and the long-term nature of the objective.

1.2 Experience Engine

Inspired by the idea of the *Experience Factory* the *Experience Engine* was developed [JHC99]. The *Experience Engine* is an approach in which communication and personal exchange of experience are the focus of attention. The *Experience Engine* concentrates on the creation and management of experience transfer. Everyone in their current project role is involved. In addition, support in analyzing local measuring programs and experiences is also a task of the *Experience Engine*. This approach can be transferred very easily and without much effort. It is not necessary to carry out large modification of the existing infrastructure. The success, however, is based on the motivation of each individual involved. Overriding successes and problems are monitored only by key persons and are not systematically observed. Also the active introduction of new technologies or techniques is not within the focus of the *Experience Engine*. When somebody leaves the *Experience Engine* their experience is lost to the entire group because knowledge and experience are not systematically structured and stored within it.

The requirements of an organizational approach for the systematic and experience-based improvement of processes and products arise from taking the two presented approaches together. The goal is to combine the positive characteristics of both approaches. The focus is to achieve an easy way to start implementing this common approach in different environments. An independent unit is created as in the *Experience Factory*. The gathered experience is only partially based on measure investigation. The experience transfer as it is described in the *Experience Engine* is a further component. For easier gathering, handling, storage and re-use of the experience, simple methods and techniques are used to support these activities.

In the next paragraph this organizational approach, the *Software Experience Center* (SEC), is described in more detail. The different areas of the SEC and the roles and functions are presented. To support the work of the SEC the concept of an experience database is described. The last paragraph describes methods and techniques to transfer experience in a simple way.

2 Software Experience Center

The following picture tries to convey an understanding of the dependencies and functions of a *Software Experience Center* (SEC). An old-fashioned grocer store is used to illustrate the SEC (figure 1). The six different areas are described briefly in the following:

- The *Shop Window* displays the contents of the SEC such as highlights from projects, short information on individual topics and the names of contact-partners, as free information for everyone on a high abstraction level.

- Within the *Self-Service* area experiences and information are available for quick direct access and independent use. The material is edited best-practice knowledge e.g. processes, support material, data, general information.

- Partners, experts and discussion-groups are presented in the *Information Network*. As in the Experience Engine such an exchange of experience on a personal basis can be structured and supported.

- At the *Project Support Counter* an individual consultation or personal discussion about different approaches and solutions takes place. This does not usually cover directly applicable, complex solutions and is often the starting point for non-standard problem solution and individual coaching.

- *On-Site Service* makes expert knowledge and personnel resources available for the analysis and solution of non-standard tasks. This involves co-operation, know-how transfer from experts as well as learning on the job.

- In the *Office* the internal information of the Software Experience Center is processed. Analysis and editing of raw material yields new findings as well as emerging trends. The project organization has the benefit of these additional results.

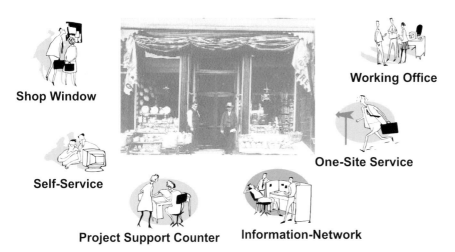

Figure 1: The Grocer Store as analogy for the Software Experience Center (SEC)

Different roles are responsible for the construction, the operation and a systematic experience transfer within the SEC. The roles in this concept are an *Experience Engineer* as well as a *Project Supporter* on the SEC Support-Team side. On the project side the *Power User* is responsible for the improvement activity. An *Experience Engineer* is responsible for collecting, analyzing and editing the experiences. A *Project Supporter* transfers the experiences and supports the daily work in the projects with his expert knowledge. The representatives of the roles are actively involved in selected development projects. This enables them to take up current problems and experiences quickly. They can bring also non-standard solutions directly to the project members. Their active cooperation ensures user-oriented editing, representation and updating of the knowledge. A broad knowledge transfer is enabled by the development and realizing of specific training concepts. The so-called *Power User* operates in the project organization and is contact-partner and engine for the active knowledge transfer within the projects. They are supported by one so-called *Experience Base*. In this Experience Base experiences and the explicit knowledge e.g. process descriptions and support material is stored. The design of an *Experience Base* is described in more details in a later section. The following picture shows the roles and their participation in the common knowledge and experience transfer.

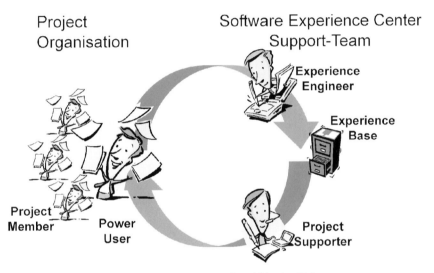

Figure 2: Roles and systematic experience transfer within the SEC

Depending upon the goal of the SEC the tasks are different. First a (pilot -) project is involved and the goal is to get a better understanding of the processes. If further projects are included, the emphasis shifts to experience handling/exchange of experience. The tasks of the *Project Support* expand accordingly. This is because of the increased number of projects, questions and topics. The goal experience handling or exchange of experience contains the tasks of the *Project Support*. From the analysis of the intra- as well as the inter-project experiences additional tasks for the controlled introduction of new knowledge arise. Here a controlled modification is prepared and initiated.

3 Knowledge-Transfer or Experience-Transfer cycle

The basis of each knowledge management is the knowledge or experience transfer cycle (Figure 3) [Fischer et.al.96]. The individual steps are described in the following briefly.

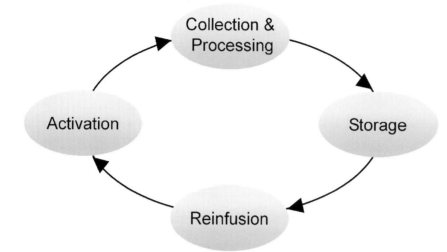

Figure 3: Cognitive Experience Transfer Cycle [Fischer et.al.96]

Activate here means the active extraction of experiences from documents, situations and also persons. It concerns knowledge which is not direct and obviously accessible ([NoHi95] implicit knowledge). The owners of this knowledge are not able to articulate their knowledge and their experiences without suggestion or assistance. They think e.g. that their knowledge is not so useful or it is to difficult to formulate. Through e.g. measuring programs, documentation of observations or discussions such knowledge can be made available for others.

Collecting and Processing means on the one hand the simple collection and making available of knowledge in its raw, rough form. On the other hand for the majority of users, it is necessary that this knowledge is adapted and edited for their specific needs. The *Experience Engineer* undertakes this task. Typically he checks the environmental factors, in which observations or experiences were made, he compares knowledge, experiences and observations and can therefore create new findings.

Storage describes more the technical aspects e.g. the representation of contents or a particular utility tool. A more detailed description of these aspects is found under the next section.

Infusion (also Reinfusion) is an often underestimated step, because the cycle does not end with the knowledge being made "available". It must be edited, on the one hand, so that it can be utilized in the daily development process. On the other hand the development process must provide for active reference of this knowledge. The user will only come to use this *Experience Base*, when there is enough interesting material available, i.e. when the critical mass of information has been exceeded.

This experience transfer cycle forms the basis for the work with the experiences. This cycle is centered around documents, knowledge and experiences which represent the current state of the art. Infusion of the knowledge takes place through its use in projects. . New knowledge is generated and documented in the form of observations and notes. The collection, evaluation and assimilation of the observations achieve systematic updating and improvement. For the support of the experience-based improvement an experience database is necessary. The next section describes an *Experience Base* concept.

4 Conception of an Experience Base to support the Software Experience Center

On the one hand experience should be stored easily with little additional editing effort. On the other hand there are users with different requirements, who all want to be able to access the experiences easily and in a way tailored to their specific needs. An *Experience Base* must support both sides, because the acceptance of both the users and the experience suppliers is the key to its success. If the acceptance and usage are small, then support is not possible and the effort for creation and maintenance can not be justified.

In order to reduce the effort of handling knowledge and experiences to a minimum a certain level of expertise is necessary on the forms and media of knowledge, experiences and information. The huge abundance of possible documents and the associated effort involved in editing, maintaining and possibly disposing of them unused can be therefore be minimized from the very beginning. Not all experiences can and should be recorded in written form. Not all information needs to be made accessible for everyone in the Internet. The *BIP-Approach* was developed [LSH99] to achieve the level of expertise required. The *BIP-Approach* explains which experiences should be represented in the head (Brain), on paper (Paper) or in electronic documents (Intranet). Criteria for allocating the experience to the individual media have been defined also. The key finding is the fact that all three media have their specific advantages and therefore the experiences can not and should not be completely stored in a tool-supported database. In the following illustration the individual statuses and their transitions are described in detail (figure 4).

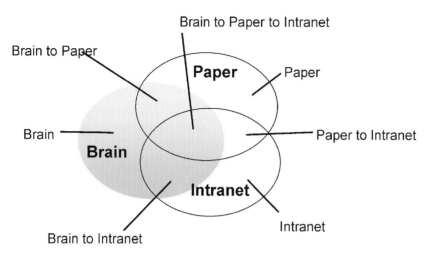

Figure 4: Knowledge and experiences are represented in different media

Brain – not all experience will be recorded in the long term. It is ok that incomplete knowledge is in the head.

Brain to Paper – Things, which one needs more frequently, which only few know or which are easily forgotten, should be written down.

Paper – Some information comes from the outside (article, forms, faxes). It is not available electronically, and none has it in their head. No reason to reject it!

Paper to Intranet – If a suitable form of electronic storage is available then use it. The more the computer can parse, the more can it help. Electronic is better than unstructured, possibly non-electronic paper. What is quickly outdated, need not be printed.

Intranet – Computers are ideal for administering different versions and variants. Also a lot of data is best stored on a computer. Printouts are always outdated.
Brain to Intranet – A lot of what a person has in their head today, is forgotten tomorrow and then it is lost to the SEC unless it has been stored elsewhere. It is often worthwhile typing things in or scanning them.

Brain to Paper to Intranet – Core contents often undergo a metamorphosis, leaving tracks across all media.

In the following Intranet-based section we will concentrate on the concept of an *Experience Base*. The steps of *collecting* and *processing*, *storing* and *reinfusion* from the experience transfer cycle are supported here. Support of the six areas within the SEC takes place in different intensity. A high level of support is possible for the *Shop Window*, *Self-Service* and *Information Network areas in particular*. The *Shop Window* is the most public part of an *Experience Base* and thus also the most frequented one. Initial questions can be answered via the Intranet including search support because the information is presented in a form that is understandable to everyone. The *Self-Service* area must ensure fast and simple access. This is possible via the Intranet with electronic search support.

The search for experts in the *Information Network* can also be very well supported by a database. Only partial support can be provided in the *Project Support Counter* and *Work Office* areas. The point of interest in these areas is storing and administrating documents and raw information. interpretation of this information to form solution proposals is the role of the *Project Supporter*. In the *On-Site Service* area the focus is on know-how and experience transfer, non-standard assistance and personal consultation. The *Project Supporter* performs these same tasks within the SEC itself. As the last general aspect the structure of the *Experience Base* should be addressed. To fulfil the requirements of high flexibility on the experience search and re-use side as well as simple data structure on the other an application-specific solution is necessary. By utilizing a flat, more general file structure and a flexible navigation network, for example by linked HTML-pages, these requirements can be fulfilled. The navigation, the representation of contents and the search for the experiences can be designed in an individual, user-oriented way.

The following illustrates the requirements from the user's point of view: *"I see the information, experiences and knowledge like a large lake. Fishing rods are used for the search. A certain bait is attached to the hook and cast out into the lake. A tree of information, experiences and knowledge hangs from the hook. It corresponds exactly with my requirements and constraints. The information is structured and processed optimally for me as a searcher"*

Three main user groups are described briefly in following example:

Accessible for *everyone* ...

... the information is presented on an abstract level in a simple, clear and appealing way. Contents include highlights, topic outlines, short information and contact partners.

For project members ...

... there are two special aspects: the view for experienced personnel and the view for newcomers. For experienced people all the material is prepared for the fast access during daily business. Side by side this material includes prepared "best-practice" processes, support material, experiences from solution approaches, complex solutions, expert knowledge and personnel support. For the newcomers the focus is on introductory material in the form of guided tours and lists of contact partners and experts.

For *Project Supporters, Experience Engineers, Power Users ...*

... the editors of the contents of an *Experience Base* make available all documents in their current and preceding variants and versions. There is also a specific work area within the *Experience Base* for this user group only.

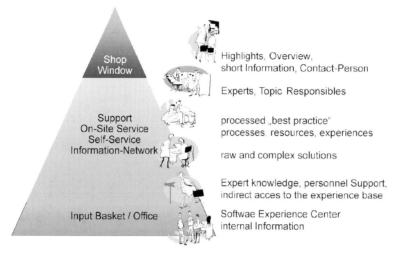

Figure 5: Knowledge access and contents of an Experience Base

The information quantity and the dependencies of the information for the individual user groups are represented in a pyramid (Figure 5). At the base of this pyramid most documents and information are available in an unprocessed state. The role of the *Experience Engineer* is to process and edit these sources to form expert knowledge. In the next step summarization and preparation for project-members is carried out. At the top of the pyramid the information is represented in an even more concentrated form. This interdependency as well as the support provided to the user groups by the individual areas of the SEC are shown in figure 5.

5 Experiences and suggestions for the implementation of an experience data base

For the implementation of a prototype *Experience Base* the Mind-Mapping method can be used [Buzan]. Mind-Mapping is employed particularly during brainstorming. The different contributions are arranged around the main topic. In a tree-like structure the contributions can be arranged and structured. The hierarchy, sequence as well as the connections between contributions are represented in graphic form, which leads to a better overview of the contents. In the implementation of an *Experience Base* the available data and documents as well as the user views and their access to the information is illustrated in an appropriate structure. With the MindManager Tool [MindMan] it is possible to create a HTML Web from this graphic structure including the appropriate contents. This HTML Web can serve as a very useful prototype. Modification and extension of the structure or contents can be implemented easily. Particularly in the starting phase, the prototype can therefore be easily adapted to the requirements of the users.

If the implementation as a simple HTML Web is sufficient, then further work on the prototype is not necessary. However if notes, reactions, observations need to be assigned directly to the documents, then further tool-support is necessary. Tools such as MS Office or Adobe Acrobat offer good support in this area, for example through their integrated comment function. The requirements can be extended in a further stage of development by the following points for example:

- Navigation within Intranet or Internet.
- Access to documents of different type with a uniform interface (Browser).
- Support for Web representation of different user-groups (store example).
- Support during the creation of the Web Site by structuring and automatic navigation.
- Support for maintenance of the link network or the entire Web Site.
- Support during the integrated input of documents and attributes.
- Search for documents and experience packages according to classification.
- Search for contents within the experience packages and further documents (full text search).
- Definition and administration of user-groups and user-rights.
- Integrated version checking.
- Management of notes on documents or sections from documents.

In the implementation of these extensive requirements the first positive results from the Hyperwave Information Server [Hyperwave] are available. This tool is a Web Server with integrated document database, an integrated attribute and full-text search as well as a link and version management.

6 Methods for goal-oriented and user-oriented knowledge transfer

In the individual areas of the SEC (shop window, self-service, project support counter, information network, on-site service and working office) the support that each user group receives is different. On the one hand the requirements from the user's perspective and on the other the preparation of contents are different. The SEC areas are assigned different information levels (figure 5, figure 6). From the base to the top of the pyramid the information and knowledge are more concentrated and are presented according to the user requirements. In order to obtain continuous improvement of the contents, a knowledge and experience transfer is necessary (figure 6). This transfer is based on the knowledge and experience transfer cycle already presented (figure 3). In the following, examples of methods and techniques are presented for an appropriate knowledge transfer.

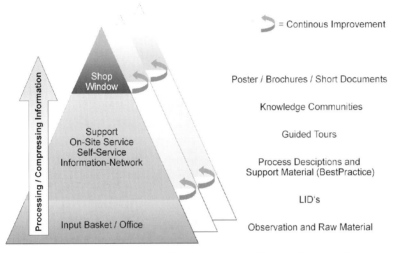

Figure 6: Methods for goal-oriented and user-oriented knowledge transfer

6.1 Poster / Brochures / Short Documents

Posters, brochures and short documents are made for everyone to understand. They represent the strongest compression and abstraction of knowledge and experiences. Here no consideration is given to the special interests of a certain user groups. The information is presented in a concise and very clear way. It is very important that contact information to individual experts or expert groups be provided in these forms of representation. The following checklist can be used for the content:

- Answer to the question: What is that (e.g. Inspections)?
- Answer to the question: When do I need it (e.g. Inspections)?
- Answer to the question: What is my benefit?
- Answer to the question: What experience from my field exists already?
- An abstract of the topic on 2–3 pages
- The naming or reference to partners and teams of experts

6.2 Knowledge Communities

These teams of experts, so-called *Knowledge Communities* is the next type of a knowledge, experience and information-exchange. North, Romhardt and Probst define knowledge communities as follows [NRP2000]:

"Knowledge communities are longstanding groups of people who share both a common interest in a particular subject and the desire to accumulate and exchange knowledge together. Participation is voluntary and personal. Knowledge communities are grouped around specific contents."

These communities can on the one hand be used to make a particular theme the subject of discussion and so to initialize a knowledge-exchange process. On the other hand they can also be used for the further development of a subject over a longer time period. The organizational foundation is not always easy to create. A certain open culture and freedom from time constraints are necessary in order to enable success. The benefit is derived particularly in the form of mutual exchange, the achievement of common understanding on different terms and approaches as well as the opportunity of leading new employees into subject areas and integrating them into expert groups.

6.3 Guided Tours / Process Descriptions / Best Practice

New employees are supported with intranet-based Guided Tours. This Guided Tour enables the initial support within the break-in period. The advantages are the independent training and the use of the same knowledge base by all new colleagues. On the other side the experienced colleagues are relieved from training and are able to answer more specialized questions. The questions the new employees ask their colleagues are on a more competent base. If the Guided Tour is integrated into the *Experience Base*, a further advantage is the simultaneous training in structure and contents. This second section is created specially for the needs of more experienced colleagues and contains descriptions of process and appropriate support material (Best Practice). They can use it for their daily work. Experience gained in the production of Guided Tours shows that a very flat structure is advantageous. To clarify terms in the Guided Tour simple hyperlinks in a common glossary are used. These hyperlinks open independent pop-up windows so that the user doesn't have to leave the Guided Tour. Links to other contents within the *Experience Base* are also shown in separate windows for easier orientation while allowing exploration of the whole *Experience Base* at the same time.

6.4 Light Weight documentation of Experiences

For the experienced colleagues in the projects and the experts on a topic so-called LID's (Light Weight documentation of Experiences) [Schn2000] are available. LID's are structured documents to record knowledge, experience and information in a simple way. The structure follows a project or a part of a project in chronological order. The ideal conditions for such LID's is a well-defined action over an approx. 2-3 month period. After this period all involved persons can document their observations and experiences as well as their recommendations for improvement. The effort of writing a LID is well spent particularly when there are several similar such actions and the knowledge, experiences and information can be reused. The following steps are involved in the creation of LID:

- Shortly after an activity is terminated the key persons should describe it from their viewpoint. This can occur either as an individual interview or in form of a workshop. A short checklist is used as a basis to get the lessons learned.
- The LID description is represented on a few pages and the most current mentioned documents are referred with hyperlinks.
- In particular pay attention to documents that were used as templates or were nearly templates. These "nearly templates" can become just as interesting in their re-use as current templates. Likewise they can mature to templates through further use.
- All documents are stored in a directory and the LID description is the only point of access to the information and documents. This LID description (the lid of the pot) covers the pot with it's contents. This ensures that no contents are lost or are reused in the wrong way. The lid therefore holds the contents together and explains their context.

The advantages of such LID's are described as follows:

- The documentation will be not forgotten.
- The effort is relatively small.
- The structure and representation is designed to re-use.
- A reflection on what happened occurs
- The available documents will viewed and re-usable ones won't be removed.
- Relationships and comments are stored before "the pot is closed".

7 Summary

For continuous and systematic process improvement in software engineering an organizational approach, the *Software Experience Center* (SEC) was presented. The basis of the SEC is the idea of the *Experience Factory* [BCR94] supplemented by the *Experience Engine* [JHC99]. One is a more measurement-oriented approach, and the other an approach based more on personal exchange of experience. The unification of both approaches took place in SEC. The areas of the SEC (*Shop Window*, *Self-Service*, *Project Support Counter*, *Information Network*, On-Site-*Service* and *Working Office*) and their interdependencies are illustrated by the example of a grocer store. The tasks in the SEC are accomplished by the roles of *Project Supporter*, *Experience Engineer* and *Power User*. An Experience Base, whose concept was presented likewise here, supports the work of these roles. In order to reach the requirements of the different user groups (everyone, project worker, expert) methods were presented to the goal-oriented and user-oriented knowledge transfer.

8 References

[SoftQuali99a] SoftQuali Konsortium: Systematische Qualitätsverbesserung durch Software-Inspektionen und Organisation von Erfahrungswissen; Session 5.3 auf der SQM1999, Köln 1999

[SoftQuali99b] SoftQuali Konsortium: Systematische Software-Qualitätsverbesserung durch zielorientiertes Messen und Bewerten sowie explizite Wiederverwendung des Software-Entwicklungs-Know-Hows; Abschlussdokumentation September 1999 http://www.iese.fhg.de/SOFTQUALI/dokument/erg_m.htm

[LSH99] D. Landes, K. Schneider and F. Houdek: Organizational learning and experience documentation in industrial software projects; International Journal on Human-Computer Studies, Page 643–661, Vol. 51 1999

[NRP2000] K. North, K. Romhardt, G. Probst: Wissensgemeinschaften – Keimzellen lebendigen Wissensmanagements, io-Management, http://www.handels-zeitung.ch/zeitschriften/io_management/artikel6.html or Arbeitsgemeinschaft Wissensmanagement Kaiserslautern http://www.cck.uni-kl.de/wmk/papers/public/Wissensgemeinschaften.pdf

[Romb2000] D. Rombach: Capitalizing on Experience, Key Note of the Profes 2000 Conference. Oulu, Finland, June 2000 http://www.iese.fhg.de/profes2000/postconf/Dieter RombachPROFES2000-KeyNote.zip

[Schn2000] K. Schneider: LIDs: A Light-Weight Approach to Experience Elicitation and Reuse, Springer, Berlin: Proceedings of the Profes 2000 Conference. Oulu, Finland, June 2000

[Buzan] T. Buzan, B. Buzan: Das Mind-Map-Buch. Die beste Methode zur Steigerung ihres geistigen Potentials, MVG; ISBN: 3478717302, 1999

[MindMan] Information in the Web www.mindmanager.de / www.mindmanager.com

[Hyperwave] Information in the Web www.hyperwave.de / www.hyperwave.com

[NoHi95] Nonaka, I.; Hirotaka, T.: The Knowledge-Creating Company. Oxford University Press, 1995.

[Fischer et.al.96] G. Fischer, S. Lindstaedt, J. Ostwald, K.Schneider, and J. Smith. Informaing system design through organisational learning. In Proceedings on the 2nd International Conference on Learning Society (ICLS), pages 52–59, Northwestern University, Evanston, 1996.

Knowledge Management: A pragmatic process based approach

CHRISTOF NAGEL

T-Nova Deutsche Telekom Innovationsgesellschaft mbH,
Development Center South West (Germany)

Abstract: The approach is pragmatic and powerful knowledge management system. The system is embedded in the business process model, which is established since several years. The processes provide the knowledge management with input and support the use of it. The information objects have a structure, conceptual based on the quality improvement paradigm. The content of the object consists of the description of knowledge, "non practices" and "best practices". Beside the usual ones (queries, ...) a new kind of accessing information objects is given by the processes, whereas the processes and their activities are attributed with links to the objects. The approach contains no concepts for knowledge trees as the effort for definition and maintenance is to high compared with the possibility to access objects by the processes which can be considered as specialised knowledge trees. A systematic analysis for improving the processes can be found by looking for accumulation points of information objects linked to a process activity. A further feature of the approach is the structure of the knowledge data base which is flat and not based on a structure tree. This article describes also how a knowledge management system can be a established in an enterprise.

Keywords: knowledge management, business process model, knowledge tree, best practices, experience packages

1 Introduction

The T-Nova Development Centre South-West has introduced a knowledge management system. The knowledge of the enterprise based on experience should be documented and represented. As the centre has a well defined system of business and engineering processes several advantages were used during introduction and development of the knowledge management.

   One of our objectives two years ago was "Let each member in the enterprise know what the "best practices" and experiences of the other colleagues are." Setting up this objective was the starting point for the development of our concept for knowledge management. During the development we had to find answers on the questions:

1. What is the input we like to have in the knowledge management system and how do we get the input?
    Chapter "Process of Knowledge Management"

2. What are the elements/objects of our knowledge management system and how is the database organised?
    Chapter "Development of the basic concept"
3. How should our users get access to the contents of the knowledge management system?
    Chapter "Development of the basic concept"
4. How must the knowledge management system be introduced and promoted?
    Chapter "Process of Knowledge Management"
5. After the introduction, is there only an acceptance of or do the members of the enterprise use the knowledge management system in order to support their own work? What are the real benefits of the knowledge management system? At the end of the article we describe the experience with our concept.

In the following of this article we give an answer to these questions in our point of view. Based on the answers we have build up a system and an approach which can be characterised as follows:

*   The objects of the knowledge management system are packages having a structure influenced by the cycle of the quality improvement paradigm.
*   The view on the data base of the knowledge management system is not structured by a knowledge tree as proposed in literature. We have not seen an advantage in developing a knowledge tree. What we use is a special knowledge tree, introduced several years ago and known by our project teams since that. The knowledge is derived from our processes namely the software engineering processes. The knowledge is also linked to the processes and these ones are the knowledge trees used in this approach.
*   Nearly all what we do in the knowledge management is supported, based or guided by the processes. The processes provides us with input for the knowledge management system and they assure that we get information about the use of the packages from the knowledge management system.

2 Development of the basic concept

Several years ago we have studied the basic concepts of the quality improvement paradigm and of the experience factory. The quality improvement paradigm is based on a cycle, an improvement cycle, consisting of the steps:

*   characterise and understand problems
*   define goals
*   select suitable process methods, techniques or tools
*   perform the methods or techniques or apply the tools

- analyse the results
- package the experiences and put it in a data base

First experiments with the quality improvement paradigm have shown, that the approach do not fit exactly for our enterprise. Our enterprise, the T-Nova Development Centre South West, has defined and uses processes covering each business. That means we have processes for example for management of customer relations, personal support, production processes for software engineering and consulting, ... An important role in this context has the improvement process. A part of this process are assessments, based on Bootstrap-method, being applied to units (projects, departments, teams) of the enterprise. By the assessment the definition, the right customisation and the usage of the processes especially the software production process are controlled.

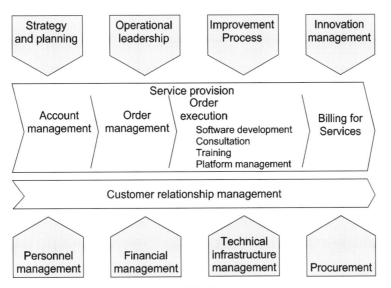

Figure 2.1: The business process model of DC SW

In the assessment metrics and characteristic numbers are analysed in order to determine whether they fit according to the goals and objectives of the unit. In the case they do not fit or in the case of other weaknesses of the unit we define improvements concerning new metrics, management or engineering practices. The unit has to work out an improvement plan and to perform the improvements. The results of the improvements are again checked by assessments. Taking the points described here into account, the different parts of the improvement process and of our assessment procedures cover already a number of steps from cycle of the quality improvement paradigm. Another part of the cycle is covered by the process for the derivation and definition of goals and objectives. Therefore there was no need to introduce the paradigm formally in departments or teams. In counterpart the introduction of the paradigm would instantiate a second and a little bit different improvement process in the enterprise.

It seems that the additional introduction of the quality improvement paradigm in an enterprise with a well defined an nearly complete business process model would lead to difficulties and conflicts concerning the existing processes and definition of goals. Enterprises with a business process model should analyse if they do not already have an implicit quality improvement paradigm or parts from it.

Another reason why we do not have introduced or used the paradigm explicitly is given by the time we needed from setting up until finishing a cycle of the paradigm. Too much time is needed in order to get input for experience packages for the knowledge data base. The number of packages as a result of this approach is too small for the experience base considering the period of a year.

The concept of T-Nova Development Centre South West uses for its knowledge management system the basic ideas from the quality improvement paradigm and from the experience factory and implements them adapted to the business process model.

2.1 The information objects of the knowledge management system

The information objects in this system are structured. A number of products bought under the name knowledge management systems have a lot function in order to handle information objects being unstructured but often no sufficient functions to handle structured objects. But a structure in the objects is necessary, as the users of the systems, that means the readers of the objects, expect to find the information they search fast and as quite as possible easy. The users like to have the same look and feel for each information object. The information object in our case are called experience packages, as they document mostly experiences made by units or members of the enterprise. Usually each experience has it own package. One package should not contain two or more experience. The structure of the packages does not allow this and the handling of the packages is difficult especially the searching.

In the structure of a package parts can be detected, which correspond to certain steps of the cycle from quality improvement paradigm.

- title:
  Each package has a title, which is build from main message of the package.
- abstract:
  The abstract gives a short summary of the package in one or two sentences. This should help the reader to decide whether the package is interesting or not.
- problem or state:
  In the most cases of an experience the people have had a problem or state of their work or their project. The problem had to be solved or state had to be improved. The original problem or state is described in this part.

- method, procedure:
  In this part of a package the methods or procedures to solve a problem or to improve a state are described.

- results:
  By setting up or introduction of a new method or procedure a result is intended. But is the result, got after performing the method or procedure, the one which was intended? Very often we have differences between the desired and the real result. The real result and the deviations are described here.

- downloads:
  During the performing of new methods or procedures useful programs, utilities, macros or templates were created and used. In the experience packages are links set to these tools, so that readers can download them, if they have a similar problem or are interested at all.

- comments
  Each reader of a package has the opportunity to write a comment to a package. The discussion of new methods or procedures will be supported by this way.

Title	Collecting of topics for status meetings
Abstract	Systematical preparation of status meetings
Problem	The results of status meetings are unsatisfactorily: Topics are forgotten or are not well prepared.
Method/Procedure	A template with the agenda is provided for team members. It is put in a directory accessible for each member. Everyone of the team write his topics in the agenda for the next meeting. It is an obligation for the project manager to prepare on the topics and to discuss them in the next meeting.
Results	The template is mostly used by the project and quality manager. The quality of the meetings was improved significantly.
Downloads	You can find the template under this link .
Contact Person	Gerd Schwantke
Comments	none
Classification (Process)	6c1QD06
ID EP_1055	Datum 12.07.2000

Figure 2.2: Example of a experience package

- characterising, identification
  Some other parts are contained in a package in order to characterise, sort the package and to identify the author. The author has also the role of a contact person in cases where a reader has questions to a package.

2.2 Access to knowledge management system

How do the users of the system get access to experience packages? A main difference between concepts for knowledge management systems described here and in the literature or discussed in workshops lies in the so called structure tree or knowledge tree.

Very often it is proposed to invest a lot of work in creation of very well defined knowledge tree. Before a lot of work is spent, it should be analysed what have to be done in order to introduce a knowledge tree and what is the probably return of invest.

What are the purposes for the construction and maintenance of tree, if the knowledge management system offers one?

- Information and contents of the packages were extracted and generalised to topics. The topics are mapped on a tree oriented structure, whereas the categories represents the levels in the tree. By that way a selection of the content from the packages is copied into a tree oriented structure. The tree structure is defined by a team. The view on the base from someone else not belonging to the team do not have to be the same, even if the team is the best one which can ever be found. First results of our prototype have shown that.
- The definition of the knowledge tree has to be reviewed or inspected at least yearly. The reason are for example:
  - The focus on the topics treated by the knowledge management has changed.
  - The user gives inputs and feedback to knowledge management which are never expected.
- In the first year after introduction of the knowledge management system it is expected that the tree must changed more often, as mentioned before. Therefore the effort for the maintenance of the knowledge tree must also be considered.

After the introduction of the knowledge tree we get two groups of users. The first ones which accept the tree and can work with it. This ones are disappointed, if the tree was changed after a while. The second group has always a different view on the tree. We think in the second group are the majority of our users.

Collecting all this facts, comparing the effort of definition, construction and maintenance with the advantages of the tree, we got the opinion that the return of invest of a knowledge tree is only minimal.

Similar analysis are made for the concepts of building key words and indexes for the knowledge management system. After that these concepts were also rejected. Our knowledge management system offers the users three possibilities to access to experience packages:

1. Navigation to the experience packages via our processes
2. Different lists of packages for example: list of new packages or list of top ten packages
3. Find the packages by using a search engine

2.2.1 Navigation to experience packages

The T-Nova Development Centre South West has as already mentioned before a well defined system of business and engineering processes. Each business and engineering activity is described in or covered by a process. The processes are described in the following manner: In level 0 the whole business process model is defined. The level 1 contains the processes itself with their refinement in sub processes. In level 2 the processes are described in detail with activities, roles and important input or output documents of the activities.

The idea, which was realised, was the use of these processes in order to represent the experiences of the enterprise. If the definition of the business process model is complete and detailed enough, the great majority of experiences the people in an enterprise made can be attached to processes and their activities. The experiences described by the packages are attached to the activities and sub-processes. In common the experiences should not coupled with the processes in level 0 as the number of experiences growths very fasten for certain processes (e.g. engineering processes). A great number of experiences coupled with a process and without tool for sorting or searching does not invite the users to read the experience packages.

Our approach has several advantages.

The processes are defined and introduced 5 years ago. They are known and used in the projects and departments of the enterprise. The degree of knowledge about and the use of the processes are monitored by audits and assessments. If someone have a problem he or she should identify which activity or sub-process is involved and can look whether there are experiences attached.

The processes cover the business and nearly each activity of the business. By attaching experiences to the processes points of problems can be detected which different teams/departments of the enterprise have in performing the process. These points are input of improvement process. This feature will be described later in detail.

By coupling of activities and experience packages we have on one side the standard description of the activities how they have to be performed and on the other side the experiences. The experiences explain how the activity can be done or offers a solution (a pattern, a tool, a macro, ...) or describes probable problems occurred during the performance of an activity. The members of the enterprise do not get only the standards of the processes and their activities they have to perform but they get also examples or solution how they can do it.

In a certain way the processes and their attachments of experience packages can be understand as a knowledge tree. But this tree was already defined and the processes are well known to the people who perform the processes. The tree is a very natural one, being build from the structure and from the business the enterprise has.

The technical realisation looks as follows. The processes are represented in an intranet. Each sub-process and each activity having at least one experience package attached has got an additional information, which express how many packages are attached to (see figure 2.3). The number is also an link to intranet server of the knowledge management system. By traversing the link a list of links to the packages itself is shown. Each item in the list consists of the title, a short abstract and the editing date of the package. The list is sorted by date. The layout of the list is very similar as the example in figure 2.4. Based on the title and on the abstract the reader can decide whether or not to navigate to the package.

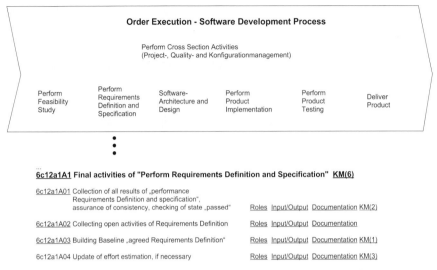

Figure 2.3: Software development process attributed with links to the knowledge management system

2.2.2   Lists of packages

Different lists are offered to the user of the knowledge management. The first one is the list of published packages. The experiences are collected until usually a number greater 5 is reached. The experiences are the packed and published together. The list of published packages is updated now and sorted by publishing dates. The new packages are inserted at the top of the list. It is recommend to the teams and departments to study the list in the regular status meetings. In a monthly rhythm they can study the list during the meeting and decide which of the new package could be interesting and should be applied. An example of the list of published packages is shown in figure 2.4. This list helps people of the teams to keep informed without a lot of effort in studying the contents of the knowledge management.

Other lists of packages offered by the knowledge management system are constructed by applying criteria's. For example a top ten list is build from the database of packages. This list being updated monthly contains the most interesting packages in the point of view of the knowledge engineer. Other top ten lists can consist of the most accessed or the least recently accessed packages. In our approach a type of list containing only packages with downloads is also interesting. Downloads in this context are patterns, tools, macros or something else which are linked to the package and which are practical results of the experience.

New put in at 4.8.2000:

"Avoiding main memory problems under Windows95/98"

| Abstract | *"- no abstract"* |

"Effective use of external forces and providing the know how transfer"

| Abstract | *"use extermal forces for coaching and not for the operative support"* |

"Framework for unit tests under C++/Java"

| Abstract | *"providing a framework for download"* |

New put in at 12.7.2000:

"Collection of topics for status meetings"

| Abstract | *"systematical preparation of status meetings"* |

Figure 2.4: List of new published packages

2.2.3   Search engines

The user of a knowledge management system should be able to access to the experiences by search engines. This engine should have the same look and feel as the internet search engines like Lycos, Yahoo or other. The way to write a query and to sent it should be so easy as it is in the well known engines. The answer on the queries should have an layout which is the same or equivalent to that ones from the internet search engines. But it is useful to have additional function in order to work with the answers on the queries. If the answers contains a great number of packages the user should have a function to sort the packages. Criterions for sorting are key words in parts (e.g. in the problem description or in the title) of the packages, dates or author names. The keywords are defined by the user in the moment in which he forms the query.

3 Process of knowledge management in T-Nova Development Centre South-West

The process of knowledge management consists shortly described of the following steps:

- At first we have different sources to get input. The sources deliver inputs in different qualities and different details to an experience.

- The input is analysed. It is determined whether the input is interesting for knowledge management. Missing details are demanded from the people who have given the input. A package is formed from all of the input to an experience.

- The packages are collected and embedded in the data base. The attachments to the processes are performed. The lists of packages are constructed.

- The packages are taken for consulting the departments and project teams in the enterprise.

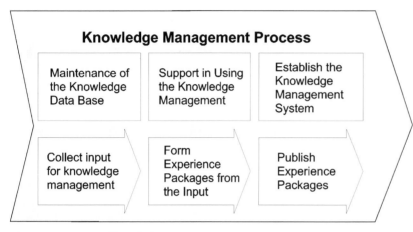

Figure 3.1: Process of knowledge management

3.1 Sources for input to the knowledge management

Different sources are used for the knowledge management. One of the sources has their origin in spontaneous inputs given by members or teams of the enterprise. Supported by a tool the experiences can be written in a very easy manner. The layout of the input form of the tool is a result of discussions with the potential users. The main points in the discussions were:

- Keep the tool easy. The tool has to be self-describing, so that the use is easy.
- Ask only for information being real necessary. For example avoid to ask for classifying details.
- Give a fast feedback what will happen with the input.

The second version of the tool and the process behind the tool fulfils these requirements. The tool is accepted in the enterprise. The number of inputs got by the tool meets the expectations. Not only experiences are accepted as input for the knowledge management, but also knowledge or know how. This source of experiences is based on a bottom up principle. The people are free to give an input or not. There is no process or standard or something else which forces the people. It is important to have this source where the using is absolute free.

Another source are project reviews. In the engineering processes of the business process model a special review type, the project review, is defined. In the project review the experiences of a project team are considered. The team is asked what are the experiences which should be documented in the knowledge management system that other colleagues can read and use them. The experiences are documented at first in a review report. In this report the experiences have a structure being very similar to the packages in the knowledge management data base. The experiences documented in a project review report can be classified as "best practices", "non practices" and information. The last ones are not experiences they are often knowledge or recommendations. But these information are also worth to be taken in the data base. It was surprising that the teams want also to document the "non practices". "Non practices" have their reason often in a mistake of someone. The packages resulting from these "non practices" are very important and leads to new improvements of the processes, as it is described later in this article. Based on the fact that the teams document "non practices" it can be followed that they want publish their experiences by the knowledge management and that the project reviews are accepted. The acceptance is necessary in order to get qualitatively high project review reports.

A third source of experiences are the assessments. During assessments the assessors detect a method or a solution which can be considered as a "best practice" and should be represented in the data base of the knowledge management system. This practice is documented in the result report of the assessment. The knowledge engineer gets a hint to the "best practice" and decides whether or not the practice can be accepted for the knowledge management. In a lot of cases the information to the "best practice" does not allow the decision so that it is necessary to ask for more details to the "best practice". Together with all information an experience package is formed and put in the data base. By this source of experiences we concentrate only on "best practices" as the "non practices" should only be published via knowledge management by the assessed team or departments itself and not by third ones (e.g. assessors). As only the "best practices" are published this source is well accepted in the enterprise.

The last two sources have a top down character. Given by the engineering process and the improvement process the teams and departments have to perform project reviews and assessments. This approach has advantages:

- The approach to get input is systematic and not based on chances.
- It is no problem to get input as great number of reports from assessments and project reviews are written yearly.

3.2 Forming experience packages from the input

The input for the data base has to be transformed in the structure of an experience package. Often the input does not have any structure. The purpose of the knowledge engineer is to form the experience package from the input. The purpose is detailed in:

- Transformation of the input into the structure of an experience package.
- After transformation there are often open questions. Typical questions are:
  What was the real problem?
  What were the results?
  Is it possible to provide a download containing a solution (tool, macro)?
  The authors are asked for further details.
- Insertion of a title and of a abstract in the package.
- Study of the processes which of them or which of their activities fit to the content of the package. The identity numbers of the processes and their activities are inserted in the package.

3.3 Publishing the experience packages in the knowledge management system

The experience packages are usually collected for a while until a significant number of packages are in the state to be published. In the next step the packages are processed in order to put them in the right form in the data base. The list of new packages will also be updated. They are now linked to the processes and the activities based on the identity numbers in the packages itself. The authors are notified and they can perform a last review before the packages are released.

3.4 Maintenance of the knowledge data base

Maintenance in the context of this article means the activities needed to keep high the quality of knowledge data base or to improve the quality. Technical maintenance of a data base is not a topic of this article.

Beside the typical activities like correction of errors three main activities are considered in this approach:

- As already mentioned the packages have a part in which comments to the package can be written. The comments are sent to the knowledge engineer by the readers of the packages. The readers can also of course sent comments to a comment of a package. Each comment to a package is inserted in this one together with the name of the author. It is the purpose of the knowledge engineer to insert the comments.

- Each top ten list represents a kind of state of the data base at a certain time. The top ten lists have to be updated in regular intervals, at least at the time where the number of packages or comments to the packages has changed very much.
- The deletion of packages is also an important activity as old or uninteresting packages prevents the readers from seeing the important and interesting packages. Possible criterions for the deletion are the age or the use of the packages. The age is measured by the creation date of the package. The use can be expressed by the number of accesses. In this approach an algorithm will be applied which is taken from the main memory administration. The algorithm is called least recently used described in books of computer organisation.

3.5 Support in using the knowledge management

It is not sufficient to implement and to introduce the system. With a knowledge management system a new medium for information is introduced in an enterprise. The assumption that the members of the enterprise have only waited on this medium and that they want use it is often wrong. What is needed, besides the introduction and establishing of the knowledge management, is a concept by which the use of the contents of the knowledge data base is supported.

At first we recommended the teams and departments to study the list of new packages monthly. This has the advantage that there information are always up to date.

A stronger support is guaranteed by our assessors. They have not only the role of giving hints to "best practices" as described in section *Sources for input to the knowledge management*. They have also the purpose to consult with packages in cases where they determine weaknesses during assessments. The consulting consists in proposing packages and their application in order to help the teams or departments to improve themselves. The assessors get always the newest information to the knowledge data base.

During the setting up process of a new project the knowledge engineer analyses together with the project managers the main characteristics of this project. A data base research is performed to find packages being helpful and interesting for the project. The knowledge engineer consults the project manager in the application of the packages. This proceeding has some advantages. The new project is supported with the newest experiences from the data base. The support is optimised by the knowledge engineer as he knows the content of the data base very well. Mistakes made in earlier projects can be avoided. But the knowledge management is also supported as the contents of the data base are used. During the consulting the knowledge engineer learns which contents of the data base are demanded and which not. This will have an influence on the topics discussed during the project reviews.

In our enterprise the knowledge engineers, the consultants and the assessors come from the same team. This constellation supports also the use of the knowledge management system, as the same team

- is responsible for the process quality in the project teams or departments,
- consults the teams in applying the processes, standards and engineering methods and
- is responsible for the content of the knowledge data base.

Having all these purposes in one team help to keep the quality of the data base high and to detect how and in which teams the content of the data base could be applied.

3.6 Introduction and Establishing of a Knowledge Management System

The title of this section express exactly what has to be done to get a working knowledge management. It is not sufficient only to introduce the knowledge management. Concepts for establishing are also needed.

At first the data base of the knowledge management system was initially filled. For that a number of project reviews were performed and the assessors were informed that they should give hints to "best practices". In the next step the knowledge management is formally introduced by email to all people of the enterprise. An additional message was placed on the portal page of the intranet. After that some roadshows were performed for the departments and teams.

After the introduction the use of the knowledge management system must be established. One method for establishing is the support of the using described in section *"Sources for input to the knowledge management"*. It is the most important and efficient method. Another method is to remember in regular intervals that the system exists. It can be done by publishing of highlights or new features. Highlights are for example the number of packages inserted in the database (100, 200, ..., 1000, ...) or very interesting packages.

4 Results

4.1 The content of the knowledge data base

Since one year working with the approach we have collected input for the experience packages. For that the three sources for getting input described in section *"Sources for input to the knowledge management"* are used. The quality and the size (measured in words of description) are very differently. The criterions for the quality concentrate in the question: "Does the experience package have a potential use or advantage for someone who is not the author of the package?" We intended to encourage the people of the enterprise to give us input via one of the three sources. Up to now we think it was the right way as:

- The data base was filled with a sufficient number of packages in an acceptable quality.
- The people in the enterprise learn that it is worth to work with the knowledge management system.
- The quality of the packages is quite good.

The topics treated in the packages were not limited to any area of interest. Although that there was no special area of interest most of the packages can be linked directly to activities of the business process model. This depends both from the sources for getting input used in this approach and that the business process model covers the whole business of the enterprise. Most of the packages describe problems and solutions for improving the performance of processes. Packages resulting from spontaneous inputs describe often new ideas.

4.2 The acceptance of the knowledge management

Each knowledge management has to show that is worth to manage the knowledge. The acceptance is one of the most important question during the establishing of a knowledge management. Only if the knowledge management is accepted the advantages of it can be demonstrated. Most the of the people in the enterprise will agree and say that they need such a system. But this is not the acceptance which is significant for the success of the knowledge management. The acceptance in our approach is measured by the number of inputs for packages got from the people of the enterprise and by the use of the knowledge in the data base.

Considering the three sources for getting input described in the sections above a great number of packages put into the data base shows that a lot of people have waited for the knowledge management. The number of packages resulting from spontaneous inputs is more than sufficient. This feedback is very important as the people are absolutely free in sending the input or not. It signals that they are willing to communicate their experiences other people without any obligation like project reviews or assessments. The data base of the knowledge management system contains as already mentioned also packages with "non practices". The number of packages documenting "non practices" got from the project reviews demonstrates also the acceptance. Our impression is that the members of the project teams have searched for a medium to communicate their experiences and they found it in the knowledge management.

The number of input or the number of packages in the data base is not the only sign of the acceptance. It should be also considered how and what of the knowledge in the data base is used. During the introduction of the knowledge management system it is necessary that the knowledge engineer give hints to project teams and departments which of the package could be interesting. This is done during the consulting of teams and departments. By this way the packages are used. The people in the enterprise must be shown that it is useful to study the content of the data base. The functions (search, list of new packages, top ten) of the system to access packages are sufficient. The most interesting package the people find and use are the ones with downloads. The downloads contain solutions or parts of solutions for example tools, macros or templates. These downloads are demanded at most in the system.

The acceptance of the knowledge management system is supported by the processes. It is not so difficult to get input as in other approaches and the use of the knowledge is also guaranteed at a certain degree. But the free use of the system is also more than sufficient. The attractiveness of the system is based on the quality of the contents and especially of the downloads in the packages.

4.3 Unexpected results

A few month after the introduction of the knowledge management system some results could be considered which we have not expected during the definition and developing of the approach. These results are very useful features of the system.

After a while of putting packages in the data base and linking them to the processes it was determined that a greater number of packages have the same topic. This determination is done by an analysis of the processes. Each activity of a process having a greater number of packages is analysed in detail together with the packages. The question is: Do the packages or some of them describe similar problems? If it is so, then there is an accumulation point of problems in the process at this activity. In the next step the problems have to be analysed and improvements to the process or preventing activities have to be performed. By performing these improvements and activities the enterprise do the step into a learning organisation via the knowledge management. This can also be determined by Bootstrap assessments.

The corresponding packages provide an input for a so called abstract package. The predicates of the packages are summarised and represented in a generally accepted form. The abstract packages have a very high value and are often a trigger to improve a process accordingly.

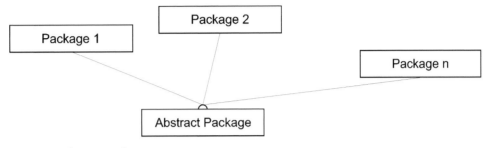

Figure 4.1: Abstract packages

Another unexpected result was got by the analysis and comparison of the project review reports. These reports show the problems of the project teams. They show how the teams act in similar situations and also the differences between the teams. Based on the reports the knowledge engineer is able to consult the teams in order to solve the problems by giving examples from the practice of other projects. Problems which have several teams in a department are discussed with the managers of the department.

5 Conclusions

In this article we have described the approach of knowledge management system defined and established at T-Nova Development Centre South West. The selected approach is a pragmatic and a process based one. It is pragmatic as existing concepts for knowledge management are adapted and mapped to our processes in a practical manner. The literature proposes for example knowledge trees and keyword building but we have replace that with linking the knowledge to processes and offering powerful search functions. Getting input to the knowledge data base is supported directly by the processes. The maintenance and the use of the knowledge is implemented in the enterprise through the processes. The introduction and the establishment of the system would have been by far more difficult without the business process model. We have adapted the concept of quality improvement paradigm and the experience factory. But in our approach they are easier to use and more fasten, what is a result of the already existing processes.

The advantages the enterprise have, given by a team being responsible for assessments, consulting and the knowledge management were used to establish the knowledge management and to keep high the quality of the contents. Our processes are improved by the knowledge management and the teams and departments have the chance to learn from the problems and experiences of others.

6 References

Probst et al. 1997 Probst G., Raub S. and Romhardt K. (1997) Wissen managen – Wie Unternehmen ihre wertvollste Ressource optimal nutzen. Frankfurter Allgemeine – Gabler

Hayes 1988 Hayes J.P. (1978, 1988) Computer Architecture and Organisation. McGraw-Hill

Gensch 1999 Gensch P. (1999) Inhaltliche Gestaltung wissensbasierter Datenbanken. Seminar: Ideen- und Projektdatenbanken, Management Circle

Rombach et al. 1997 Rombach D., Bomarius F. and Birk A. (1997) Workshop Experience Factory

Basili and Green 1994 Basili V., Green S. (1994) Software Process Evolution at the SEL. IEEE Software, 58–66

Integrating Knowledge Management and Quality Management

ROB BALTUS
Comma Soft AG (Germany)

Abstract: In this paper the integration of knowledge management and quality management is discussed. First of all a proper understanding of knowledge management is necessary and it is pointed out what learning in this perspective means. Also the need of quality management for effectively carrying out knowledge management processes is emphasised. Learning from experiences is the basis for process improvement. It is illustrated how knowledge management can support building a quality system through organisational learning and that you can start with it even if processes are at a low maturity level. Then the technological aspect of building quality systems is discussed – the advantages and disadvantages of using intranets and the solution that Comma Soft AG provides for effectively using knowledge management: infonea®. It is shown how the Visual Search™ technology can be used to enable learning while searching by interconnecting the available information in the knowledge management system. Finally, it is described how infonea® is used internally for building a software quality management system and the experiences that were made.

Keywords: knowledge management, knowledge cycle, organisational learning, visual search, infonea.

1 Introduction

Controlled and well-defined processes are an essential part of a quality system. It is common practice that these processes are to be derived from practical experience by using an appropriate assessment method. The processes are then continuously improved through feedback of their practical use.

In large organisations, there still is the problem of providing the right information at the right time and at the right locations. Everybody is familiar with questions like "This process description tells me to create test plans. Didn't John already create such a plan in his last project? Where can I find an example of this test plan?" or "I still have problems with these memory leaks. Which available tools can I use und who has used them already?". What comes on top is that software development underlies an evolutionary paradigm, especially when using the newest technologies. As a result, learning and feedback are natural activities in software development. Reusing process and product experiences is essential for improvement, i.e. reusing knowledge is the basis for improvement.

2 What Is Knowledge Management And What Do We Mean by It?

2.1 The Intangible Asset Knowledge

Knowledge is the key asset in many companies nowadays. Especially companies in the service sector have to rely on the knowledge of their employees. For these companies, it is essential to have a quick and effective access to the knowledge of their employees in order to use it purposefully. Projects should be able to use the knowledge that has been created in other projects. That means a kind of knowledge pool should be available where projects can get the information they need quickly and effectively. The problem is that the knowledge normally is available somewhere in the organisation. But, until it is found and after asking the tenth colleague the wheel is reinvented. In this case you could say "if the organisation knew what it knows…."

Like stated before, knowledge is an important aspect in many companies. Knowledge is necessary to create new innovative products, to keep one step ahead of competitors. Knowledge is a very important non-material resource of an organisation. Perhaps up to 40 percent of the value of an organisation is made up by knowledge. The problem is that knowledge still is an intangible asset, that cannot be found on any balance sheet yet.

2.2 Learning

Let's go deeper into our understanding of knowledge. Take a look at following question: "what do you know about your information or what information do you have about your knowledge?" If you repeat this question often enough, you suddenly don't see the difference anymore between knowledge and information. If you take a look at all the products that are connected with the word knowledge management it proves to be right. But there is a big difference: information can be copied, knowledge has to be learned.

Let's take a look at figure 1. If a person possesses information about subject A and another person about subject B, they both can copy the information of the other person. Both now have information about both subject A and B. If this procedure continues a person gets overwhelmed with information. Of course at the same time he will learn something, but the moment arrives where the amount of information is so big it cannot be coped with. A human being has no infinite storage capacity with very fast access times. In this case only information is exchanged until a certain limit is reached.

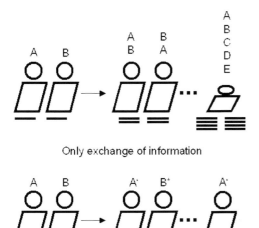

Only exchange of information

Integrate knowledge, understand and use it

Figure 1: What is learning?

How does reality look like? The knowledge that people possess is altered or created from recognising the connection between different information. If a software developer – in his context – understands what somebody from the sales department does, that's enough; he just needs his view on the knowledge of the other person. So, knowledge is created by learning, because it is understood what the other person knows.

Thus, it's important to integrate and interconnect knowledge so that a person can understand it from his perspective and is able to use it.

3 Building A Quality System Using Knowledge Management

3.1 The Usage Of Process Models

It is well-known that mature processes are a prerequisite to achieve a high product quality. In addition to that, the experience and the knowledge of the employees are very important.

In order to achieve a high process maturity often following path is followed: a process reference model like ISO 9001, CMM, ISO 15504 is used to diagnose to what extent the processes in the own organisation cover the requirements from these models. The results from this analysis are used to identify adequate improvement measures. Continuous improvement is very important in this approach. An ideal model cannot be defined and declared as a law of how to perform processes in the organisation. It is better to take small steps and learn from the experiences that are made implementing the process improvement measures. This top-down approach is very common nowadays. If we take a look at the amount of software process assessments that are performed around the world nowadays, there is a huge increase compared to ten years ago. Certainly international standardisation efforts like ISO 15504 and the associated trials have contributed enormously to this process assessment "awareness".

3.2 Learning From Experiences

Learning from experiences can already start when processes do not have a high maturity or even aren't implemented yet. In this approach, knowledge and experiences that are made in the single software projects are analysed and made available to other projects. That means, processes are created from existing knowledge and experience, instead of implementing an ideal model. And that is exactly where knowledge management can contribute. If you are the project manager of a software project and are able to get a quick access to experiences that similar projects have made or knowledge that they have created, it helps you to manage your project better.

It is important though that a process framework is identified, so that experiences and knowledge can be related to those processes. If you want to share your experience you have to know to what processes they relate.

From my point of view, a mixture of both approaches is optimal. The knowledge (best practices) of the software engineering and quality management community, like it is documented in the reference models, should be mixed with own knowledge and experiences.

In ISO 9001 it is required to provide the right information at the right moment to those employees that need this information. Let's take a look at software development. This is a highly innovative field, with new techniques and trends almost every day and where constant experiments are necessary. That is why recently an iterative approach in software development where a software product is produced in several iterations gains more and more acceptance. Because requirements are diffuse at the beginning of a project, learning and feedback are natural activities in software development, and with that reuse of knowledge, i.e. knowledge management is a basis for improvement.

3.3 The Knowledge Cycle

If we concentrate for a moment on continuous improvement. What does it mean? Continuous improvement is learning continuously. And to learn faster, and not to wait until the software project is ended and than see what can be learned from it. These lessons learned might have become obsolete or they might have helped another project very much, if they only had known about it!

While software projects are carried out, an intensive exchange of knowledge is necessary in order to create experience and knowledge faster.

When discussing quality management and continuous improvement, the plan-do-check-act cycle (PDCA-cycle, Deming 1994) is used very often. Since we are talking about knowledge management we will use the knowledge cycle (Probst et al. 1998) that has some similarity with the PDCA-cycle.

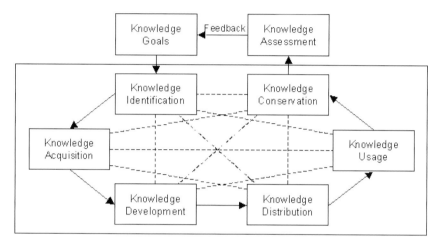

Figure 2: The Knowledge Cycle (Probst et al. 1998)

This knowledge cycle indicates the core processes of knowledge management.

Knowledge Goals – What direction do I go?

Knowledge goals guide the knowledge management activities. They state on what levels what knowledge has to be built. Knowledge goals – like quality goals – have to be integrated into the organisational strategy because knowledge management – like quality management – is a management responsibility.

Knowledge Identification – How does available knowledge become transparent?

It is necessary to analyse and describe the knowledge environment of the organisation. You could compare it to carrying out a software process assessment in order to analyse the process environment of the organisation. There are a lot of organisations that do not have an overview about their data, information, and capabilities. This lack of transparency leads to inefficiency and uninformed decisions. An effective knowledge management has to establish this transparency.

Knowledge Acquisition – How do I buy external knowledge?

Organisations import a great part of their knowledge from external sources like clients, subcontractors, suppliers etc. Knowledge can be "purchased" by recruiting experts or acquiring highly innovative companies. A systematic knowledge management has to take this potential into account.

Knowledge Development – How do I build new knowledge?

Knowledge development is complementary to knowledge acquisition. The target is to create new capabilities, new products, better ideas and more mature processes. Of course knowledge development is integrated into research and development and market research, but knowledge is developed in other areas of the organisation as well. That is why dealing with new ideas and using the creativity of the employees is important.

Knowledge Distribution – How do I bring the knowledge to the right place?

Distributing experiences or knowledge across the organisation is a prerequisite to use isolated knowledge or experiences throughout the whole company. Not everything has to be known by everybody. Therefore you must identify who needs to know what and to what extent. Knowledge management has to facilitate this process of knowledge distribution.

Knowledge Usage – How do I assure the usage of knowledge?

The main goal of knowledge management is to use the organisational knowledge to benefit the organisation. Just identifying and distributing knowledge does not assure the usage of knowledge (just think about classic intranets). Usage of knowledge has to be assured for a successful knowledge management.

Knowledge Conservation – How do I protect myself from losing knowledge?

Once knowledge is acquired, it is not automatically available for the future. It has to be analysed what knowledge is worth to be conserved. Also it has to be organised how knowledge is stored and regularly updated.

Knowledge Assessment – How do I measure the success of my learning processes?

It is necessary to define and use methods to measure the defined knowledge goals in order to get insight into the success of knowledge management. The problem here is – and again we see an analogy to quality management – to define measurable goals. Here methods like GQM (Van Solingen/Berghout 1999) can help.

3.4 Learning At A Low Maturity Level

The knowledge cycle can be used to achieve an effective distribution and usage of knowledge and experience even if processes are still at a low maturity level. This is supported by the idea of the learning organisation or experience factory (Basili et al. 1994).

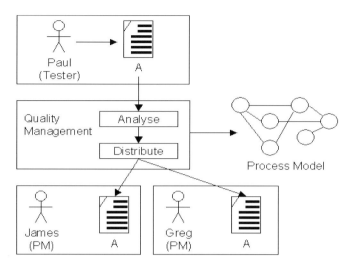

Figure 3: Learning from experiences

If a tester creates a document "A" with experiences about test techniques, this experience is then analysed and perhaps abstracted by quality management so that other projects can use this experience. But also this document can influence the process model if analysing the document shows that there is improvement potential or even new processes have to be defined.

Discussing the knowledge cycle we saw that conserving and assessing knowledge is very important. A separate instance is needed that assesses the quality of the *contents* of the knowledge management system, improves it if necessary and uses this information to define and improve processes. This is definitely a quality management task, so that we now have closed the gap between quality and knowledge management.

4 The Pros And Cons Of An Intranet-Based Quality System

A technology that allows information and knowledge to be put at somebody's disposal quickly is web-technology. There are some reasons for documenting and realising a software quality system with this technology:

- The paperless office, no shelves filled with folders; the information about the quality system (process descriptions, procedures, guidelines, standards, experience packages etc.) is at somebody's disposal in his own work environment, at his fingertips.

- The web-platform is independent from operating systems.
- New versions of quality system documentation can immediately be published, and therewith an important requirement of ISO 9001 is met.
- The Intranet-based quality system can be used as a software engineering portal, with links to other websites that concern the quality system processes.

There are some problems that shouldn't be underestimated. If printed material is transferred 1:1 to online text the result is poor. Actually, the text should be rewritten and restructured. What is the result normally? Documents that are in an online system are printed. If we look at a process description for example, roles would be connected with the activities they perform and the activities would be connected with artefacts that are produced or needed in order to carry them out. If this information were stored in one document, then the people that have to use this process description would print the document rather than trying to read it on-line.

A second problem that we see when using an intranet is that the information in the intranet can lead to confusion ("lost in hyperspace") and cognitive overload (too much information).

Although the tools for programming web applications have improved strongly in the past years, it still is a big problem to keep an intranet up-to-date with the latest information and newest or changed documents. If you use an intranet in your organisation you'll know what I mean.

The easy-to-use web programming tools and the usage of so called homepage wizards, do not require investing much time in user interface design. But the user interface design and the usability of web applications are extremely important. It should be possible to present the contents of the intranet-based quality systems in different ways with different views. The people in an organisation need different access possibilities to the quality system. Every person has different knowledge and a different background and needs his own access to information and knowledge. A developer will need different information from the requirement analysis process than a system analyst. The developer needs to know what artefacts are the result of this process so that he can start working, the system analyst needs to know what activities have to be carried out, what methods can be used in order to create a software analysis document that enables the developer to implement the software.

5 infonea® – An Infrastructure For Knowledge Management

Comma Soft AG has created an infrastructure for knowledge management: infonea®. It would go too far to explain this powerful tool in detail but it is necessary to understand its philosophy and key elements.

5.1 Knowledge Through Interconnection

A very important element of the infonea® philosophy is "knowledge through interconnection". Dead data of the intranet becomes alive by interconnecting it with people and processes. Let's explore following situation: "This test procedure document was created by John, what's John's job? I see, he is the quality engineer responsible for the *help*LINE® product. What is John's responsibility? He is responsible for the software-testing process and his role in this process is test designer. That explains why he created this document." We see that the experiences that are made, or the knowledge that is created, is derived from recognising the logical connection between different information, in this case connecting documents with persons, processes, and products.

5.2   Learning While Searching

Another key element of the infonea® philosophy is "learning while searching". By searching for information, the user should get an overview, he should be able to recognise the context, and his attention should be awakened: he should learn something. But he also should have the possibility to rate that what he just learned. In above example it should be possible to rate the test procedure document in order to make it more or less valuable information for other employees and roles.

The infonea® Visual Search™ technology plays an important role. If you use a common search engine, you only have a short learning success. You'll find the right information but there is a certain phase of frustration where you only are searching for information but do not learn anything.

Perhaps you can use some kind of "better" full text search, e.g. with a semantic analysis, but you still will have this phase of frustration. The problem is, the next time you search for information, you start all over again. If there is more information on a certain subject, it will take you longer to find the appropriate information.

Just try to find something in the internet about this search term: "integrating knowledge management and quality management". You'll probably find nothing ("sorry, no results were found"). The frustration starts. Then only search for "quality management". Now you'll find something, the only problem is, you have found more than 400,000 hits. Perhaps you'd better try "knowledge management". The same problem, here you will also find more than 400,000 hits. Some search engines offer the possibility to narrow your search, so you can try that. The point is, it will take some time to find the appropriate information.

When using Visual Search™ the time you need to find the appropriate not only is shorter. While you are searching, you experience a lot and you will not have this phase of frustration because you intuitively combine available search objects.

5.3 Visual Search™ In Detail

Let's consider we have only six documents in infonea® and only four object types: process, topic, author, and role. The following table shows these documents:

Table 1: Documents in infonea®

Document	Process	Topic	Author	Role
A	Software Test	Test Techniques	Paul	Tester
B	Software Test	Test Automation	John	Test Manager
C	Project Management	Cost Estimation	John	Project Manager
D	Project Management	Budgeting	Peter	Project Manager
E	Software Test	Versioning	Paul	Software Engineer
F	Configuration Management	Versioning	Paul	Software Engineer

We will use this example to explain Visual Search™. There are two different people searching for information: project manager James and project manager Greg. When they both start searching they have the following view:

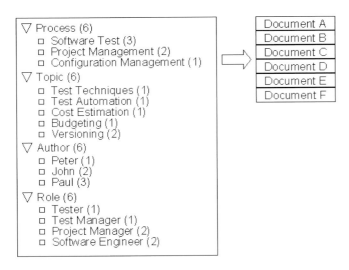

Figure 4: The view on the information in infonea®

The number behind the object type indicates the number of information objects that are available for this object type, in this case the six documents A through F.

James first starts selecting the process Software-Test. infonea® automatically checks what other object values are valid for this selection and James has following reduced view on the information:

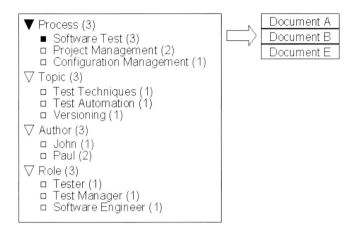

Figure 5: Reduced view after selecting process "Software Test"

Note that only those object values and documents are displayed that are available for the process "Software Test". The topics "Cost Estimation" and "Budgeting" as well as the author "Peter" have been removed. In this case infonea® avoids that you get frustrated because "no matches were found".

Now James selects the Role Tester. His view is reduced again:

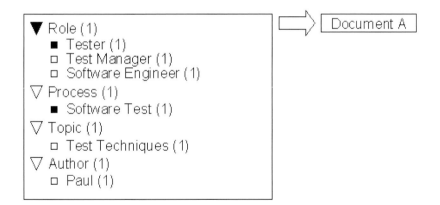

Figure 6: Reduced view after selecting process "Software Test" and role "Tester"

This means that James has found document "A" by reducing the search criteria by and by. His search has been visualised.

Remember Greg was also looking for information. His Visual Search™ path is displayed in following figure:

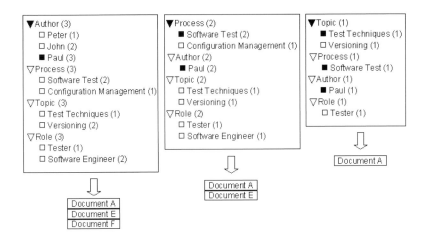

Figure 7: Visual Search™ path: Author – Process – Topic.

Greg first selects the Author "Paul". The documents that Paul wrote are displayed and the view is reduced to those object values that are valid for the author Paul. Then he selects the Process "Software-Test". His view is reduced again. Finally he selects the Topic "Test Techniques". He also found document A.

Can you see the difference? infonea® only offers to you those search criteria and values that are valid for your personal path through the knowledge system. Although both James and Greg finally found the same document, they went their own way through the system and learned different things.

James' starting point was the "Software Test" process. On his search path he learned what topics were related to Software Test and what people created information for this process. Greg's starting point was Paul. He learned for what processes Paul created information and on what subjects.

They used the time until they found the appropriate information for learning. If you have insight into the search, if you are able to create knowledge through interconnecting available information, the learning success is on a long-term basis.

Figure 8 shows that the experience that Paul made on test techniques was analysed by quality management and then stored in infonea®. The project managers James and Greg used their own search path to use the experience that Paul has made.

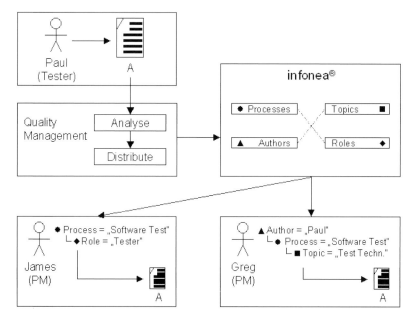

Figure 8: Using infonea® to learn from experiences

Although this was a very simple example, you could see the power of infonea®. In this example we also only used documents as object types. But also other object types, e.g. teams, people, topics, can be stored in infonea®. Imagine how you are supported with Visual Search™ when thousands of information objects and numerous object types are stored in infonea®.

5.4 Feedback

One of the core processes of knowledge management is knowledge assessment – how to measure the success of the knowledge management. Although Visual Search™ eases your search for information, the quality of the search result must not necessarily be very high. Therefore you have the possibility to rate the information that you have found. This has also to do with knowledge conservation. The rating of available information helps to analyse what information is worth to be conserved or what information has to be updated.

5.5 Publishing Information

What do authors have to do in order to create and publish their information and create references to existing information without high editorial expenses? Authors can publish their process experiences and knowledge at the click of a mouse, create references to other information (e.g. processes, contacts, tools, experiences), becoming immediately available at all relevant locations within the company. To make this possible, a sufficient description of the information that is put into the system is necessary. This information is stored in attributes or logical connections that belong to a specific object type. These logical connections can be followed in both directions, e.g. the connection *authorship* can be "author of " or "written by". infonea® provides adequate guidelines for the input of the information and checks t also. Information that already electronically is available is used (e.g. user data, title of the document, keywords etc.) so that no redundant input of data is needed. There are variable guidelines dependent on author, type of information, department, and subject area etc. because each object type has its own attributes. What is behind that is a maintainable rule system, because not everybody is allowed to publish everything. For example, only members of the quality management team are allowed to publish process descriptions and guidelines.

It must be possible to easily modify published information. A process description that is published is not valid for an indefinite period but will change frequently – if the continuous improvement cycle works. infonea® supports this with a version control mechanism with checkin and checkout.

5.6 Maintenance

A very cost-saving aspect of infonea® is that a lavish maintenance isn't needed anymore. Your corporate user interface design is only defined once and always used when information is published and prepared to be displayed. The information that you publish is immediately at the disposal of all authorised people in the correct design and presentation.

To illustrate this, see figure 9.

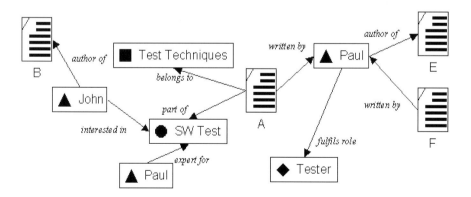

Figure 9: The information network made visible.

Figure 9 is a visualisation of a part of the information network in infonea®. Suppose you would add the information that Paul also is a software engineer. infonea® knows that the role "Software Engineer" is connected to the process "Configuration Management". The process "Configuration Management" is connected with the topic "Versioning". The topic "Versioning" is connected with the author "Paul", the process "Software Test", and the documents "E" and "F".

Not only the new information automatically is available but also the information network is expanded (figure 10).

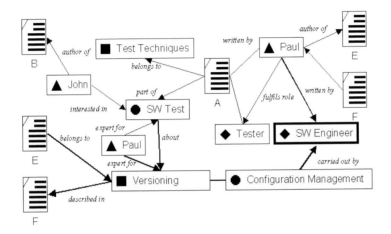

Figure 10: A new information element automatically is available

5.7   Application Areas Of infonea®

infonea® is an "operating system" for knowledge management and there are several solutions that can be considered as applications for this operating system. Summarising, infonea® is a solution that supports information and knowledge management in the intranet, internet, or extranet with different solutions for a large range of applications. It also is an architecture that software developers can use to build their own solutions. The range of applications contains :

- corporate portals / personal portals
- yellow pages / skill management
- best practice pool
- information systems
- project / process / organisational knowledge
- visualising structures
- knowledge about knowledge
- product catalogues

6 Building A Intranet-Based Quality System With infonea®

After discussing knowledge management, building a quality system, intranets and in-
fonea® these four topics are integrated now and it is explained how we have built an
intranet-based quality system with infonea®.

6.1 The Object Model

The infonea® solution that is discussed here is the solution that we at Comma Soft internally use. The object model that we used for this quality management solution has
following structure:

It is important to stress that you can start searching for information at any object.
Let's start with the processes. Like in every quality system processes depend on or refer
to other processes. There are certain roles that are involved in the execution of the process. Also there is certain information that is part of a process (i.e. process descriptions,
templates, artefacts etc.). This information can refer to other information, for example
a process description would refer to guidelines and templates that can be used. This is
the classic modelling of a process model: processes, roles and artefacts.

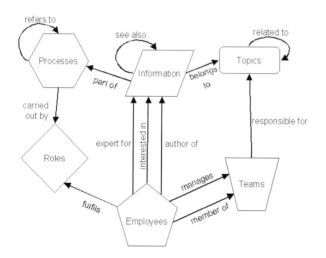

Figure 11: Object model of the quality system solution

But it is interesting to become more concrete, which roles are fulfilled by what employees? For which information are they experts or where are they interested in or did
they even publish information? To which teams do they belong? In this context, a team
should be understood as a group of persons that are responsible for certain topics. Often teams are organisational units but also project teams or cross-section functions like

quality management. The topic that a team is responsible for can be related to other topics. And to close the circle: information belongs to a certain topic.

An example makes this clear (figure 12).

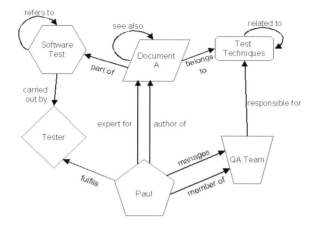

Figure 12: Using the object model of the quality system solution

Imagine, you are new at Comma Soft and are test manager in the infonea[®] team. The software test process would then be of interest for you. In this process your role as a test manager is defined but also the role of a tester. You would like to know which people are testers. You see that Paul is a tester and he also is a member of the QA team and is sitting in the same office as you are. You would like to know if Paul is an expert for something so that you can ask him if you need some information. Paul wrote several documents about test case determination. You also find the document that has been rated as the most valuable by your colleagues. You will have a closer look at this document later on. The document belongs to the topic "test techniques". To the topic "test techniques" there are several other documents that could be interesting. The QA team is responsible for the topic "test techniques" but also for other topics. Since you are new in the company and leading this QA team, you would like to know for what topics your team is responsible for. And that is how you navigate yourself through the system according to the maxim: "learning while searching".

6.2 Feedback

When discussing the knowledge cycle, we saw that it is important to get feedback about the success of the knowledge management system. In a quality system, feedback and the evaluation of feedback is an important task to keep continuous improvement going. That is why we have integrated several feedback mechanisms into infonea[®].

6.2.1   Content Feedback

First there is a direct feedback on the content, the rating of information like we have seen before. The analysis of the feedback can lead to changing or updating the contents or even deleting it. It must be clearly stated here that this is a procedure that can not be automated. This needs a human interaction. And when talking about a quality system, analysing feedback on the contents of the quality system information (processes, roles, artefacts etc.) can lead to changing and improving processes. Thus, continuous improvement is supported.

6.2.2   Application Feedback

Also a direct feedback on the application is possible. The user can give comments like "I don't like the layout in this list" or "When I click on this button, nothing happens". These change requests and defect reports can then be taken into consideration by the infonea® change control board in order to plan further releases.

6.2.3   Benefit Feedback

A third feedback possibility is perhaps the most important one: a feedback about the benefit of the knowledge management supported quality system. For this we developed a GQM model. The majority of the metrics are subjective ratings by the users but also objective measures, e.g. the average number of new documents for a given topic.

Before infonea® was introduced internally in January 2000, all users had to fill out a questionnaire that we developed using the GQM model. The results of this survey showed that most people felt that the information they received was incomplete and unconsidered. They also criticised the information transparency, i.e. the quality of the information and the path it went. As we discussed the knowledge cycle, we saw that knowledge development is very important. In the questionnaire there were some questions about motivating people to use and to provide information. Interesting was that the majority said that they would benefit from using information but not enough from providing information. Another question that dealt with information distribution confirmed this. The rating of the question "Do you think that all people that need the information are informed about it" was very poor.

In any case the results of the survey showed that there was a need to implement an effective knowledge management system. The survey will be repeated after the people have been using the system for a year to see if the knowledge management has improved. Using these kind of questionnaires and repeating the survey in regular periods, allows it to measure the benefits of the knowledge management supported quality system. This is the first step in making the intangible asset knowledge transparent and finding its way to the organisation's balance sheet.

7 Summary

We have seen that knowledge management can support quality management, since it supports continuous improvement and enables a reproduction of the quality system in the knowledge base. But also quality management is necessary to effectively use knowledge management; the quality of the contents as well as the quality of the structure of the knowledge management system has to be managed.

Building software quality systems using modern web-based technologies is the only way to provide a quick access to all relevant quality system information. If using an intranet for this, it's a step in the right direction but there are some disadvantages that should not be overseen. infonea® is able to cope with these disadvantages but also supports learning through Visual Search™ and improvement of the quality system. infonea® can be used to implement an intranet-based quality system. But having invested once in the system, its usage can be expanded to other application areas, e.g. skill management, product catalogues, etc. and can it be used to manage the knowledge of the whole organisation.

8 References

Basili et al. 1994 Basili VR, Caldiera C, Rombach HD (1994) Experience Factory. In: Marciniak JJ (ed) Encyclopedia of Software Engineering, Volume 1. John Wiley and Sons, New York, pp 469–476.

Comma Soft 2000 Comma Soft AG (2000) Profitable Wissensvernetzung – Knowledge Management bei der Commerzbank ZIT. In: SQL Server Magazin, Volume 02/2000, H&T, Munich, pp 50–51.

Deming 1994 Deming, WE (1994) The New Economics: for industry, government, education. MIT CAES, Cambridge.

Probst et al. 1998 Probst GJB, Raub S, Romhardt K (1998) Wissen Managen. Frankfurter Allg. Zeitung für Deutschland, Frankfurt. Gabler, Wiesbaden.

Röscheisen 2000 Röscheisen E (2000) Wissen im Umlauf. In: Screen Business Online, Volume 08/2000. MACup, Hamburg, pp 42–47.

Van Solingen and Berghout 1999 Van Solingen R, Berghout E (1999) The Goal/Question/Metric Method. McGraw-Hill, London.

A Cost-Benefit Model for Software Testing

Rudolf Göldner

RZF NRW – IT centre of Northrine Westphalia's Finance Department (Germany)

Abstract: This article attempts to illustrate the economic viability of quality assurance measures such as software testing by comparing the costs of such measures with the costs that the user incurs when errors occur at the workplace. Since there are hardly any empirical studies on these costs, with the exception of Compaq's "Rage against the machine" study, this article seeks to estimate these error-induced costs. Obviously, the more users there are, the greater the benefit provided by quality assurance. In other words, quality assurance is worthwhile, irrespective of all other beneficial aspects, as soon as the number of users exceeds a critical figure. Finally, the formula for estimating the error-induced costs incurred by the user is applied to the data from two projects.

Keywords: quality assurance, software testing, cost benefit model, error-induced costs

1 The status of quality assurance in the software development process

Quality assurance measures, such as testing during the software development process, are recognised software engineering methods and are included in every software process model. Software development is based on four conflicting dimensions: *functionality, quality, deadlines* and *costs*. The scope for solutions on any given project is restricted with regard to these dimensions. Thus, if the costs and deadline are specified in advance, the functionality and/or quality assurance have/has to be limited (Figure 1). So, quality assurance is restricted by the dimension of costs on the one hand and time-to-market requirements on the other.

For software producers, quality assurance especially in the form of software testing entails effort which, in turn, affects the release date for the software product. Moreover, the effort required to detect and correct errors does not really depend on whether these activities have to be performed before the product is used or when it is already being used – with the exception of analysis errors. This is why it is often doubted that the effort invested in quality assurance is necessary. However, the economic viability of quality assurance has to be measured using other criteria, e.g. at the user level, where the software is in productive use. There is no doubt that system crashes and malfunctions cost more effort on the part of the user (Figure 2).

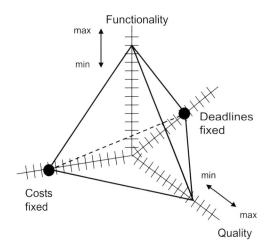

Figure 1: Tetrahedron of software development: the solution space is limited

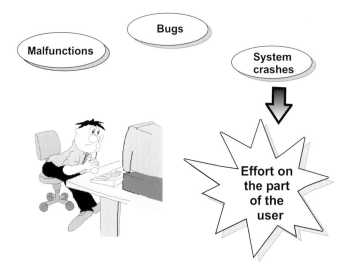

Figure 2: User centric view of software bugs

Unfortunately, there are hardly any representative studies on this issue. One of the few that do exist is Compaq's "Rage against the machine" study. An extract from this study was available on Compaq's website from May 1999 [1] but has since been removed.

2 Compaq's "Rage against the machine" study from the point of view of quality assurance

2.1 Technology-related anger

In March and April 1999 a representative survey of 1,255 employees who use computers at work was carried out in Great Britain. The amazing and worrying result was the "technology-related anger" (TRA) detected by the survey. This type of anger is much more common than the much better known phenomenon of traffic-related anger and results in outbursts of rage that can go as far as actual physical attacks against the computer.

The survey questions referred to IT as a whole, i.e. hardware, software and networks. The responses showed:

- there is a high level of stress, anger and frustration caused by computer problems;
- this leads to substantial costs for the company;
- 23 per cent of those questioned said that their work was interrupted at least once a day; and
- 20 per cent of those questioned said that they spent up to three hours per day solving IT problems.

The damage for the company is not only caused by the fact that staff spend time on computer problems themselves, but also by the psychological stress exerted for the individual employees. Although they may react differently according to their disposition, their reactions as a whole have a negative influence on the atmosphere and productivity within the company.

2.2 CBI statistics

Statistics compiled by the Confederation of British Industry (CBI) show that, on average, it takes one hour per day and user to solve IT problems . (These figures are quoted in the Compaq study, too [1].)

This figure is more or less the same as the result of the Compaq study with regard to the 20 per cent who said that they spent up to three hours per day solving IT problems. Thus, if this figure is transferred to all of the users (i.e. 100 per cent), an average of 0.6 hours per day is used for this purpose.

The CBI concludes that these breakdowns cost £ 25,000 per person per year. Since 9 million people in Great Britain have a computer at their workplace, the macroeconomic damage caused by the breakdowns comes to almost £ 225 billion per year.

The Compaq study focuses on the psychological effects rather than the costs of IT breakdowns. It also makes no distinction between hardware, software and network failures. But our experience shows that the computer hardware (even the desktop printer) and the network hardware rarely break down in a stable system and certainly not on a daily basis. This means that the main cause is the software.

3 The cost-benefit model

3.1   Error-induced costs incurred by the user

As software testing is one of the most important measures in quality assurance I will restrict my reflections to software testing, now.

The costs incurred during use are defined as downtimes in person days [PD], with one PD equalling eight hours. Only serious errors, i.e. those errors that cause the user effort, are taken into account. There is a link between *the costs (C) during use, the number of errors (ER) in the software* and *the number of users (U)*. If *the average effort during use per error and user* is defined as B_m the following is true:

$$C = B_m * U * ER \quad [PD]$$

3.2 Optimistic estimate of the error-induced costs incurred by the user

The next step is to attempt to produce an optimistic estimate of the average effort B_m per error and user. This process does not cover follow-up effort of the type necessary in the case of data being lost due to software bugs. Though this follow-up effort can take on huge dimensions, it can hardly be calculated without empirical studies. The average effort per error and user is determined as follows:

$$B_m = e * p \quad [PD \text{ per error and user}]$$

where *e* is *the average effort in PD per error* and *p* is *the proportion of users that is actually affected by the error*. For e, i.e. the effort invested by the user per error, empirical values can be quoted. Users hardly ever spend more than half a day dealing with an error. However, the minimum time required is normally not less than half an hour. In this case, the following is true:

$$0.0625 < e < 0.5 \quad \text{[PD per error and user]}$$

The proportion p of users affected by an error should really be 100 per cent but this is not the case because:

- 30 per cent of users may be absent or may perform another task
- 10 per cent may hear about the error from other users and do not use the erroneous function
- 10 per cent may get an error message from the hotline in time and do not use the erroneous function

Thus, p could be said to equal 50 per cent or 0.5.
The result would be

$$0.03125 < B_m < 0.25 \quad \text{[PD per /error and user]}$$

and the minimum costs would be
$$C_{min} = 0.03125 * U * ER \quad \text{[PD]}$$
and the maximum costs

$$C_{max} = 0.25 * U * ER \quad \text{[PD]}$$

The expected value is

$$EX (B_m) = 0.14 \quad \text{[PD per error and user]}$$

and the average costs
$$C_m = 0.14 * U * ER \quad \text{[PD]}$$

Table 1: Costs during use in Person Days depending on the number of users U and the average effort B_m per error and user. The figures in brackets are the costs in Person Years.

ER = 20			
B_m [PD/error and user]	U		
	400	2,000	10,000
0.03125	250 (1.25)	1,250 (6.2)	6,250 (31.2)
0.14	1,120 (5.6)	5,600 (28)	28,000 (140)
0.25	2,000 (10)	10,000 (50)	50,000 (250)

If a software system that has ER = 20 serious errors is delivered and then used by U = 400 people, the minimum costs will be C_{min} = 250 PD, average costs C_m = 1,120 PD and maximum costs C_{max} = 2,000 PD (Table 1, Figure 3). If there were U = 2,000 users, the costs would be 5 times as high. The average costs would then come to C_m = 5,600 PD or 28 person years and, as said, this model calculation doesn't even cover the considerably larger effort required when data is lost due to software bugs (Table 1).

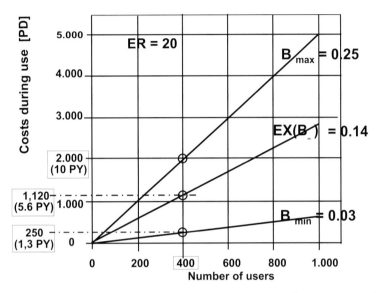

Figure 3: Costs depending on the number of users and the effort per error and user. Example for a software product shipped with 20 errors.

3.3 Financial benefits of software testing

It is now possible to compare the costs incurred by the user with the costs of software testing in order to assess the efficiency. Obviously, the software testing costs C_{ST} must be lower than the costs incurred by the user if no software testing is done. ER_{ST} stands for the errors detected through software testing.

$$C - C_{ST} = B_m * U * ER_{ST} - C_{ST} > 0$$

In other words, software testing is also worthwhile if the number of users exceeds a certain, critical level U_{crit}, as follows:

$$U = U_{crit} > C_{ST} / B_m * 1 / ER_{ST}$$

We shall now use data regarding two projects in North-Rhine Westphalia's finance department to conduct a model calculation. The developers' test (software developers' white box test) was followed by user acceptance testing, during which ER_{ST} serious errors were discovered. The effort was defined as C_{ST} (Table 2, Figure 4).

Table 2: Financial benefits of software testing C - C_{ST} and critical level of users U_{crit} calculated from two projects

	Project A			Project B		
ER_{ST}	386			604		
U	200			200		
B_m	0.03125	0.14	0.25	0.03125	0.14	0.25
C	2,413	10,808	19,300	3,775	16,912	30,200
C_{ST}	1,820			1,362		
$C - C_{ST}$	593	8,988	17,480	2,413	15,550	28,838
U_{crit}	151	34	19	72	17	9

 ER_{ST} = 386 errors were detected on Project A and the effort involved came to C_{ST} = 1,820 PD. The product is used by U = 200 people. The average costs incurred by the users due to this error would have been C_m = 10,808 PD. Thus, the benefit from using user acceptance testing totalled 8,988 PD. Or, to put it another way, user acceptance testing would have even been worthwhile if only U_{crit} = 34 people had been using the product (Figure 5).

On Project B (Table 2, Figure 4) the results were even more drastic. ER_{ST} = 604 errors were discovered and the effort required came to C_{ST} = 1,362 PD. This product is also used by U = 200 people. The average costs incurred by the users due to this error would have totalled C_m = 16,912 PD. This means that the benefit from using user acceptance testing was 15,550 PD. Or, in other words, user acceptance testing would have even been worthwhile if only U_{crit} = 17 people had been using the product (Figure 5).

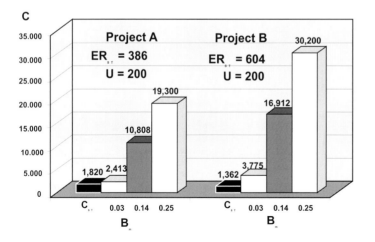

Figure 4: Costs of software testing C_{ST} compared with costs incurred by the user calculated from to projects

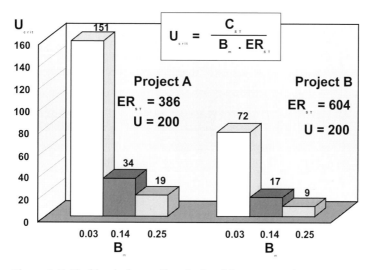

Figure 5: Critical level of users U$_{crit}$ calculated from two projects

On both projects the costs of user acceptance testing were less than 20 per cent of the total costs. The method used to perform the user acceptance testing was "SQS-TEST" [2] by Software Quality Systems AG, Cologne.

4 Outlook

It is clear that the *U* (user) value is the significant factor. The higher *U* is, the greater the benefit and the justifiable effort that can be invested in systematic software testing and quality assurance respectively.

If the average value is used for B_m, the justifiable effort for software testing can be calculated as follows:

$$C_{ST} = 0.14 * ER * U \quad [PD]$$

It is not as easy to estimate the effort incurred by users when software bugs lead to data loss or corruption. Such estimates necessitate company-specific, empirical studies, which, in view of the rationalisation potential that could be tapped using error-reduced software, are really crucial.

If, for whatever reason, empirical studies cannot be carried out, the only real alternative is the "minimum marginal costing" method presented here.

Acknowledgements: Special thanks are due to my colleagues Ursula Masznicz and Carsten Thomas, and to Petra Bukowski from SQS AG who developed some basic ideas for this model in a brainstorming session. Furthermore, I want to thank my colleagues at QuiS – the SQS-TEST User Group [3]- for their lively discussions of the model.

5 References

[1] Compaq Computer Ltd: Rage against the machine http://www.compaq.uk/ rags/find.pdf, May 1999 There is a summary in German at http://www.heise.de/tp/ deutsch/inhalt/te/2892/1.html

[2] Software Quality Systems AG http://www.SQS.de/tools/index.htm

[3] QuiS – Arbeitsgemeinschaft der SQS-TEST-Anwender SQS-TEST User Group http://www.sqs.de/tools/tool_quishome.htm

An Example Cost/Benefit Analysis for Quality Management Systems (QMS)

GREGOR JAHNKE
ARGE ISKV GMBH (Germany)

Abstract: ARGE ISVK GMBH is a software and systems company that specialises in developing information systems for statutory health insurance schemes. Almost 90% of all requirements and business events in the field of statutory health insurance are currently covered by "IS KV" (Health Insurance Information System). ARGE ISKV GMBH's sophisticated *IS KV* now offers the most up-to-date products in the field of statutory health insurance. *ISKV* is currently deployed at around 25,000 workstations throughout Germany, with customers including company and guild health insurance schemes plus some private health insurance companies.

In the 1990s, ARGE ISKV GMBH joined forces with SQS AG to develop a company-specific QM system. Pilot projects are currently underway to explore alternative testing methods and tools for quality management purposes. The main project is dealing with test automation for batch applications and it is this project that will serve as the basis for the following detailed examination of cost/benefit analyses in the field of quality management.

Keywords: Software, Systems, Quality Management, Quality Assurance, Testing, Cost/Benefit

1 ARGE ISKV – a company profile

ARGE ISVK GMBH is a software and systems company that specialises in developing information systems for statutory health insurance schemes. Originally embedded in the public structures of statutory health insurance as the IT department of the "Bundesverband der Betriebskrankenkassen" (Federal Association of Company Health Insurance Schemes), in 1994 ARGE ISKV GMBH began to be spun off to form an independent company. This move to the free market and the increasing competition in the health insurance sector from the mid-90s increasingly raised the question of the costs/benefits and the economic feasibility of information systems (in the sense of administration costs) and their development.

Almost 90% of all requirements and business events in the field of statutory health insurance are currently covered by "IS KV" (Health Insurance Information System). The development platform and the run-time system are based on a UNIX platform and the INFORMIX database system. The dialog applications are developed in 4-GL form using UnifAce and the batch applications are developed using C. ARGE ISKV GMBH's sophisticated *IS KV* now offers the most up-to-date products in the field of statutory health insurance. *ISKV* is currently deployed at around 20,000 workstations throughout Germany, with customers including company and guild health insurance schemes plus some private health insurance companies. ARGE ISKV GMBH presently employs approximately 200 staff. The first-line customer support is guaranteed by around 15 independent *IS KV Service Centres (ISC)* together with ARGE ISKV GMBH.

In the 1990s, ARGE ISKV GMBH joined forces with SQS AG to develop a company-specific QM system. Pilot projects are currently underway to explore alternative testing methods and tools for quality management purposes. The main project is dealing with test automation for batch applications and it is this project that will serve as the basis for the following detailed examination of cost/benefit analyses in the field of quality management.

2 Principles and prerequisites

2.1 Background to and reasons for the development of a cost/benefit model

With regard to consideration of the economic feasibility and the related cost/benefit analysis of QM systems, requirements and necessities became apparent at ARGE ISKV GMBH and led to more consistent investigation of the subject and the initiation of a cost/benefit analysis. Examination of the economic feasibility of work processes and QM measures is usually triggered by evidence of inefficient processes and the aim or result usually involves making changes to the existing situation. It goes without saying that, in our experience, there is no one universal model for assessing the costs and benefits of a QM system but that each company has to draw up its own conditions and criteria in line with a few basic rules. This paper aims to present and communicate these basic rules, based on ARGE ISKV GMBH's experiences, in order to provide an example and food for thought for other companies.

As is most certainly the case in other companies, ARGE ISKV GMBH's software development and QM strategies are influenced by factors, e.g. company-specific and strategic reasons concerning customers and/or partners, that preclude new measures and decisions (e.g. automation of test processes) even if their economic feasibility has been proven in mathematical terms. These factors include

- the employees being 100% behind and feeling responsibility towards their own products and thus the requirement that products be tested by the staff responsible for the product.

- customer involvement in QM measures (customer testing).

Consequently, economic assessments have to be seen in a different light from the very start.

To begin with, it is important that the company studies its own software development processes, the associated QM structures in general and the operative QM in particular. Relevant figures drawn from the current QM measures are crucial in securing success and allowing subsequent comparison in order to identify the benefit of changes to the QM system. Simple measurement of the tasks, activities and quality results plays an elementary role, especially in the field of software development, in the preparation of an economic feasibility analysis as well as serving as the basis for any decisions resulting from it but such measurement is often difficult in practice. Industry realised this problem some years ago and introduced relevant standards but such standardisation is not so easy in the field of software development. One reason might be the high degree of individuality and creativity in software development compared to "standardised" industrial production. Nonetheless, it is only be keeping quality records and being motivated/setting oneself the goal to examine in more detail and, where appropriate, "optimise" certain recurring, standardised activities or steps within them that one can form a basis for dealing with this issue and bringing about change.

2.2 What action should one take? Or "less is better than more"

The action to be taken will depend on the maturity of the company's QM system. In our case, the aim was to examine more closely a QM model that had been in existence for many years, to develop and test suitable changes and optimisation measures and, whilst doing so, to concentrate on the aspect of economic feasibility or, to put it in basic terms, "Is the expense really worth it?"

Thus, to tackle this subject in line with the conditions and expectations mentioned, it is advisable to define a pilot project that underlines not only the purely theoretical expectations, but also the results of previous assumptions and economic feasibility analyses and verifies them where appropriate. Such a project should also help, in unclear situations, to generate the results by testing the measures in order to be better able to implement and enforce them later on.

The pilot project should also place more emphasis on gathering information than on inordinate values. In this case, *less is definitely more*. Even if the practical results do not confirm the assumptions, it is better to make a better decision based on these findings with less money lost in investing in a clearly structured project and to not do certain things as planned than to be faced with the painful situation of having to justify spontaneously initiated measures with high investment and little to no success.

3 A cost/benefit analysis model for ARGE ISKV GmbH

3.1 Software development at ARGE ISKV GMBH

Software development and thus quality management at *IS KV* are performed on the basis of a classical phase or "waterfall model". This means that the quality management measures (quality measurements, tests, audits or reviews) are conducted in parallel with the phases or at the point of transition to the next phase.

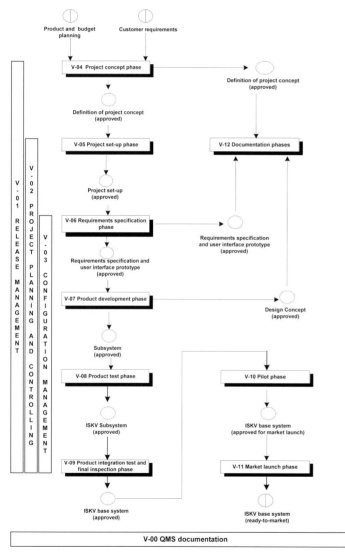

Figure 1: V-Model of ARGE IS KV GMBH

The company's QM area is based in a central department, with the staff, "quality officers" in the case of test management and "quality managers" in the case of operative QM, acting as "service providers" for maintenance teams and projects in a traditional matrix structure. These service providers implement the company's QM specifications in the field of software development.

With regard to quality management, ARGE ISKV GMBH attaches particular importance to the following factors:

1. The employees convince themselves of the quality of the products they design by examining the products realised.
2. It is crucial that the customer is involved in QM measures.

Together with ARGE ISKV GMBH's guidelines, these two principles are defined as clear company aims. They influence the structure of the software development process and the form and procedure for QM measures (also as an impact of a cost/benefit analysis). At the moment, most of the tests are conducted manually.

Since the development of the *IS KV* largely consists of maintenance projects, any analysis of the economic feasibility of the QM system will automatically ask, *"How long with the software continue to be used?"* and *"What additional investment is the company willing to make to implement measures as a result of the findings of a cost/benefit analysis?"* Although it is often no problem to gain acceptance for investment in, for example, tools for producing and developing software, it is not always so easy in the area of quality management. One of the reasons is that the term "quality management" is now so frequently used by everybody but people do not bother to measure it using strict methods and procedures that would make its meaning clear to everyone. But here too, the rule is "No economic feasibility without transparency, clear rules, procedures and processes."

3.2   Prerequisites for the pilot project

ARGE ISKV GMBH needed to assess, in a structured manner, the possibilities for automating certain test processes in defined quality management phases and calculate the economic feasibility of such a measure. This necessity arose from various factors and insights, including the following:

*   insufficient qualified human resources,
*   inadequate flexibility and throughput in certain QM phases,
*   insufficient test standardisation and thus time-consuming evaluation of the test results and the actual quality of the test.

The pilot project was also intended to deliver criteria, procedures and measures for any change processes necessary. The aim was to assess the economic feasibility of existing and potential changes in the QM phases, to produce a cost/benefit analysis and make the need for investments easier to understand.

In light of previous findings and experience in the field of test automation, only *ISKV* products with batch applications were used on the pilot project. The project did not cover automation of dialog applications.

4 Cost/benefit analysis for or economic feasibility of a QMS

4.1 Base figures

Firstly, we determined the factors that served as the basis for calculating investments and subsequent returns.

The extent of necessary changes ensuing from a feasibility analysis of a QM system can be determined by answering the following simple question:

what useful QM measures have to be defined, structured and consequently invested in to keep the volume of errors and thus the costs of correction and fixing low?

Of course, many details and nuances could be derived if one were to change the number and type of the factors but such a balancing act shouldn't even be attempted. The important thing is to be able to discern the trends that form the basis for a medium-term or long-term decision. In the ARGE ISKV GMBH pilot project, the cost/benefit analysis for the implementation of test automation focuses on the effort and cost involved in fixing errors. This involves:

- error rates,
- effort and cost involved in error fixing per error,
- effort and cost involved in error administration,
- cost unit rates for resources (day/hour) and
- cost centres.

Table 1: Cost centres

Cost centre	Task/activity
General	
Customer	• Reports errors • Provides support during the analysis • Plays a consultative role to varying degrees
ISC	• First-line support • Provides support during the analysis • Plays a consultative role to varying degrees
ARGE ISKV GMBH	• Second-line support • Administers the trouble tickets • Informs customer and ISC
Maintenance project	
Business department	• Analyses the error in the software • Requests error-fixing • Informs customer and ISC
Implementation	• Corrects errors • Development test
QM	• Organises testing • Tests and evaluates

Table 2: Cost unit rates

Assumed cost unit rate in €	
Daily rate	511.00
Hourly rate	64.00

The cost per error to be fixed are provided in the form of QA-metrics experienced by former projects within ARGE ISKV GMBH.

Table 3: Cost per error to be fixed

Error administration costs for • the customer • ARGE ISKV GMBH • the IS KV Service Centre	€ 1,530.00
Effort involved in fixing error incl. implementation and testing	€ 2,045.00
Total cost of fixing an error	€ 3,575.00

The figures for the cost of fixing an error are the basis upon which the economic feasibility or benefit of the planned measure (in our case, test automation) must be measured later. Ultimately, the more differentiated the individual values, the more detailed the assessment and the expected result will be.

4.1.1 Investments

The pilot project aimed to identify the effort and costs that would arise from individual steps/activities to implement and operate test automation measures and to calculate the expected return on investment (ROI). From the very beginning, it was clear that it would not be efficient to use test automation for all batch applications. Consequently, criteria were defined with regard to the importance and significance of the software products for the customer and ARGE ISKV GMBH (degree of availability, risk in the event of incorrect functioning, product for finance transfer) in order to allow a pre-selection and to immediately steer subsequent investments in a particular direction.

Table 4: Investments

Investments
One-off investments
• Pilot project costs (at least prorated because utilisable results from the pilot project should be included)
• Licence agreement costs for tools
• Staff training costs
• Cost per batch application of changing over to test automation
Ongoing investments
• Ongoing maintenance costs for tools
• Expected costs for maintenance and modification of test automation measures due to software and data structure changes
• Costs for any additional technical environment such as test computers, etc.

4.1.2 Return on investment (ROI)

The test automation for batch applications was intended to generate the following two returns:

1. time-saving in individual work steps and
2. a reduction in the percentage of errors by improving the QM measures.

The first of these was also the goal of the pilot project. It was thus considered that the investment in the pilot project should be accepted even if there was a certain risk because it might otherwise not have been possible to calculate values of similar validity. The actual ROI was deemed to be the time saved during the testing. In certain work steps and activities, the test automation measures on the pilot project saved on resources, which could be used more efficiently elsewhere.

The error reduction and the resulting ROI due to quality increases was estimated at 5% and an increase over three years because it must always be seen in relation to the density and distribution of test automation within the entire *IS KV* product range. It is also a factor used to measure subsequent successes and failures of changes in procedure and make them transparent.

4.1.3 Variable influencing factors

It is difficult to estimate variable, but key factors such as *frequency of use* of test auto-mation in the testing field, *number of corrections* in the batch applications due to errors or normal modifications and *temporal distribution of investment and return* due to the time taken to implement the necessary measures.

On average, *IS KV* supplies 4 releases per year to the customer (or ISC). The fre-quency with which test automation is used also determines the increase in economic efficiency and product quality due to the rise in stability through improved, standard-ised quality management. The pilot project decided to always test highly important products as standard whether or not changes had been made. The importance of a product is based on whether it is dependent on or integrated into neighbouring prod-ucts within the *IS KV* information system.

It is important to establish the time frame for the implementation of the measures and to estimate how many of the defined tasks for implementing test automation can be scheduled for or carried out in the coming months and years. It is not possible to come up with precise values without experience.

The time frame for implementation at ISKV was calculated over three years as fol-lows:

Table 5: Temporal distribution of investments and return

	1st year	2nd year	3rd year	4th year
Investment (distribution)	45%	45 %	10 %	
ROI capacity cost	35%	70 %	100 %	
ROI quality increase		1%	3%	5%

Rather than coming about as soon as the measures are introduced, the expected in-crease in quality occurs later or to a lesser extent compared to the investment within one time window/period. However, for the implementation at ARGE ISKV GMBH it was important to ascertain the economic feasibility and effectiveness of introducing test automation so a time lag of one year was assumed for the expected quality in-crease.

Table 6: Comparison of investments and return

One-off investments	€ 470,00
Ongoing investments (annual)	€ 74,000
ROI (annual)	€ 335,000

The results for the pilot project on the implementation of test automation were ap-proximately as follows:

4.2 The result of the cost/benefit analysis

The following chart shows a comparison of the calculated factors and figures for investments and ROI.

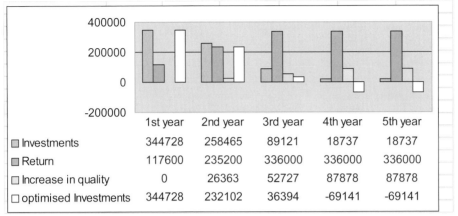

	1st year	2nd year	3rd year	4th year	5th year
Investments	344728	258465	89121	18737	18737
Return	117600	235200	336000	336000	336000
Increase in quality	0	26363	52727	87878	87878
optimised Investments	344728	232102	36394	-69141	-69141

Figure 2: Investments and Return on Investments (ROI) in €

An analysis of the results shows that the return from introducing test automation almost reaches the level of the investment by the second year of use and considerably exceeds it by the third year.

If the calculated increase in quality is considered as an investment-decreasing factor, the relationship between that "optimised investment pillar" and the ROI appears in a different, improved light.

With regard to ARGE ISKV GMBH's cost/benefit analysis, this means that the investments pay off in defined framework conditions provided that the *IS KV* system's remaining runtime is at least three years.

It is vital to realise what the financial and strategic effects of implementing the necessary measures will be. The gap between the investment and the return in the second and third years of use differs to that at the point of introduction. The aim of providing figures, in the form of a feasibility analysis, to support a decision in favour of the measures has therefore been achieved.

Under these defined conditions, the pilot project demonstrated the feasibility and sense of introducing test automation. This was also emphasised by comparing the cost and benefit of such a measure.

Quality management can also, through test automation measures, react flexibly to the increasing requirements for more effective and more efficient use of time and resources.

5 What do we learn from all this?

Feasibility analyses and cost/benefit analyses of QM systems are very individual, company-specific processes. The rules that apply to ARGE ISKV GMBH may not always be completely relevant for other companies. The figures used as a basis for decisions concerning the introduction of test automation are specific to ARGE ISKV GMBH and might be different for other companies.

The *quality indicators, investments* and the *ROI* must be examined individually. The type of cost/benefit analysis used also depends greatly on the individual objective which the company seeks to pursue with it. The more precise the basis for the decision has to be, the more detailed the base figures and influencing factors that have to be deduced. This in turn means that *QM must be measured* when gathering those base figures in order to achieve good quality so that the quality of the results (the basis for the decision) is also good.

Even if the economic feasibility has been demonstrated and perhaps verified using a comparison of costs and benefits, the decision to implement test automation depends on other factors too. Although ARGE ISKV GMBH has clearly shown the advantages of test automation, it will not, for example, be introducing an automated testing procedure for all batch applications. Instead, it will use certain rules to make selections in order, for example, to fulfil the following company goals:

- the employees being 100% behind and feeling responsibility towards their own products and thus the requirement that products be tested by the staff responsible for the product.
- involvement of customers in QM measures (customer testing).

Part II

Certification and Testing

Scalable Acceptance Testing

PAUL KEESE

SQS Software Quality Systems AG (Germany)

Abstract: This paper describes a scalability model for the user acceptance testing of business-oriented software systems. The scalability model is based on the test specification. The specification of a user acceptance test has two aspects that are scalable: the approach to test case design and the definition of test completion criteria. Different combinations of approaches to test case design and test completion criteria require varying amounts of effort and lead to varying levels of quality. The adequate combination, i.e. test approach, depends on the business risk of the business process and the probability of error in a new or changed function within that business process.

Keywords: acceptance testing, test case specification, scalability, business processes, business risk, probability of error, test completion criteria

1 Introduction

Although "scalability" has become a tired corporate buzzword in recent years, its importance in software testing – and especially in connection with user acceptance testing (UAT) – is in-creasing. Different aspects of user acceptance testing can be handled in a scalable manner. Project organization, staffing with subject-matter experts, and test automation are just a few examples [1] [2]. The following model of scalability is based on the specification of a user acceptance test. The test specification as a "blueprint" for test execution plays a decisive role in determining both the costs and the benefits of a test.

2 A UAT Model

2.1 User Acceptance Testing Defined

During *user acceptance testing*, a user representative tests the integration of one or more newly developed or changed functions in a business process. The main objective of acceptance testing is to validate the implementation of a business process with respect to correct-ness. Other quality characteristics such as robustness can also play an important role. In the V model of software testing, user acceptance testing is normally preceded by functional and technical integration testing at the least.

2.2 Scalability in Testing

A test approach is then *scalable* if it can be adjusted easily to specific project situations and product characteristics by varying effort and quality. Cost, time, and quality still compete in software projects. Time and budget restrictions, though, differ from project to project. The software products to be tested vary also, both in terms of the level of quality demanded and the probability that a software product still contains errors. A "one-size-fits-all" approach to user acceptance testing is therefore not economical; what is called for is a scalable test approach.

2.3 Business Processes as Testing Context

Acceptance testing is conducted within the context of business processes. A *business process* is a sequence of work steps that begins with an external input or action and ends with an external output or action. Each non-manual step of a business process is supported by a business function of a software application. From the perspective of software testing, a business process can therefore be seen as a chain of business functions.

   An example for a business process is the purchase of stock. The business process begins with an external action: a customer orders 100 shares of General Motors. Several business functions are executed (for example the order is forwarded to a broker, positions are reconciled, and the deal is settled), before the business process ends. The shares are credited to the customer's securities account; the costs are debited to his cash account; and the customer receives confirmation of the stock purchase.

2.4 Test Case Components

The expected behavior of a business function in a business process can be described with the help of a functional test case. Each functional *test case* consists of the same *basic components* (Figure 1):

- At the center is the *function* or functionality to be tested.
- The functionality has prerequisites or *pre-conditions* in tables and files.
- Depending on the function under test, online inputs or *parameters* might be necessary.
- The processing of pre-conditions and parameters results in a new state in tables and files or *post-conditions*.
- In addition, the functionality can produce results that are not relevant for further processing or *external effects*. Examples of external effects are error messages or printouts.

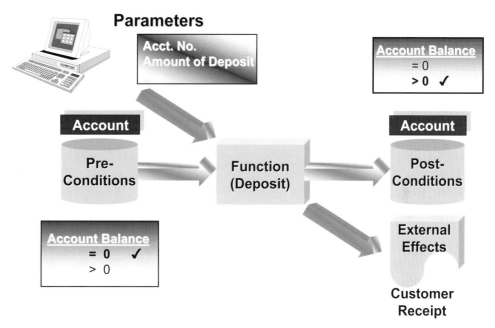

Figure 1: Test Case Components

2.5 Business Processes and Test Case Sequences

A user acceptance test case is the description of a particular path through a business process. A test case for acceptance testing can therefore be viewed as a sequence of individual function test cases.

A business process begins with a function, for example a function in a front-end application. This function has certain pre-conditions in tables and files and requires on-line inputs or other parameters. The first business function in the business process changes the state of data in tables and files; in other words, the function also has post-conditions. These post-conditions are at the same time the prerequisite or pre-conditions for next function in the business process. This chain of function test cases is continued until the final function of the process is reached (Figure 2).

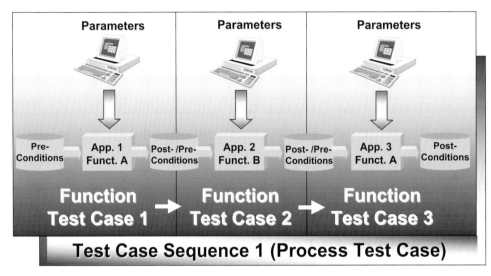

Figure 2: Business Process as Test Case Sequence

3 Scalable Test Approach

The approach for the specification of a user acceptance test has two aspects that are scalable: the approach to test case design and the definition of test completion criteria.

3.1 Approach to Test Case Design

Testers can invest different amounts of effort and achieve different levels of quality (test coverage) when specifying test cases for user acceptance testing. At the bottom end of the scale there is *ad hoc testing*, in which the tester simply starts testing with little or no planning or documentation.

The next step up in terms of effort and quality is *intuitive testing*. In the intuitive approach to test case design, the tester writes down the test cases beforehand, often with the help of a document template. The test cases are derived from the tester's daily business and experience, especially those areas or situations where the tester believes errors are most likely to be discovered (error guessing).

At the other end of the spectrum is *systematic testing*. Here the tester specifies test cases with the help of one or more methods (e.g. equivalence class analysis) [3] [4]. Tool support is useful and often necessary for the systematic approach to be efficient.

3.2 Test Completion Criteria

The definition of when a tester is finished with testing is likewise scalable. Test completion criteria can be defined at the level of business processes, at the level of functions within business processes, and at the level of pre-conditions and post-conditions for individual business functions (Figure 3).

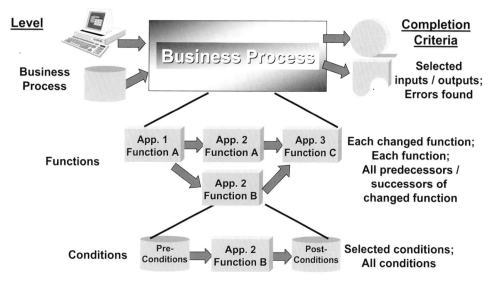

Figure 3: Test Completion Criteria

3.3 Influencing Factors for Test Approach

A concrete test approach for UAT is determined by:

- The selection of an *approach to test case design* (so that the tester knows how to specify test cases)
- In combination with one or more *test completion criteria* (so that the tester knows when she is finished with test case design)

The task at hand is to choose from the many possible test approaches the best approach for a business process that uses a new or modified business function.

This decision is risk-driven and is influenced by two factors:

- The *business risk* of the business process
- The *probability of error* in the new or changed function

3.3.1 Business Risk

Business risk has both monetary aspects, for example the revenue directly lost if a business process fails, as well as non-monetary aspects, such as loss of image if a failure becomes public.

Quantifying business risk can be an extremely difficult undertaking. It is possible to define objective criteria such as the opportunity costs per day of a business process that cannot be executed. The measurement of the actual costs (not to mention the non-monetary effects) of a failed business process can still be a formidable task. The techniques and results of the risk analysis performed in Year 2000 project work might help here [5].

3.3.2 Probability of Error

The probability that a business function still contains software bugs when it enters user acceptance testing depends on three categories of factors:

- The *characteristics of the software*, e.g. the complexity of processing rules (algorithms) and interfaces, e.g. the number of interfaces, the number of fields that are updated or only read, etc.
- The *extent of changes* made to functionality and the structure or semantics of interfaces
- The *quality (coverage) of the tests*, especially function testing, already carried out

4 The Adequate Test Approach

4.1 ABC Analysis

ABC analysis can be applied to both the business risk of a business process and to the probability of error in a new or changed function within that process in order to determine the adequate UAT approach in a given situation.

The result is a three-by-three matrix in which each cell represents a combination of low, medium, or high probability of error for a new or changed function that is used in a low-, medium-, or high-risk business function. Each cell is assigned a suggestion for the approach to test case design and one or more possible test completion criteria. The matrix can then be applied to each new or modified business function to be tested within a project (Figure 4).

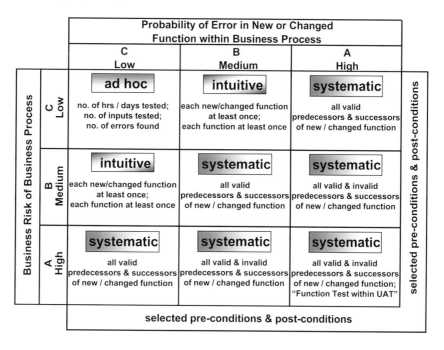

Figure 4: Test Approach and ABC Analysis

4.2 ABCs of Test Case Design

In the absence of empirical data, it is debatable where one test approach should stop and the next should start, but ad hoc testing is most certainly the most efficient approach for the low-risk corner of the matrix.

Moving in the direction of higher risk and higher probability of error, ad hoc testing is replaced by intuitive testing.

Finally, in all situations where both business risk and error probability are deemed to be not low, systematic test case design is probably the right approach.

4.3 ABCs of Test Completion Criteria

4.3.1 Completion Criteria for Ad-hoc Testing

By its very nature, ad hoc testing lends itself only to organizational test completion criteria. Examples of completion criteria that can be used are:

- Time-boxing, e.g. test for a predetermined number of hours or days
- Execute the business process at least a certain number of times
- Test until a predetermined number of total errors have been discovered (in combination with time-boxing) or until the number of errors discovered within a certain time frame has fallen below a predetermined value

4.3.2 Completion Criteria at Function Level

The simplest test completion criteria at the function level are:

- Test each new or modified function in at least one test case sequence
- Test each and every function of a business process, whether changed or not, in at least one test case sequence

Both of these completion criteria can be measured manually and are therefore also suitable for intuitive testing without tool support.

More rigorous completion criteria consider the sequence of functions tested within a business process. A matrix can be used to analyze all pairs or immediate sequences of functions within a business process. Each function of the business process is both in a row and in a column of the matrix. The functions in the rows are interpreted as predecessor functions; the functions in the columns are interpreted as successor functions. Each cell thus represents an immediate function sequence in the sense of "successor function Y follows predecessor function X".

Possible values for each cell are:

- "+" if the function sequence is valid
- "-" if the function sequence is invalid and leads for example leads to an error message
- " " if the function sequence is not relevant for testing, for example two functions which do not process any common data

Function pairs or pairs of function test cases can be used to construct different test case sequences for user acceptance testing.

A test case sequence can contain valid function pairs in which the pre-conditions of the successor function are equal to the post-conditions of the predecessor function. In this case the post-conditions of the successor function are also created.

It is often possible to execute a business process in different ways; in other words, there are alternative flows. The alternative flows of a business process are described in separate test case sequences.

A test case sequence can include invalid function pairs. In an invalid function pair, the post-conditions of the first function do not correspond to the pre-conditions of the following function. Therefore, the post-conditions of the second function are not produced. Instead, for ex-ample, there is an error message. The test case sequence can still be continued, though, for example with a valid function pair (Figure 5).

Valid Function Pair: Post-Conditions = Pre-Conditions

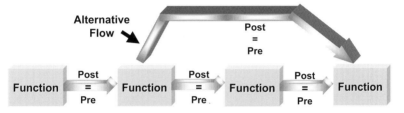

Invalid Function Pair: Post-Conditions <> Pre-Conditions

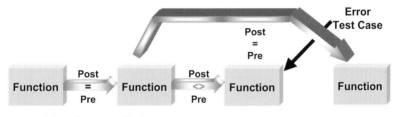

Figure 5: Test Sequence Variations

Examples of possible test completion criteria based on function sequences within business processes are:

- Test only function pairs in which the predecessor function modifies data needed by the successor function. Here the focus is on update functionality because it is generally more complex and thus more error-prone than read-only processing.
- Test only valid function pairs. This completion criterion can be justified if error situations were adequately covered in function testing or if a mature business process is involved.
- Also test all invalid function pairs. Here the accent is on testing the robustness of the business process, for example if the business process is new or if error test cases were not part of a function test.

Completion criteria defined on the basis of function pairs are suitable for systematic testing and generally necessitate the use of a test design tool.

4.3.3 Completion Criteria at Condition Level

Finally, completion criteria at the level of conditions involve testing pre-conditions and post-conditions of a business process or of an individual function.

On the one hand, it is possible to cover only selected pre-conditions and post-conditions. The emphasis here is on error-prone or mission critical inputs or outputs of a business process. Examples of selected pre-conditions or inputs for a business process are certain types of products or customers. Examples of selected post-conditions or outputs of a process are documents sent to the customer or data sent to business partners.

Selected pre-conditions and post-conditions can be used as supplementary completion criteria for all types of testing (ad hoc, intuitive, systematic), for example in the form of a checklist.

On the other hand, if warranted by risk, all relevant pre-conditions and post-conditions of a new or modified function within a business process can be tested. This entails considerable effort due to the resulting number of test case sequences but also leads to very high coverage. For the function involved this approach could be thought of as a "function test within user acceptance testing". However, integration aspects are still not neglected, because the input data for the function is created by the preceding functions and the function's output data is processed by the functions that follow it in the business process.

A function test within UAT can be suitable for very complex functions, functions for which no (trustworthy) function test has been performed, as well as functions in mission-critical business processes.

5 Outlook

Although selecting the suitable test approach remains an inexact science with the help of any matrix, the ideas set forth here are meant to be a first step toward picking the size of user acceptance testing that fits the particular situation. Practical experience with the catalog of possible test approaches is necessary in order to gather metrics on the costs (effort) and benefits (quality achieved) of each approach. Then it becomes possible to select those test approaches that produce a given level of quality and at the same time are efficient and easy to manage, with or without tool support.

6 References

[1] Humphrey Watts S.: Managing the Software Process. Addison-Wesley, New York, 1989

[2] Fewster, Mark, Dorothy Graham: Software Test Automation: Effective use of test execution tools. ACM Press, New York, 1999

[3] Beizer, Boris: Software Testing Techniques. Van Nostrand Reinhhold, New York, 1990

[4]Marick, Brian: The Craft of Software Testing. Prentice Hall PTR, Englewood Cliffs, 1995

[5] Hartmann, Wolfgang: Integration Testing in a Very Large Project. In: Conference Proceedings. 1st International Conference on Software Testing, 2000

Usability Testing – The DATech Standard[1]

WOLFGANG DZIDA AND REGINE FREITAG
GMD German National Research Center for Information Technology,
Institute for Autonomous intelligent Systems (Germany)

Abstract: The DATech Standard Usability Test is devoted to the conformity and nonconformity of software with usability standards (ISO 9241 Parts 10 and 11). The methods are intended for usability experts. The professional tester of software is guided to restrict the test effort to those requirements that can be derived as being objective and valid. A statement on conformity is thus confined to the list of such requirements. On this basis the results achieved with a test are reproducible. A complete product test, as suggested by the verification approach of ISO 9241, can hardly be put into practice cost-effectively. Therefore, according to the DATech approach a product's conformity with standards is being presumed until the reverse has been verified (so-called falsification approach). Such a proof is always linked to objective requirements derived from the context of use and user performance. Adhering to this test approach a product can be claimed as usable. If a deviation from the standard is suspected, it has to be proven by means of a separate procedure. In this case the impact of a suspected deviation on user performance is looked into. The virtue of this approach is not only seen in the stated defects and related impacts but also in its constructive contribution to quality improvement. Every ergonomic improvement helps save usage costs. Nowadays, it is not the purchase costs that "gives the user a headache" but the mostly underestimated usage costs. The application of the test method can therefore contribute to reduce these costs and simultaneously improve the quality of work.

Keywords: usability, software, standards, conformity, quality, test

1 Introduction

The usability of a software product is a main factor when assessing the quality of interactive software. Functional and software-technical characteristics are considered as far as they have an impact on the use of software. Therefore, not the technical quality of product characteristics is evaluated but their effects on the workplace and on the user. The product is judged above all by whether it works properly and reliably at the user's workplace and by the extent to which it does so (ISO 9241 Part 11).

[1] The development of the DATech Standard Test was supported by the research project F 1693 of the German "Bundesanstalt für Arbeitsschutz und Arbeitsmedizin". Partners of the project were GMD German National Research Center for Information Technology, Redtenbacher Software, TÜV Rheinland and TÜV Informationstechnik Essen.

The internationally agreed upon concept of usability enlarges the traditional obligations of software quality management. It does no longer suffice to satisfy pure software-technical requirements as stated in ISO/IEC 12119. Please note that the traditional concept of usability as defined in this standard turned out to be too narrow a concept. Figure 1 includes the concept of "usability in context", which requires an more circumspective usability-engineering approach.

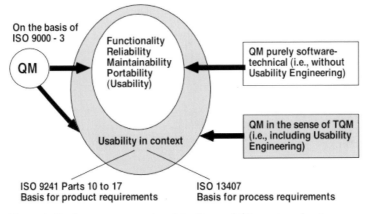

Figure 1: Quality management enriched by usability engineering to ensure usability

Testing software products for usability can be conducted in various ways and by a variety of methods (Nielsen and Mack 1994; Dumas and Redish 1993). However, test results depend on the method employed. Consequently, the application of a test method is basically subject to an agreement between partners (manufacturer and customer). A standard usability test, however, ensures that conformity with international usability standards (ISO 9241) is being confirmed. A standard test is a means to avoid any dispute regarding the methodology upon the evaluation of test results. The conformity of software (i.e., conformity with standards) should rather be judged on the basis of a methodically agreed upon approach. The practical experience gained by usability test laboratories in Germany could be used to develop a method which is consensual and whose application and further development makes the test laboratories work on a comparable basis, which is the DATech Standard Usability Test[2]. DATech accredited laboratories are obliged to use this guideline as a reference model for the development of their own test approach.

Target groups of the DATech standard test are also manufacturers and customers since it enables them to better prepare themselves for the collaboration with the usability test laboratories. If customers and manufacturers agree on the application of the standard test for testing software products they can commission a test laboratory to conduct the tests.

---

[2] DATech is the German organization for accreditation of laboratories in information technology and other fields of technology. The DATech Standard Usability Test is identical with the DEKITZ Standard Usability Test. The DEKITZ organization became integrated into DATech during summer 2000. This may be confusing for those who already know the DEKITZ test.

Providing a service for usability product testing does not suffice to ensure the usability of software products, since one cannot test usability into the product subsequently. Industrial practice in usability engineering revealed that usability of software could only be achieved by improving the manufacturer's engineering capability (Landauer 1995; Mayhew 1999). In particular, quality assurance for usability requires managing the early analysis and prototyping processes. Usability test laboratories also provide a service to make software manufacturers and their customers ready for utilizing state-of-the-art usability engineering methodology. Although the service will be primarily offered to software developers it is evident that the core activity of a mature usability design process is developing usability requirements. This process invites the prospective users to participate in usability prototyping as required by ISO 13407. Currently, DATech is going to accredit usability laboratories for testing the maturity of the manufacturer's usability-engineering process.

The development of both, product and process test, is in response to the European Council Directive (90/270/EEC) concerning the work conditions of computer supported work places. Along with the Directive a series of usability standards (ISO 9241) were developed and have been accepted with the European Union. With the complete publication of these standards (Parts 10–17) in the late nineties software industry should be ready for testing products for compliance with the standards.

The practice of software use shows that many usability requirements can only be identified by practical use of a product in the product's context of use. The DATech test also provides a questionnaire to enable the customers and users of software products in analyzing mismatches at the workplaces of software users. In all European member states customers of software in their role as employers are obliged to observe software users at their workplaces to prevent them from undue mental strain caused by poor software.

Customers of software are increasingly becoming aware of the disadvantages poor software is bringing about (Minasi 2000). For a long time, software products were primarily purchased on the basis of functionality and purchasing costs. When the software worked and the purchasing costs were low the product was regarded as acceptable. However, after having learned that the product's usage costs are usually three times the purchasing costs, the product's usability came into play. Usage costs can be diminished, when the sources of usage problems are considered more carefully and the usability defects are removed (Bias and Mayhew 1994). It turned out that most of the defects could be traced back to organizational needs or user issues, which are implied in the product's context of use but have not been sufficiently analyzed and tested in the beginning of the design process. The DATech approach can be utilized to systematically develop context-dependent usability requirements.

The test methods do not require expensive laboratory technology. Unlike a merely software-technical product test, the DATech standard test works from the viewpoint of the actual use of a product in its context so that even functional and reliability tests do not require a costly test environment. The cost of the test is also reduced considerably by the falsification approach adopted. In contrast to the standards (ISO 9241 Parts 10 to 17) which suggest a complete verification for proving the conformity of a product with the relevant requirements of a standard, the DATech test guideline recommends to falsify only the test criteria derived or to be derived from Part 10 of the standard. These test criteria are assumed to be fulfilled by the quality of the characteristics of the product or by user performances to be actually executed at the system. Testing means to attempt falsifying this conformity assumption for every test criterion. A falsification indicates a suspected nonconformity whose impact is judged separately and whose significance is to be examined by an evidence test.

In the practice of test laboratories, the verification approach suggested by ISO 9241 turned out to be too costly. Software testers were always confronted with the unanswerable question where to begin with a usability test and where to terminate it. In the case of a test conducted in parallel with the design process of a software product, however, the verification approach is still to be recommended because the conformity question is being asked for each individual design solution.

2 The empirical basis of usability testing and evaluation

Being faced with a software product a software tester is rarely in a position to test the product's quality. This fact has been ignored so far. One and the same product may have different qualities (usabilities) depending on the context of use. The user including his or her characteristics and experiences pertains to the context. Compare the usability of a Unix shell for two user target groups. Imagine a user who is well experienced in the Unix world and a user familiar with Windows. The latter will find a Unix shell horrible. Not so the Unix user. Further context attributes may have an impact on user performance and user satisfaction. In particular the task characteristics determine user performance. However, it is not just functionality that matters. The interaction with the system within its context also influences the quality of software use. Hence, it is indispensable to know the user and the flow of task performance before testing a product's usability. A complete basis for evaluating usability includes the characteristics of the context of use, the derived context-related usability requirements and the identified usage problems. The evaluation basis is valid if users and usability experts agree upon these facts.

Users are not prepared to assess the usability on the basis of standardized requirements, since users do not know the definitions and terms. Experts, however, do so. Standards are not suitable for serving as a common evaluation basis. Nevertheless, both partners can develop a common understanding of the conditions of usage and the needs implied. While experts interpret these needs in terms of the standards, it is obvious that the users describe the conditions and requirements of use in terms of their own "language", which is task-dependent. This approach strictly complies with the notion of requirement in an international standard (ISO 8402): "Expression of needs and/or their translation into stated requirements for the characteristics of an entity" (par. 2.3). Hence, a defined usability requirement is always expressed in both terms, a required user performance and a suitable, enabling product attribute.

The DATech standard usability test applies a model to acquire the basic data necessary for testing and evaluating a product's usability (figure 2). From this model it becomes evident that usability requirements cannot be developed without inviting the users to participate.

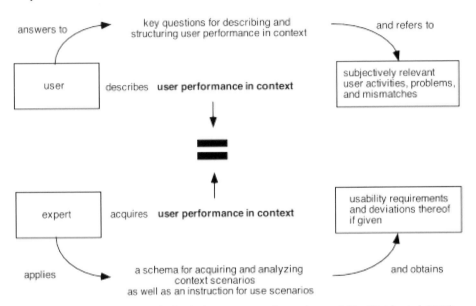

Figure 2: Model for acquiring the basic data necessary for testing usability (Dzida et al. 2000)

Figure 2 illustrates that the empirical basis for usability testing is a validated understanding of the "user performance in context". The DATech test guideline introduces into the application of this model to provide for a sound basis of usability design and testing. Unexperienced usability testers ignore the empirical basis and merely focus on the usability of product characteristics. However, taking the ISO definition of requirement into account, a product characteristic can only be tested for its usability if the corresponding user performance needs have been clarified. Quality is always relative. The usability of a product characteristic is relative to the required user performance in context.

3 Structure of the DATech Usability Test

The test procedure is divided into three sections:

- Test preparation:
  Analyze both the context of use by means of context scenarios and the task performance by means of use scenarios. Then systematically derive or develop usability requirements; ultimately transform the requirements to test criteria (using ISO 9241 Parts 10 to 17 and sections of ISO/IEC 12119). These preparatory steps are used for the operationalization of a requirement in terms of a test criterion. It can be defined as a user performance or as a product characteristic. If the standard contains a user performance requirement, the test criterion has to be interpreted from the viewpoint of the implied needs of the context of use. Interpreting test criteria means to put the standard requirement in more concrete or precise terms considering the implied needs of the context of use.

- Executing a conformance test:
  Test the effectiveness of the product (using sections of ISO/IEC 12119) and then its efficiency; select the suitable product characteristic for each test criterion or identify the required executable user performance; verify the conformity with standards (using ISO 9241 Parts 10 and 11). Here, the test criterion is tested for conformity by means of the given product characteristic or the user performance executed at the visual display screen.

- Evaluation of nonconformities:
  Evaluate the effects of a suspected nonconformity with the aid of a decision table and verify nonconformity (using ISO 9241-11) if the reduction of efficiency is significant and if the defect can neither be satisfactorily corrected, nor relieved, nor compensated. The communication about a verified, significant nonconformity should be constructive; in particular parts 12 to 17 of ISO 9241 contain characteristics or performance requirements to be referred to in the communication.

The methods of scenario-based context analysis and user observation are preferably used for preparing a conformance test. The context attributes recommended in ISO 9241-11 are analyzed and described in a narrative way, so as to motivate the user to validate the acquired context data. The scenario method is assisted by a structured interview guideline to ensure the objectivity of data acquisition. Also, a requirements development schema, the objectivity of which has been empirically verified, assists the derivation of usability requirements. The user-performance requirements are derived from use scenarios. The scenario methods adopted in the DATech approach are extensions of what has been published in (Carroll 1995, McGraw and Harbison 1997, Dzida and Freitag 1998) as well as in (Jacobson et al. 1992).

3.1 Test preparation

The test procedure has been developed for detecting nonconformities. This is to examine and evaluate the non-fulfilment of a minimum requirement (test criterion) derived from the standard (ISO 9241-10). This test is the most important application of the test procedure. For preparing this test a test criterion has to be specified.

If the standard contains a performance requirement, the test criterion has to be interpreted from the viewpoint of the implied needs of the product's context of use. Interpreting test criteria means to put the standard requirement in more concrete or precise terms considering the implied needs of the context of use.

Each conformance test requires that test criteria be defined. Four steps describe the path from the analysis of the context of use (ISO 9241-11) to the definition of test criteria (see also figure 3).

1. Context scenario:
    Use key questions of a structured interview for acquiring the context scenario.
2. Requirements:
    Extract implied needs and context-related requirements from the result of step 1. Use key questions for verifying implied needs before deriving requirements. Clarify any unclarity still left with the inquired user. Let the context scenario be validated by the inquired user.
3. Use scenario:
    Every key tasks identified in the context scenario should be described in one use scenario each specifying the complete sequence of user activities and system responses at the display. Further requirements are derived from the use scenario if the tester identifies a problem of use indicating a suspected nonconformity.
4. Test criteria:
    Test each recommendation of the standard (ISO 9241-10) for both applicability and concretisation regarding the context of the results of the first three steps. This produces the list of test criteria. Note that this list is a checklist specifically created for the conformance test. There are no generally available checklists for this purpose.

3.2 Test execution

The conformance test terminates the test procedure. The test requires that test criteria be defined by means of the preceding methodic steps (cf. figure 3). Test criteria can be defined as product characteristics or as user performances. The formulation as a required, executable performance is to be preferred over a formulation as a characteristic, particularly, if the characteristic suggests a specific implementation.

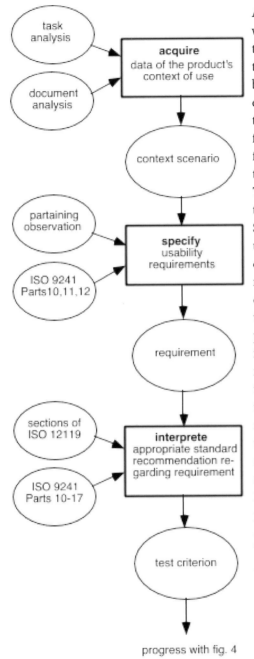

Figure 3: Definition of a usability test criterion (The figure contains logical, no temporal, dependencies between states and actions.)

Acquisition: Since a product's usability within context of use always depends on the implied needs of the context of use, these are to be elicited first. This therefore begins with a task analysis and the evaluation of documents about the context of use and describes the context in the form of a context scenario. Key questions for data collection help ensure the objectivity of the data (acquisition objectivity). The scenario form is well suited to have the data validated by the inquired users.

Specification: Requirements for the product are derived from the context scenario considering task requirements and user needs. Key questions for deriving requirements help ensure the objectivity of the requirements (objectivity of appraisal). If problems of use are identified, further requirements are determined by means of observation at the dialogue system and documentation of the observation data in a use scenario and these requirements are specified considering the dialogue principles (Part 10 of the standard) and the principles for the presentation of information (Part 12).

Interpretation: The requirements for the product are formulated in a context specific way while the requirements specified by the standards are context neutral. Test criteria are defined by interpreting the neutral formulations from the viewpoint of the context-specific requirements. Depending on the type of the requirement, all standards (Parts 10 to 17) can be used for interpretation to formulate the criterion as precisely as possible. The criterion is preferably formulated as an executable user activity/performance.

During the execution of the conformance test (figure 4), the test criterion is compared with the given product characteristic or user performance. If the test criterion is defined as a characteristic, an inspection of the product is usually sufficient to determine conformity with the characteristic. If the test criterion is defined as user performance, observation during runtime of the system is the preferred method.

The methods of inspection, observation, user inquiry and document analysis are preferably used for executing the conformance test

– to determine the fulfilment of standard requirements or
– to inquire into a suspected nonconformity and its reasons.

If there are indications of nonconformities, inspection and observation are to be complemented by user inquiries. This is to learn about the impairment of the user by the suspected nonconformity or to follow up indications of disturbing factors in the context of use. To speak about a "suspected" nonconformity results from the falsification approach underlying the test procedure: every product characteristic or every executable user performance is assumed to be in conformity with standards (zero hypothesis) until this assumption is refuted through the empirical proof of negative effects. The effects of a defect are to be judged separately (see next section: evidence test).

The standards contain both user performance requirements and requirements embodying product characteristics. The methods mentioned in figure 4 are not equally suited for these different requirements. The methods should not be used independently of each other but should complement each other. Examples: An inspection of the dialogue can lead to unambiguous results on account of a preceding task analysis; a user inquiry or an observation which contributes to the explanation of a problem of use can be complemented by the inspection of a related product characteristic.

Since usability within the context of use of a software product always depends on the real operating conditions of the context of use, its analysis is indispensable (see ISO 9241-11) and must not be restricted to task analysis. The methods of the test procedure can also be used for the restricted test of usability as specified in ISO/IEC 12119. A test according to ISO/IEC 12119 does not replace the test according to ISO 9241-11; however, the test of task-specific functionality, reliability, adaptability as well as user documentation is indispensable to examine effectiveness / efficiency in the sense of ISO 9241-11.

Furthermore, usability within context of use of software depends on the satisfaction of the target user group so that statements about the conformity with standards in the sense of usability within context of use always require a test of user satisfaction by means of adequate methods (e.g. user inquiry). Objective indications of insufficient user satisfaction should be followed up, for example, unanimous complaints of users about software.

Effectiveness test: The test of the conformity of a product with ISO 9241-10 requires that the product be effective in the sense of ISO 9241-11. For this purpose, the results of the work tasks derived from the context scenario are compared with the product's performance (i.e. inspection of functionality for effectiveness and reliability as well as the user documentation.

Suitable product attributes or user performances: The "key tasks" of the users are represented in the form of use scenarios; the characteristics of the product or executable user performances of the user, which comply with the test criteria (i.e., which are comparable) are derived from these scenarios by means of inspection, document analysis or observation.

The **conformance test** is a comparison of each test criterion with a corresponding characteristic of the product (and/or the actually executable user performance). In case of insufficient conformance, the assumed conformity with standards is questioned (suspected nonconformity). The comparison requires an inspection of the dialogue system or a document analysis (with respect to the characteristics) or an observation (in particular with respect to the user performances) and an inquiry of users if nonconformities are suspected.

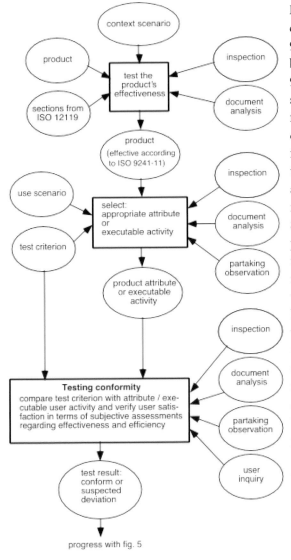

Figure 4: Executing a conformance test
(The figure contains logical, no temporal, dependencies between states and actions.)

The documentation of a conformance test is to provide evidence whether the following quality criteria have been fulfilled:

— Has the test criterion been formulated as a product characteristic or as a user performance requirement?
— Has the minimum requirement of a standard been tested for applicability?
— Have the standard performance requirements been interpreted from the viewpoint of the implied needs of the context of use?
— Has the fulfilment of performance requirements been tested during runtime of the system and within the product's context of use?
— Have nonconformities been analyzed with respect to their relevancy for impairment of users and disturbing circumstances within the context of use?
— Does the conformity statement differentiate between the identified ergonomic quality within the context of use intended by the manufacturer and the user's real context of use?
— Has the satisfaction of the target user group been examined?
— Has the impact of a suspected non-fulfilment of a test criterion been examined (evidence test)?

3.3 Evidence test: evaluating suspected non-conformities

The conformance test consists of a comparison of the test criterion with the relevant product characteristic or the relevant executable user performance. According to the falsification approach, conformity is assumed for every executable user performance (and/or for every characteristic). A detected suspected non-fulfilment of the test criterion is to be subjected to an evidence test.

With the support of the user, the tester walks through the use scenario at the workplace. Here, complete work tasks which are typical of user performance are examined for whether the product fulfils the test criteria. In this test the knowledge acquired from the survey of the context scenario is to be utilized. The observation at the user's workplace delivers a (possibly empty) list of nonconformities. If suspected nonconformities are detected, they are entered as problems of use ("critical incidents") into the use scenario; these are to be subjected to an evidence test where appropriate.

The evidence test verifies for each suspected nonconformity, whether it is

(a) an actual nonconformity and whether it is
(b) significant.

A suspected nonconformity is to be subjected to an evidence test which evaluates the impact of a nonconformity (cf. figure 5). The test is to apply the decision rules of the evidence test.

When examining detected ergonomic defects for their causes, we should consider that the causes can be given not only in the tested software but also in characteristics of the hardware or in other conditions of the context of use. An assessment of the working environments (in the sense of § 3 of the Council Directive on work with display units or on account of ISO 9241-2) can be useful if this reveals the causes of the shortcomings.

A decision table (drawing on the German standard DIN 66271) is used for finding out whether the suspicion of a nonconformity can be verified. This is primarily based on assessing the effects of a nonconformity (figure 5).

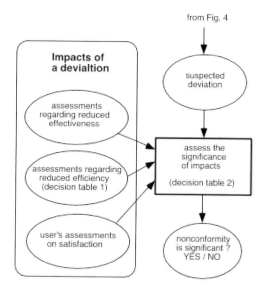

If the conformance test detects a deviation of the product characteristic (and/or the actually executable user activity) from the test criterion, a suspected nonconformity is stated. This is then a reason for falsifying the suspected nonconformity of the product with respect to this characteristic. The significance of the impact of the suspected nonconformity is examined by an evidence test which looks into the effects of the nonconformity on task processing (reduction of effectiveness and efficiency) and on the user (diminished user satisfaction).

Figure 5: Evidence test: evaluation of impact of non-conformities
(The figure contains logical, no temporal, dependencies between states and actions.)

The following steps are required for executing the evidence test:

Step 1:   A suspected nonconformity was observed.

Step 2:   Verification: "Is the nonconformity actually a violation of
   a)   the standard recommendation from which the criterion was derived;
   b)   the dialogue principle the standard recommendation is based on?"

Note: If a design alternative to the standard characteristics is detected, it is admitted according to ISO 9241 and should not be classified as nonconformity if it reduces neither the performance (effectiveness and efficiency) nor user satisfaction.

If no: Nonconformity is insignificant. End.

If yes : Continue with step 3.

Step 3:   Judge effect of nonconformity; the basis is ISO 9241-11, i.e., the impact of the nonconformity is examined with respect to effectiveness, efficiency and user satisfaction.

a)   How high is the reduction of effectiveness caused by the nonconformity (i.e. missing functionality)?

First of all the following question needs to be answered:

"Which goals of product utilization cannot be attained properly (completely and correctly) due to this nonconformity?"

Key questions for a):
– "How great is the importance of the non-attainable results?"
OR
– "How often are the non-attainable results required?"

The tester ranks the reduction of effectiveness by means of these two questions on a two-level scale: high, low.

If the reduction of effectiveness is high, the nonconformity (verfied in step 2) is significant and the evidence test for this nonconformity is terminated (cf. decision table 2 below). Therefore, a high reduction of effectiveness (= relevant goals of product utilisation cannot be attained even when trying to work around) always appears in the overall judgement.

b)   How high is the reduction of efficiency caused by the nonconformity?

This is divided into three sub-judgements:

ba)   Significance of impact (unnecessary effort and cost etc.):

Key questions for ba):
– "Are working steps required which are not due to the actual work task (but due to characteristics of the product)?"

or if the nonconformity leads/led to errors of use:
– "How high is the effort required for correcting the errors?"

Ranking on a two-level scale: high, low

bb) Percentage of affected users:

Key questions for bb):
- "Which percentage of the target user group is affected?"
- "How often occurs the reduction of efficiency during typical product use?"

Ranking on a two-level scale: high, low

bc) Possibility of working around, compensating by the context of use or alternative design:

Key questions for bc):
- "Is it possible to bypass the problem by using other functions than those provided?"
- "Is it possible to compensate the nonconformity by an appropriate adaptation of the context of use?" (Example: additional user training can compensate for missing or bad documentation; a supplementary program can complement missing functions etc.)

Ranking on a two-level scale: easy, difficult

In the first decision table, the evaluation criteria (ba, bb, bc) are arranged transparently to measure the "height" or "significance" of the reduction of efficiency identified by key questions on the basis of the incarnations given by the table.

Decision table 1:
Overall ranking for reduction of efficiency[3]
(two-level result: high, low)

ba)	Severity of impact	high	–	–	low
bb)	Percentage of affected users	–	high	–	low
bc)	Possibility of bypassing	heavy	heavy	easy	–
	Total reduction of efficiency	high	high	low	low

---

[3] Reading of the decision table: A suspected deviation is judged according to three assessment criteria (lines of the table). Entries for judgements are "high/low" or "easy / heavy" (colums of the table). In the last column the judgements are summarized.

Therefore, the reduction of efficiency is regarded altogether as high if the severity of the impact or the percentage of affected users is high and if there is no easy way to work around.

Comment on an economical approach to evaluation:

The effort required for decision making can be reduced if the evaluation of the possibility of bypassing is done first since in the case of "easy" bypassing, the further evaluations in decision table 1 are no longer required. We can immediately continue with decision table 2 to evaluate whether the easy bypassing is regarded as satisfactory by the users. If a high diminishment of user satisfaction is detected, the nonconformity is significant in spite of easy bypassing.

If bypassing is ranked as "heavy", the ranking of the two further criteria in decision table 1 is of decisive importance. Determining the "severity" of impact or the "percentage" of the affected users is differently complicated depending on the specific case. Hence it is recommendable first to do the ranking which is easier to operationalize, since its result may make the more difficult ranking unnecessary.

If efficiency reduction is high, nonconformity is significant (see decision table 2) and the evidence test for this nonconformity is terminated.

> c)   How great is the reduction of user satisfaction caused by the nonconformity?

> **Note:** This is to judge the subjective impairment of users who use the product for a sufficiently long time, i.e., who are beyond the initial learning phase which is to ensure a temporal stability of the judgement.

> **Key questions:**
> – "How satisfied/dissatisfied are the users with the use of the product for task accomplishment?" (e.g. rating scales)
> – "How high is the percentage of users who experience/express a subjective impairment?"
> **Ranking** on a two-level scale: high, low
> (as a weighted mean for a representative sample of the target user group)

The second decision table provides a survey of the assessment criteria (a, b, c) to measure the "height" of the efficiency reductions identified through decision table 1 and through the key questions predefined in the table.

Decision table 2:
Procedure for significance rating: Overview
(two-level result: Is the nonconformity significant? Yes/No)

a)	Effectiveness reduction	high	–	–	low
b)	Efficiency reduction	–	high	-	low
c)	Diminishment of user satisfaction	–	–	high	low
	Nonconformity is significant	Yes	Yes	Yes	No

Therefore, a suspected nonconformity is altogether a significant nonconformity if it (a) can be verified as a deviation from the standard recommendation and the dialogue principle and (b) leads to a high reduction in at least one of the three categories effectiveness, efficiency and user satisfaction.

According to decision table 1 (efficiency reduction), this means that insufficient effectiveness or insufficient user satisfaction "comes always through"; lack of efficiency, however, can be compensated by easy bypassing.

To get a constructive outcome from the evidence tests, the following measures might be taken if sufficient resources are available:

– insufficient effectiveness is remedied, e.g. through maintenance,
– insufficient efficiency is remedied by the modification of the characteristics, e.g., by adaptation to the characteristics required by ISO 9241, Parts 12 to 17,
– user satisfaction is achieved by modification of the characteristics or by a compensating design of the context of use.

4 Accreditation and certification

DATech is an authorized German organization for accrediting usability test laboratories. DATech supervises the accredited laboratories for their capability to provide test services on a mature and comparable level of expertise. Up to now, five organizations have been accredited for their usability test laboratories: SIEMENS, IBM Germany, TÜV Rheinland, TÜV Informationstechnik Essen, and the Physikalisch Technische Bundesanstalt (PTB) in Berlin. The SIEMENS and IBM laboratories provide in-house services for usability testing. The TÜV laboratories and the PTB test software products of software producing companies. If a product's usability is acceptable according to the standards' requirements the laboratories certify the compliance of the product with the international standards. The accreditation of laboratories is periodically observed by DATech assessors who check whether the laboratories still provide best practice test services.

5 References

Bias and Mayhew 1994 Bias R G, Mayhew D J (1994) Cost-Justifying Usability. Academic Press, Boston

Carroll 1995 Carroll J M (ed) (1995) Scenario-Based Design. Envisioning Work and Technology in System Development. Wiley & Sons, New York

Council Directive 1990 Council Directive (1990) On the minimum safety and health requirements for work with display screen equipment (fifth individual Directive within the meaning of article 16 (1) of Directive 89 / 391 / EEC). Official Journal of the European Communities, no L 146/14

Dumas and Redish 1993 Dumas J S, Redish J C (1993) A Practical Guide to Usability Testing. Ablex Publishing, Norwood, N.J.

Dzida and Freitag 1998 Dzida W, Freitag R (1998) Making use of scenarios for validating analysis and design. IEEE Transactions on software engineering, vol 24, no 12, pp 1182-1196

Dzida et al. 2000 Dzida W, Hofmann B, Freitag R, Redtenbacher W, Baggen R, Zurheiden C, Geis T, Beimel J, Hartwig R, Hampe-Neteler W, Peters H (2000) Gebrauchstauglichkeit von Software. ErgoNorm: Ein Verfahren zur Konformitätsprüfung von Software auf der Grundlage von DIN EN ISO 9241 Teile 10 und 11. Schriftenreihe der Bundesanstalt für Arbeitsschutz und Arbeitsmedizin, Forschung F 1693, Dortmund, in print

ISO 8402 ISO 8402. Quality management and quality assurance – Vocabulary. Second edition: 1994

ISO 9241 ISO 9241. Ergonomic requirements for office work with display terminals (VDTs)
Part 10: Dialogue principles (First edition: 1995)
Part 11: Guidance on usability (First edition: 1998)

ISO/IEC 12119 ISO/IEC 12119. Information technology – Software packages – Quality requirements and testing. (First edition: 1994)

ISO 13407 ISO 13407. Human-centred design processes for interactive systems. (First edition: 1999)

Jacobson et al. 1992 Jacobson I, Christerson M, Jonsson P, Övergaard G (1992) Object-Oriented Software Engineering. A Use Case Driven Approach. ACM Press, Reading MA

Landauer 1995 Landauer T K (1995) The Trouble with Computers. The MIT Press, Cambridge MA

Mayhew 1999 Mayhew D J (1999) The Usability Engineering Lifecycle. A Practitioner's Handbook for User Interface Design. Morgan Kaufmann Publishers, San Francisco

McGraw and Harbison 1997 McGraw K L, Harbison K (1997) User-Centered Requirements: The Scenario-Based Engineering Process. Lawrence Erlbaum, Mahwah, NJ

Minasi 2000 Minasi M (2000) The Software Conspiracy. Why Software Companies Put Out Faulty Products, How They Can Hurt You, And What You Can Do About It. McGraw-Hill, New York

Nielsen and Mack 1994 Nielsen J, Mack R L (1994) Usability Inspection Methods. John Wiley & Sons, New York

Ensuring the quality of Web Sites and E-commerce applications

GUALTIERO BAZZANA
ONION S.p.A. (Italy)

Abstract: The presented work focuses on the peculiarities of Web-based applications explaining their effects on testing practices. Moreover, the work will deal with testing management aspects that are fundamentally affected by the nature of Web applications. Testing solution will then be presented, both for static aspects (related to HTML, pictures, XML) and dynamic aspects (ASP, CGI, Proxies, Cookies, etc.). Room will be devoted also to commercial tools available in order to give the audience an overview of the existing technologies.

Keywords: Internet-Test, Internet based applications, Web testing

1 Background

The last years have seen an explosive growth in the WWW. Currently the Web is the most popular and fastest growing information system deployed on the Internet, representing more than 80% of its traffic.

Additional trends are:

- Interaction of Web-based solutions with large DBMS;
- Web-portals;
- Usage of Web-based interfaces for Intranet/Extranet applications that directly interface the company legacy system;
- Usage of Web-based approaches for critical applications (e.g.: on-line stock trading)
- Access to the Web by different media (e.g.: mobile phones, TV)

- Need to allow equal opportunities to Web access also for impaired or disabled people, in order not to exclude them from the new "Information Society".

This has increased the complexity and criticality of applications, requiring the adoption of systematic testing activities also in the Web-based realm that is far too often wrongly considered an application domain populated mostly by hackers. The increasing importance and reliance of Web applications ask therefore for more and more testing levels to be applied.

As of date, we can say that Web-based applications deserve a high level of all software quality characteristics defined in the ISO 9126 standard, namely:

- *Functionality*: Verified content of Web must be ensured as well as fitness for intended purpose
- *Reliability*: Security and availability are of utmost importance especially for applications that required trusted transactions or that must exclude the possibility that information is tampered
- *Efficiency*: Response times are one of the success criteria for on-line services
- *Usability*: High user satisfaction is the basis for success
- *Portability*: Platform independence must be ensured at client level
- *Maintainability*: High evolution speed of services (a "Web Year" normally lasts a couple of months) requires that applications can be evolved very quickly.

In the experiences of the author, Web-based applications are characterised by notable project management.

Development is managed in accordance with Rapid Application Development (RAD) approach where Round-trip engineering is followed, by which we do not have a waterfall model but rather we: "design a little, implement a little, test a little" several times on incremental versions; this implies that analysis and design are scarce when compared to "standard" applications: the goal is to sketch-out an innovative idea into a service, rather than to build a product starting from very precise specifications and architectural design. Henceforth, proof of concept presentations are the normal way to set-up "live" specifications and limited formalisation of analysis and design automatically implies that usage of defect prevention techniques can only be marginal: most of things to be checked are thus let to dynamic testing.

Such characteristics have marked the success of the Web; hence we do not think that Web development has to be adjusted in order to fulfil traditional software engineering practices, but rather testing techniques and tools have to be capable of operating within such innovative approach.

The following aspects further complicate the picture:

- Designers are often not professional software developers or at least are not aligned with conventional software engineering practices;
- The turnaround of people involved in Web projects is extremely high
- Compressed deadlines for services are normal considering the pace of innovation in the field;
- Evolutionary maintenance is a must; we can say that Web-based products seldom reach a mature status, since they are replaced by newer version when they still are beta-tested;
- Underpinning technologies are changing very quickly;
- There is a close contact with users in field which can give immediate feedback, but at the same time users may be unknown, especially for Internet/ Extranet applications, where there is no possibility of doing training distributing user manuals and following the standard practices for deployment of conventional applications.

2 Testing of Web-based applications: technical peculiarities

In addition to project-management challenges, we have to take into account also technical peculiarities, notably:

- Web-based applications consist of a large degree of components written by somebody else and "integrated" together with glue and application software;
- User interface is often more complex than many GUI-based client-server applications;
- Performance behaviour is largely unpredictable and depends on many factors which are not under the control of the developers
- Security threats can come from anywhere
- We do not have only HTML, but also: Perl, Java, VRML, Visual Basic, C++, ASP, PHP4, etc.
- Browser compatibility is mandatory but is made difficult by layers and multi-platforms
- Reference platforms are brand new and are being changed constantly
- Interoperability issues are magnified and thorough testing requires substantial investments in software and hardware.
- Regression testing is a headache: if we have an application which references external links we shall perform regular regression testing even if we do not change a single line of code, to ensure the hyper-links validity
- Usage of separated environments is not widespread; whereas the adoption of separated environments for development – test – production is a standard prac-

tice in "conventional" software development, this is not always the case in Web-based applications, at least according to the experience of the author.

3 Testing of Web-based applications: the proposed methodology

In the following sections, we try to cover the distinguishing features of Testing for Web-based applications

3.1 Test levels

The following test levels have been defined depending on whether the Web-based application is dynamic or only static.

Table 1: Test Levels

	Dynamic Web applications	Static Web applications
Before Shipping	Module testing Integration testing Security testing Functional testing Performance testing Load/ Stress testing	Basic correctness/ adherence to standard and guidelines: • Syntax testing • Stylistic testing • Lexical testing User interaction • Link testing • Fast Loading testing • Compatibility testing • Usability testing Structural aspects: • Integrity testing • Portability testing
After Shipping	Regression w.r.t. changes Performance monitoring End to End operational testing	Regression w.r.t. changes Regression w.r.t. external links Regression w.r.t. new technologies

The remainder of this document covers such levels in more details.

4 Testing of Static Web-based applications

4.1 Static test levels

Test levels of Static Web Sites are briefly summarised in the following.

4.1.1 Basic correctness/adherence to standard and guidelines

Basic correctness/adherence to standard and guidelines refers to *Syntax, Stylistic and Lexical testing* that have the goal to check the basic correctness of Web Sites. In order to have a pragmatic approach to Web syntactic testing, a standard checklist, containing more than 100 checks, was devised by ONION to be applied both for acceptance purposes and for regression testing activities. Such checklist covers the following aspects (for each class the number of tests is given, together with some of the aspects checked):

- syntax problems
- stylistic problems
- lexical problems

A precious source of information for this test level comes from the W3C Web Accessibility Initiative (WAI) guidelines. These guidelines explain how to make Web content accessible to people with disabilities. The guidelines are intended for all web content developers (page authors and site designers) and for developers of authoring tools. The primary goal of these guidelines is to promote accessibility. However, following them will also make Web content more available to all users, whatever user agent they are using (e.g., desktop browser, voice browser, mobile phone, automobile-based personal computer, etc.) or constraints they may be operating under (e.g., noisy surroundings, under- or over-illuminated rooms, in a hands-free environment, etc.). Following these guidelines will also help people find information on the Web more quickly. These guidelines do not discourage content developers from using images, video, etc., but rather explain how to make multimedia content more accessible to a wide audience. This document includes an appendix that organises all of the checkpoints by topic and priority. The topics identified in the appendix include images, multimedia, tables, frames, forms, and scripts. A separate document, entitled "Techniques for Web Content Accessibility Guidelines" explains how to implement the checkpoints defined. The Techniques Document discusses each checkpoint in more detail and provides examples using the Hypertext Markup Language (HTML), Cascading Style Sheets (CSS), Synchronised Multimedia Integration Language (SMIL), and the Mathematical Markup Language (MathML). The Techniques Document also includes techniques for document validation and testing, and an index of HTML elements and attributes (and which techniques use them).

4.1.2 User interaction

User interaction covers both Link, Fast loading, Compatibility and Usability testing.

Link testing
Concerning Link testing activities the following principles should be taken into account:

- ensure that all hyper-links are valid and keep to do so, by means of continuous checks when the site is operational;
- consistency check of internal and external links, as well as anchors;
- internal links shall be relative, to minimise the overhead and faults when the Web site is moved to production environment;
- external links shall be referenced in absolute URLs;
- external links can change without control: thus automated regression testing shall be promoted;
- remember that external non-home page links are more likely to break;
- avoid links that require parameter passing.
- Concerning the *site map*, link testing foresees to analyse navigation maps and look at broken links as well as unlinked pages, with regular regression testing in operation to check that Site Map is consistent with actual structure and for static parts, taking advantage of Site Mapping tools.

Content aspects should be respected as well as:

- be careful at links in "What's New" sections: they are likely to become obsolete;
- check that all "key" pages can be reached within a predetermined number of clicks (e.g. 3);
- check that content can be accessed by means of: search engine, site map, navigation structure;
- check accuracy of Search Engine results as well as results on peculiar queries;
- link testing can be extended to the testing of the information structure/ flow of typical user-paths

Link Testing extends also to *Re-directs*; in this case it mainly implies to check that the Web Site Error Code 404 ("Not found") is managed by means of a user-friendly page, as well as other most frequent Error codes (400: Bad Request, 401: Unauthorised, 403: Forbidden, 500: Internal Error, 502: Overloaded Temporarily).

Web Page Description used for book-marking must as well be checked to ensure it is accurate and attractive, other to consider the cases when bookmarking secure pages, password and login requirements are met.

Fast loading testing

Fast loading tests are concerning with aspects like the weight of web pages (especially for the home page), the presence of a fast loading abstract/index, the presence of WIDTH and HEIGHT attributes for every IMG tag. Fast loading testing is very important if we consider that 85% of Web Users indicate slow loading times as the reason for avoiding further visits to Web Sites. Moreover, a survey made by Zona Research Inc. in April 1999 highlighted very high bail-out rates for pages with a weight resulting in more than 8 seconds to wait; 1 second load-time improvement brought to a reduction in bail-out rates from 30% to 7%!

Two approaches have to be followed:

1. reduce the size of transferred data
2. optimise rendering and HTTP management.

The following rules related to the page weight should be established as support to fast loading testing:

*   Home page weight should be less than a specified size (e.g.: 45k).
*   Every page weight should be less than a specified size (e.g.: 50k)."Graphical sugar" pictures should be less than 3K (e.g. bullet headers).

Moreover for protocol optimisation the following checks must be made:

–   every IMG tags must have WIDTH and HEIGTH attributes;
–   no duplicated/linked image shall exist;
–   the same image shall always be referred with the same canonical-translated URL.

Concerning images all photographic images must be in "jpg" format whereas computer created images must be in gif format; other tests to be made are must check the adoption of correct design rules, such as: do not reduce the number of colours on "jpg" format; check the jpg compression (min. 70%); reduce the numbers of colours on gif format; check that all gif images are in interlaced format and finally GIFs shoud be sized in multiples of 8 pixels (they are downloaded in blocks of 8x8 pixels).

Similarly, we have to test that "graphical sugar" images are as small as possible, colour must be similar to background pic and the background should be the same for all pages (except for functional reasons).

Tables are managed dynamically and the browser displays the content when the WHOLE information has been retrieved. This has a big impact on fast loading and on the achievement of the "8 seconds threshold" for turn-around time on the Web. Testing shall check that while drawing a table the following rules were followed:

- Keep table text size to a minimum (e.g.: less than 5000 characters)
- To reach greater sizes, use multiple tables separated one from the other
- Avoid nested tables - when a table contains another table, the size to compute is the size of the outer table (the container).
- Minimise pictures within tables and always specify width and height
- Every page should contain text or other information before the first <TABLE> tag.

Compatibility testing

Compatibility testing concerns cross-Browser compatibility that checks for site behaviour across industry standard browsers and their recent versions. It checks that pages conform to W3C standards for HTML and other languages. It checks the site behaviour for Java applets and Active X controls. The main issues involve how different browsers handle tables, images, caching and scripting languages, JavaScript in particular. *Cross-platform Java compatibility* checks for the site's behaviour across industry standard JVMs. *Desktop compatibility* checks for site behaviour across industry standard desktop hardware and operating systems.

Usability testing

Usability testing refers to coherence of look and feel, navigational aids, user interactions and printing. These aspects must be testes with respect to normal behaviour, destructive behaviour and inexperienced users. A high number of tips are available as support to usability testing likewise: establish an information architecture, consider cross-architecture views, define categories in terms of user goals, name sections carefully, think internationally, observe cultural conventions etc…

Printing issues have also to be taken into account, considering that font management on the Web is cumbersome (printers and monitors do not always display the same font exactly the same way) and knowing that many people just surf and print (reading on screen is 25% slower).Web inventory validation foresees to verify whether each page has the right images and alternate text for the images, to ensure that each page has the links, tables, buttons, fields, applets and other controls in the correct position and with the right properties and to verify that the application downloads right components - Java applets, Active X and presentations for usage.

Usability Lab testing can be applied also to Web based application. Typical checks / questions are:

- Describe the first items you notice on the page.
- Identify which elements on a page are actionable/clickable.
- What do you expect to find behind this link?

4.1.3 Structural aspects

Structural aspects regard both portability and integrity topics. For internal design portability at server side requires that Server side (to ensure we can move a Web site with little nuisance) all file names must be in lowercase, a file name must contain only [0-9] [a-z] _ , links to URLs outside the web site must be in canonical form and links to URLs into the web site must be in relative form.

Moreover it must be checked that every directory must have an index page, every anchor must point to an existing page, and that there are no limbo pages.

4.2 Tools for Testing Static Web Applications

In the following the most known tools for Testing Web Static Applications are quickly examined.

This does not imply any endorsement by the author of any of the listed tools. Information on listed tools might not be always fully aligned with their latest version, owing to the fast evolution pace.

In general we can say that no one is fully comprehensive in its coverage, and is best used in combination with additional tools. For most tools, coverage improves with every release.

The World-Wide Web Consortium (W3C), has been committed from its beginning to the development of a neutral, open forum for the evolution of Web Technology. Like its partner standard body, the Internet Engineering Task Force (IETF) W3C is committed to developing open, technically sound specifications, backed by running sample code.

As a consequence W3C has developed various tools for Web Testing including:

- An HTML Validator, which allows HTML documents to be validated against the DTDs for HTML, including HTML 4.0
- A CSS Validator, which allows the user to validate the CSS style sheets used by HTML and XML pages
- HTML Tidy, a free utility for correcting HTML syntax automatically and producing clean mark-up. Tidy can be used to convert existing HTML content into compliant XML
- Bobby, a validator to the adherence to WAI (Web Accessibility Initiative).

All W3C software is Open Source and can be retrieved from http://www.w3.org/

Other tools for testing static aspects of Web Sites are:

- Doctor HTML
- Web Lint
- Web Site Garage
- CSE
- Etc.

Several Web testing features are also embedded in Web editors, for instance:

- Web-Edit Professional includes a multi-lingual *Spell Checker* that corrects the spelling of your documents directly within WebEdit using built-in spell checker. The spelling checker currently supports American English, British English, Dutch, French, German, Italian and Spanish. Portuguese, Finnish and Swedish will be available soon; moreover, it includes also an *HTML tag checker* which validates your HTML to ensure the correctness of your pages; supporting various HTML, Netscape and Internet Explorer versions;
- Hot Dog includes a syntax and spelling checker as well as a *Width Checker* which you can use to see how pages will appear to users whose monitors are running with different screen widths;
- Web Suite includes a *Load Manager* that provides size and download information for components created in the Component Editor. It determines download times for the different connection speeds, and lets you keep the download time in mind while you are creating your components.

When you use Java development you can of course take advantage of static and dynamic analysers, which can be assimilated to the same tools available since long time on the market for C language. Among the various development/ test environments offering such features it is worth remembering at least: SUN's Java Test Tools, TCAT for Java, White Box Deep Cover for Java and RST Test tools (inclusive of: Deep Cover for coverage analysis; Assert Mate for pre-conditions, post-conditions and data assertions testing; Total Metric for static analysis).

5 Testing of dynamic Web-based applications

5.1 Module testing

Testing of Dynamic Web-based applications deserves much of the challenges of client-server applications, with additional constraints posed by the underlying architecture.

Dynamic WWW development can be done, at the current level of technology, with two main approaches: CGI Programming (Perl, C, TCL..) or Server Extension Programming (ASP, PHP, Apache Server API, Netscape Server API, ..) It has to be noted that the risk level associated to the two techniques is utterly different, as clearly highlighted by the following pictures.

In fact, whereas when a CGI call fails just a program fails, when a server extension fails, the whole server might crash!

For Testing Server Side, an approach similar to client-server testing has to be taken, covering (as depicted by the following pictures) either GUI Testing or HTTP Testing.

Besides the well known techniques for client-server testing, you should beware of complexity from included software layers; it has to be remembered that often more than 90% of the software is out of the developers' control, being re-used from other sources.

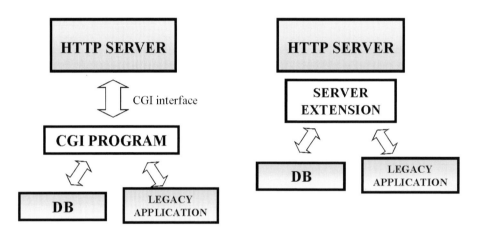

Figure 1: Two Approaches of Dynamic WWW Development

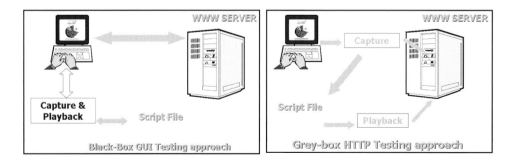

Figure 2: Testing Server Side

5.2 Integration/Security Testing

Integration/Security tests for Web applications must take into account Web specific issues likewise: included components and proxies/ caching.

A peculiar aspect of the testing of dynamic WWW applications is testing of cookies. The web is a memory-less system, with no concept of session. To overcome these issues you can use cookies: a small piece of information sent by a web server to store on a web browser so it can later be read back from the browser. This is useful for having the browser remember some specific information. The problems related with testing are that cookies expire and that users can disable them in browser.

Besides the basic Security checking performed during the previous test level, specific security testing has to be performed when Web applications make usage of sensitive data.

First of all it shall be clear that on the WWW there is no silver bullet for absolute security, likewise in real life, and that security techniques and checks shall be tailored depending on the value to be protected. Moreover, it is important to underline that security enforcing involves both organisational and technical issues; namely organisational issues are often much more important than technical ones, at least in Intranet and Extranet applications. In such cases, the approach is to define a "Security Policy" at company level and then to tailor it for the risk level associated to the various services. Security testing will thus focus on checking that those Policy rules that rely on technical aspects have been correctly implemented. For Web-based application intended for Internet usage with security constraints, specific tests will have to be devised on a case-by-case strategy remembering that at the time being Internet is a so called "open net" without any central management. It derives that availability of any service cannot be guaranteed and that confidentiality and integrity of not encrypted communications cannot be guaranteed.

In general, aspects to be covered by security testing will include: Password security and authentication.; Encryption of business Transaction on WWW (SSL, Secure Socket Layer); Encryption of e-mails (PGP- Pretty Good Privacy); Firewalls, Routers and Proxy Servers; Web Site Security; Virus Detection; Transmission Logging; Physical Security and Backups.

Testing can take benefit of available facilities and tools that are listed at CERT Web Site.

5.3 Functional testing

Functional testing can be applied at both component and system level and refers to capture and replay of users' interactions, testing from the user's perspective: black-box using state-transition diagrams, typical user interactions and boundary conditions tests.

5.4 Testing Web Performance

Aspects to be tested with care for performance include: searches on database, turn-around time of custom applications embedded in the WWW, verification of server response. This has to be done with respect to: platforms, browsers, network connections.

Aspects to be tested with care for loading include: support to many connections and users, management of message peaks and resource locking. This has to be done with respect mainly to server load.

5.5 Load/Stress testing

Failure to deliver Service Level Agreements, or in general flawless performance ultimately translates into lost customers, lost business and lost revenues are the main causes for load test. Unpredictable user loads, enormous application complexity and a lot of new and unproven Internet technologies are the main issue. Finally load testing must be performed both during and after application deployment.

Stress tests use the definition of maximum number of users that can be supported offering acceptable service (SLA) and the maximum number of users that can be supported before denial of service. Location of architectural bottlenecks, impact of hw/sw changes and scalability of the solution are some of the tests input.

5.6 Testing Tools for Dynamic WWW

Some of the most used tools for dynamic Web applications testing are: Test Works/eValid; Rationale Test Suite; Webstone; WebLoad; RSW Tool-set; Radview's WebLoad; Load Runner; Silk Test Suite; CA Test solutions

The goal of such tools is to answer to questions like: "Will my WWW work? How fast will it work? What's the server maximum capacity?" and thus to be sure that your application will behave ok when thousands of people are using it at the peak hour of the busiest day.

Such tools support web Specific testing features, including: cookies, proxy servers, user authentication, session Ids, CGI scripts, API calls, HTML forms, etc.

6 Testing ERP and WWW integration

Future Intranet/Extranet applications will require more significant work and more sophisticated skill set. In fact, Intranets will evolve into a component of the IT infrastructure making distributed computing more open, simpler and more manageable.

This will make possible the delivery of more flexible, manageable distributed business processes.

From a technical point of view, Web-enabled business applications will be based on transaction-oriented business processes; hence Intranet based applications will merge with Extranet-based business-to-business transactions, EDI and electronic commerce transactions.

Already today, to multiply benefits, companies need to integrate Web technology with transaction-oriented business applications, group-ware and infrastructure services, integrating Web-based application and MIS and setting-up simple, cross-platform applications on top of a simple-to-manage and more centralised IT infrastructure.

As far as testing is concerned, challenges are on load testing and security (user authentication, server authentication; connection privacy; message Integrity; payment security).

Tool providers are performing certified integration with ERP systems.

7 Future challenges

Future challenges are related to the evolution of the WWW, namely:

- New Generation HTTP Protocol (HTTP-NG)
- Integration between TV and the Web
- Emergence of XML
- New references for User Interfaces: evolution of HTML (for publishing documents), on MathML (for publishing Math), on SMIL (for multimedia presentation), on SVG (for publishing diagrams and vector-based graphics)
- Mobile access to the WWW as well as techniques for using voice interaction for accessing the Web
- Privacy issues
- Digital signatures
- Micro-payments

These and other emerging technologies and services will require Internet testing approaches to be continually fine-tuned, to guarantee the reliability and quality of service required by the global Information Society.

Pair Programming and Testing in a Medical Web Project

Michael Timpe

MED medicine online AG (Germany)

Abstract: The Internet is placing in the hands of the medical community a host of exciting new ways to manage and exchange medical documentation and the Net of nets is making possible the development of new services and products. The scope and potential of the Internet's reach extends from an in-house network in the MD's practice to the exchange of medical data between the laboratory and the handling physician, to posting a patient's complete medical record on a network linked with other practices, to providing the patient him/herself with access via the Internet to his/her own medical documentation. The simple exchange of information via the Internet between doctor and patient can eliminate trips to the doctor's office for unnecessary examinations on the part of the patient and provide him/her with an immediately accessible complete overview of his/her physical condition.

The purpose of this paper is to present the special testing activities which derive from the unique needs and requirements for managing and administrating medical information on the Internet. MED medicine online GmbH developed MedWinner's, an efficient and effective application covering the above aspects as well as the administrative daily work of the doctor. For reaching a substantial market share time, however, is of the essence, because Med medicine online must quickly overtake with its new and original Internet based technology the lead already enjoyed by established applications The necessity to respond rapidly to the potential of the Internet effects MedWinner's development and its testing. This paper focuses on the structuring of our development team and how some aspects of the extreme programming approach lead to a better integration of the testing and the programming staff of the development team.

Keywords: medical services, testing, pair programming, extreme programming, web testing

1 MedWinner's Application Architecture

The following figures present an overview of the integration of MedWinner's in the Internet landscape and the core architecture of the application.

MedWinner's is a pure browser application, that is to say, it runs entirely under MS's Internet Explorer. MS's Internet Information Server is employed on the server side, which in turn employs XML and SQL-Server for maintaining data. Programming languages employed are:

- JavaScript (for client side script code)

- VBScript (for server side script code)
- Delphi for implementing individual controls and components
- Visual basic for implementing individual components

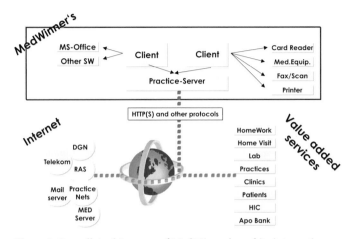

Figure 1: Overall Architecture of MedWinner's and its integration

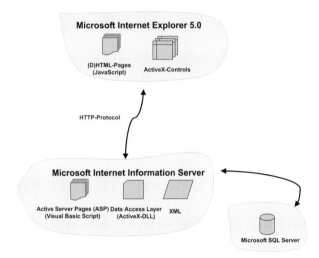

Figure 2: Technical Architecture of MedWinner's

2   MedWinner's Quality Goals

A definition of the quality goals that an application intends to achieve stands at the start of any application testing process. The testing process must make available adequate procedures and methods in order to achieve these quality goals.

- **Usability**
  With regard to usability MedWinner's is a standard product in the classical sense of "product," the application must be designed for and tailored to heterogeneous user groups. The application must cover both the requirements of those employed in doctor's office, examples being the doctor's assistant and medical technicians, as well as the needs of the doctor in the differing areas of his/her practice such as patient admission, billing the health insurance carrier, statistically analysing data, and patient marketing.

- **Performance and robustness**
  The application's performance is also an important quality goal (see [5],[7]). In the usual doctor's practice a wide variety of sequential operations must be handled in a short timeframe. An assumption can be made that the doctor has only approximately five minutes for the documentation of the patient's visit and his/her initial examination. In this period all the events associated with the visit, such as patient admittance, and the documentation of findings, diagnoses, and services performed must be taken care of.

- **Security**
  Medical data are among the most sensitive data maintained about an individual and such data therefore requires special protection against potential misuse. The provisions of the laws pertaining to data protection must be strictly adhered to. The doctor's commitment to medical confidentiality and the confidentiality of patient information must at all times be guaranteed.

- **Actuality**
  The billing procedures of the health insurance carriers and the sheer number of medications on the market constantly change. They are prime examples of the necessity for the standard practice to actualize routinely its information.

Each of these aspects brings in its wake differing activities and tasks in relation to assuring quality in any given Internet project. Because of the extremely short program design and enhancement cycles, these tasks and activities must be grounded in very pragmatic solutions.

3   Influences on the Test and Development Process

The main aspects of the applications architecture influencing the test process are:

- **Tough scheduled release policy**
  MedWinner's is introduced in a market with about 250 competing well established software systems supporting the billing process of practices and German health insurance carriers. To place the system into this market, very short release cycles are necessary to provide the customers with the necessary functionality. For each release there are about 5 weeks of development and about 2 weeks of

testing and finalising activities. This tough schedule needs a complete integration of the test team and the development team.

- **Employment of Microsoft's Internet Explorer**
  MedWinner's runs completely within IE. This has the advantage of making possible the smooth integration of medical Internet information systems in the application. A disadvantage is, however, that much self understood mechanisms, such as operating the application simply by means of keyboard short cuts or hot keys, must be manually programmed and they must be given special consideration during the test phase. Another aspect is the lack of availability of test automation tools for highly complex applications running within the internet explorer.

- **Employment of the script languages javascript and visual basic script**
  The script languages javascript and visual basic are employed to implement dynamic Web pages. These languages are integrated into HTML pages and implement the dynamic behaviour of HTML pages. These languages are so-called interpreted languages and are translated and interpreted only at run time. As a result even simple syntax errors are recognised only at run time and they can lead to terminating the application. This must also be taken into consideration during the test.

4 Pair programming and testing

Because the short development cycles for each release, one of the main aspects of bringing quality into the product is the straightforward integration of the test team into the development team. Testing is an analogous technique like programming. Hence it is not useful to split the team into two separate parts – test and development.

The medicine online development team uses some techniques of Extreme Programming but implements these techniques not only in the development group. It uses these techniques to reach a better integration of the development and of the testing team.

Some main aspects of Extreme Programming are:

- *The Planning Process,* sometimes called the Planning Game. During the planning process the planned functionality for the release are defined through user stories. They describe in a simple manner the main work flows or main courses of the functionality.

- **Small Releases.**
  Already simple systems are brought into production early, and are updated on a very short cycle.

- **Testing.**
  XP teams focus on validation of the software at all times. Programmers develop software by writing tests first, then software that fulfills the requirements reflected in the tests. Customers provide acceptance tests that make sure that the features they need are provided.

- **Pair Programming.**
  XP programmers write all production code in pairs, two programmers working together at one machine. Pair programming has been shown by many experiments to produce better software at similar or lower cost than two programmers working alone.

There are some other basic factors like refactoring, on-site customer, continuous integration, collective ownership but this paper focuses on the aspects described above and shows how the integration of the test team into the development group could work.

Medicine online does not set up teams of two programmers in the original sense of the extreme programming approach. The team is set up of one tester and one programmer in order to mention the task of building test cases as an integral part of the programming of a functionality. Setting up the teams of even one tester and one programmer keeps the balance of business know how and technical aspects of the implementation. As the main difference to the original approach of extreme programming the permanent acceptance testing is not only based on unit tests designed by a member of the programming staff. The pair-programming-team has a collective responsibility for the coding and the test case determination. The results of this team consists of the implementation and of the test case determination for the required user stories. They always work like a team and they report their results as a team.

The complete process looks like this:

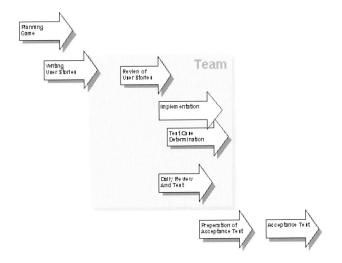

Figure 3: Testing and implementation tasks of the pair-programming-team

During the planning game the main user stories are identified and written down.

Afterwards the team starts to implement the user stories, that means, the programmer is developing the code and the tester is developing the test cases. "Daily review and test" means a permanent review of the implemented code and the user stories by the testing member of the team. The daily review and test is done every day and does not depend on builds of the complete software system as a formal handing-over of the system to the testing team. So the testing can be done without interference with the progress of the other parts of the project. Changes in the user stories or problems in the implementation are uncovered very early and the reaction times are very short.

The tasks of the testing member of the team is to maintain the user stories and to reflect these user stories to the requirements of the customers. This increases the stability and the actuality of the logical specification of the system. From these specifications the testers derive the test cases for the final acceptance testing for the release.

To ensure an independent acceptance testing, the testing member of the team should not do the final acceptance test. He passes his test cases to another member of the quality assurance team to ensure an independent acceptance test of the implemented user stories.

5   Functional Testing – Procedure

5.1 Test case determination

The test team consists of permanent and temporary employees. The temporary employees during the test cycles will be drawn from the technical support area (hotline) and the users area (doctors and their assistants). A quality control manager will coordinate the test.

During the functional testing the test of individual functions is omitted in favour of integration tests. It turned out that especially for the temporary members of the test team that they were able to work more easily with the test scenarios of the integration test than with the individual test cases of the functional tests, which were often too far way from the concrete office transaction practice. To carry out the test special test databases are provided. Each step of a test script consists of a description of:

- an initial situation, i.e., what data must be present in the database and what values the individual parameters must have,
- an action, i.e., what data the tester must input on the graphic user surface and which action he/she must then carry out (examples are click on a button, follow a link, etc.),

- and a result situation, i.e., what results he/she expects in the database and at the graphic user interface.

5.2 Test environment for functional testing

A testing laboratory with attendant periphery is currently under construction. The test laboratory will make possible the simulation of all practice types, such as the individual practice, community practices, interdisciplinary community practices, and practice communities. The test laboratory consists of a server and a varying number of clients with which to simulate the real life, every day procedures of a practice. The computer configurations will be stored on CD-ROMs, which will make possible a fast transfer from the prevailing development version to the actual end product version. In this way the test laboratory can also be utilized to simulate and reproduce real world problems arising in the practices and is also used to support the hotline.

6 Conclusion

Given the press of time pragmatic ways of proceeding had to be devised to test the application. The majority of errors in the application had to be found as soon as possible. Given the absence of automated possibilities to support the testing for the developed application, focus was directed on simple manual test cases and a team structure that accomplished the needs of a project under a tough time schedule.

Some aspects of the extreme programming approach within the development process were successfully implemented. Mixed teams of members of the development and of the quality assurance group focus on reaching the quality goals. Failures or misunderstandings of requirements were uncovered in very early development steps. The permanent daily test results in stable designs and implementations of the user stories.

The described process was implemented in the development and test of some components of the software. All components implemented in the described manner have shown a much higher stability and less field failures than the components developed in a "classical" manner with "classical testing". The task of the next months will be to set up such teams for all components of the system.

7 References

[1] Bazzana, G., Fagnoni, E.: *Testing Web Applications*, 1ˢᵗ ICSTEST – International Conference on Software Testing, Bonn 2000.

[2] Beizer, B., *Software Testing Techniques*, Second ed., Van Nostrand Reinhold, New York, 1990

[3] Meyerhoff, D., Timpe, M.: *Vom Entwurfs- bis zum Systemtest: Objektorientierte Anwendungsentwicklung verändert die Testprozesse*, in: OBJEKTspektrum 01/99.

[4] Meyerhoff, D, Caspers, S.: *Performance and Robustness Test – Factors of Success for Development and Introduction of Commercial Software*, Conquest 1999, ASQF – Arbeitskreis Software-Qualität Franken, 1999

[5] Liggesmeyer P., Rüppel P.: *Die Prüfung von objektorientierten Systemen*, in: OBJEKTspektrum 6/96, S. 68–78.

[6] Anderson, M.: *The top 13 mistakes in Load Testing Applications*. Software Testing and Quality Engineering Magazine, Volume 1, Issue 5, 30–41, 1999

[7] Dustin, E., Rashka, J., Paul, J.: *Automated Software Testing*, Addison Wesley, Reading, 1999

[8] Fewster, M., Graham, D.: *Software Test Automation*, Addison Wesley, New York, 1999

[9] Beck, K.: *Extreme Programming Explained: Embrace Change. Addison Wesley, 1999*

[10] Kund, D.C., Hsia, P., Gao, J., *Testing Object-Oriented Software*, IEEE Computer Society, Loas Alamitos, 1998

Testing Web-Based Home Banking Applications

Dirk Meyerhoff and Dirk Huberty
SQS Software Quality Systems AG (Germany)

Abstract: The rapid growth of the Internet has led to massive investments in web-based software. This is also true for the banking world, especially for web-based home banking software. Currently a large number of software companies as well as banks offer different home banking solutions. In Germany a standardised protocol (HBCI) allows the use of a wealth of combinations of home banking clients and home banking server solutions.

Compared to traditional client server testing, the architecture of the Internet provides new challenges for testers. From a bank's point of view every customer, regardless of the PC type, operating system, browser, or Internet service provider used, should have error-free access to the service. In practice, these and other Internet architecture components must be tested in the relevant combinations since many of them are not compatible. For test execution, all of the different hardware and software components must be available. Thus test planning and test automation become key success factors for reaching the desired quality of service.

However, time to market has been and still is the driving factor for development. Thus quality must be balanced with the time that the whole development project is allowed to consume. Balancing time and quality is not an easy task. Many web platforms have only limited success. Failure may in some cases be caused by software being introduced in the market too late. However, some early adopters have suffered from severe quality problems and the related damage to their public image. In this article we try to highlight the essential aspects of quality for web-based applications and give insights in how to balance these aspects.

Keywords: Internet-Test, Home Banking, HBCI, Internet based applications

1 Quality requirements for web-based banking applications

The following overview is not complete; however, the main quality factors identified in the project we supported so far were:

- Functional correctness
- Availability (24/7), accessibility, from all over the world
- Security, authentication of user and bank
- Usability

- Performance
- Overall hardware and software compatibility

In the following we will highlight the main quality requirements and describe how they are addressed in software development projects.

1.1 Functional correctness

For money transactions the users / bank customers demand functional correctness. This means correct processing of the input transactions, correct handling of different currencies (especially DM and EURO and their automatic conversion), but also satisfactory behaviour when transactions are cancelled or entered incorrectly. Testing functional correctness is usually done at different levels. Firstly, the requirements and design documents are reviewed. Document types often used for this purpose are storyboards, site maps, textual specifications and object-oriented analysis and design documents. After a thorough review, in which the conventional review process is applied, the user transactions or functions are tested individually based on the requirements and design documents (for a general introduction to testing please refer to [3]).

Regarding the task of test automation, the functional test for web applications requires new tools in some cases. Often, the capture/replay tool for standard GUI interfaces does not work with web technology. However, today there are many tools on the market that do work, provided that not too many individually programmed controls are used on the GUI (see [4, 5, 6, 12, 15, 16]).

1.2 Browser and platform compatibility

Most banks do not consider providing their customers with a single specific platform, a pre-installed operating system (OS) and browser, a modem and an Internet connection through a specific ISP (Internet service provider). Rather, they expect their customers to already have such equipment, regardless of manufacturer, brand, version and age. Therefore they willingly cope with an infinite number of combinations of browsers, browser versions, browser configurations, operating systems, modems, Internet service providers, and additional hardware and software components that connect (or separate) the customer to (or from) the bank.

Since the banks do not wish to limit access to their service to just a few customers they attempt to build upon standards and generally accepted approaches as much as possible. However, especially with new applications and technologies, there are always some pitfalls that should be avoided. With regard to HBCI ([7, 8, 11]), some providers were not able to support this technology for quite some time. With regard to browsers, there are many technologies still not supported by major browser providers. Accordingly it is recommended that all software packages used in the web-based banking application are verified against at least a reasonable selection of hardware/software combinations that customers are expected to use. We have seen many projects go back to architecture design after identifying during testing that their software approach would make use of the application impossible for more than 10% of their potential customers (see figure 1).

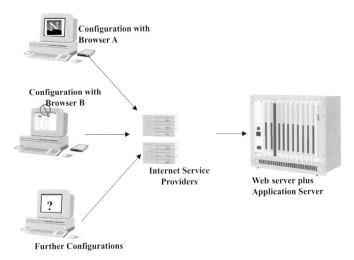

Figure 1: A Sample Architecture Design

The task of testing browser and platform compatibility is best seen as a risk management task. Depending on the similarities of some hardware and software versions, a reasonable number of specific test PCs should be defined, each containing a single OS version, installed software, browser, browser setting, an Internet connection through a modem to a specific service provider etc. Depending on how much risk (of excluding users) the project is willing to accept, between 5 and 25 PC configurations should be included. With the help of clever scripts it is possible to test several PC configurations using just one PC (hardware) (see also [2, 10, 11])

1.3 Availability

Compared to conventional client/server applications the actual availability of the application from the end user's point of view is much more difficult to assess. Due to the inability to control all hardware and software or to obtain automated reports on broken backbone networks in the Internet, the task at hand is to actually test availability all the time. For web-based banking applications a 24/7 (24 hours, 7 days a week) availability is desirable. In order to assess the availability the first task is to check whether the server is online. This can be done by automating a test user's access and letting it run repeatedly, e.g. every 15 minutes. Whenever the simulated user cannot start his desired test transaction a qualified report should be generated for the system administrators and an alarm should be generated. Based on such an alarm a specialised service team can take on the task of debugging and fixing the situation.

If we look at all the external sources of possible problems ,however, we see that this is not enough. Test users should not only test from within the server's own network but also run from different locations using different types of access. This leads to alarm reports also when, for example, the web site cannot be accessed via a specific provider or from a specific country. In some cases it might not be possible to solve the problems; however, it is essential that all problems are known by technical people from the hotline as well as from the development side. As an example, a software update made by a provider can lead to non-availability of the server due to bugs in the update. Users will connect the problem with the bank first, so the bank hotline must be aware of the situation. Generally it is a good idea to run the tests from different locations; however, test control and test result tracking should be done centrally. Management is always keen to have summarised availability reports (e.g. giving figures of more than 99.99%, which is required in some environments). The detailed reports are also the basis for discussions for example with Internet service providers in case actions must be taken.

It is best to fully automate availability tests. All tests, evaluations, and even a part of debugging can be included in an automated procedure. However, manual actions are still required in most cases for solving the problems or taking actions to circumvent them.

1.4 Security

The security of a bank web site is a critical issue. There are many facets of security, e.g. a user expects that he is the only person outside the bank that will be given access to his account and transaction data. On the other hand, the user does want complete access to all data and functions related to his account. In this respect the access control system has to be safe. In the age of hackers and denial-of-service attacks it is essential that the user's account and transaction data cannot be unlawfully changed. A transaction transferred via the Internet from the user's home to the bank may be eavesdropped on by a hacker. However, today's encryption (e.g. SSL) ensures that it cannot be understood. Signature mechanisms also ensure that an encrypted transaction that has been communicated to the bank will not be accepted a second time. Thus a wiretapped transaction cannot be modified and reused by a hacker.

External changes to the web server of the bank must also be prevented. Since all business offers made by the bank in the Internet are binding, it could be very costly, for example, to have the service fee information changed by a hacker. Flooding or denial-of-service attacks use the PCs of users to generate a huge amount of trivial and useless requests. Due to the huge number of generated requests the web server typically breaks down. This means that real users can no longer access the server.

Generally, security tests and hacker prevention mechanisms involve highly technical knowledge that must be updated daily in order to cope with the newest hacker tools, viruses and denial-of-service attacks. This is why – at least in the banking area – most larger organizations have set up security teams who deal with nothing but web security, setting up security policy, building fire walls, and the related testing tasks.

1.5 Usability

The goal of usability testing is to ensure that users receive a web application that best suits their needs and expectations. Since needs and expectations are difficult to determine the tests are executed by people with different backgrounds from different departments. Feedback from such different user groups is then channelled into an optimisation step. Usability tests starts with the documentation of GUIs, whereby users assess prototypes, demos, or just paper descriptions. These demos can, for example, be implemented with tools such as Microsoft Powerpoint®.

In banks, the first usability testers are often recruited from the departments that work directly with customers. This ensures a good understanding of end-users' needs. Later, usability tests try to involve representatives covering all possible user groups.

1.6 Performance

The performance behaviour, i.e. system response time, is a decisive quality aspect also for home banking applications. Performance testing and tuning are major activities for managing performance aspects in software development. Performance testing itself does not make an application faster. However, it reveals the effects of performance engineering, makes an application's run-time behaviour more transparent, and allows forecasts for the run-time behaviour in production (see also [1, 9]). Figure 2 sketches the situation where a number of test users is simulated.

Performance test preparation starts from the detailed functional and technical specification. Minimal requirements for response times, the maximum data volume, and relevant functional values need to be delivered by business units. Tools and a production-like test environment including mass data should be available.

In order to ensure a goal-oriented test process it is recommended that performance-critical functional transactions be identified together with key persons from the business units. Performance test results based on those critical transactions can be well understood because end-users can compare test results with their intuitive expectations. This also facilitates the final assessment of the test results, because recommendations on performance improvements can be expressed in terms of possible performance gains for those critical user transactions.

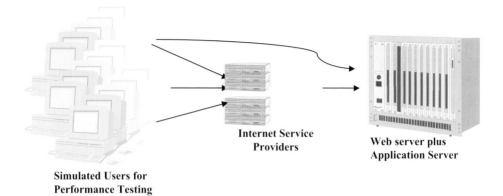

Simulated Users for
Performance Testing

Internet Service
Providers

Web server plus
Application Server

Figure 2: Simulated Users for Performance Tests

During system analysis, performance-relevant parameters are identified for each transaction. Test cases are then derived through systematic variation of those parameters.

In practice, test results show that only between 50% and 70 % of the transactions that are initially identified as not performing adequately are actually problematic. The other transactions are affected by real bottlenecks lying elsewhere – so they seem to be badly performing themselves – or they are identified as problematic based on personal psychological pre-judgement by users.

For home banking applications, security aspects and restrictions limit the possibilities for testing. Capture/replay tools that operate on the level of TCP/IP are difficult to use because all traffic on this level is encrypted. Therefore individually programmed test tools, e.g. HBCI-Testsuite®, which either understand encrypted traffic or capture input before it is encrypted, enable the automation of these tests.

In order to begin with performance analysis and test execution, the core functionality of the application must achieve a minimal level of maturity with respect to stability and correctness. Otherwise, result comparison will fail early. Test automation for performance testing is provided by many suppliers, tools for this can be found for example in [4, 12–18].

1.7 Overall hardware and software compatibility

Home banking applications are generally not entirely new applications. Rather they are implemented in an environment in which many legacy applications are already in place. These must be connected to the home banking systems. As an example, usually the back-end systems that manage customer data are already well established and running on a mainframe. In order to use the customer data bases this legacy software might be adapted, and new networks and queries might be developed. From our experience, it is very important to analyse the surrounding software and make a specific compatibility test that actually uses the target systems in the target environment. Often it is in this late stage that testers identify major misconceptions in the application. With regard to HBCI home banking, older home banking applications have to be handled very carefully. A single user might have to establish competing connections, e.g. one based on HBCI and the other based on BTX.

The overall hardware and software compatibility test is also a major task on the planning and management side. Often the test environment is very difficult to set up, because hardware and software has already been planned for use elsewhere, e.g. for production.

2 Challenges and enhancements

As we discussed above, there are a number of additional tasks for web-based applications. There is significant overhead involved in planning, preparing and executing these new tasks. Due to the usual budget restrictions the first management task is to analyse where the main quality risks lie for the specific project at hand. Based on the risk analysis and the estimated budget for test tasks, the tasks and challenges should be budgeted. This means high-priority tests should be given more attention and budget than lower-priority tasks.

Obviously, if there are more tasks to be addressed with the same budget the management and organisation of testing becomes more complicated. Especially the task of building and maintaining test environments or the testing infrastructure needed for executing the tests becomes more complicated. Given the total project time – for a web project typically somewhere between 3 and 12 months – building the test infrastructure becomes one of the first project tasks.

In many cases, general test tools can be used. In the case of HBCI home banking applications there is even a prefabricated test suite on the market. This test suite includes predefined test cases, test data, and part of the test archiving and administration procedures. In many projects, tools like this have proven to substantially speed up the test and thereby the complete project. Use of the test suite actually lowered overall testing costs by reducing testing effort and improving the quality of the application tested.

3 Summary and perspective

In this article we showed that the World Wide Web poses a number of new challenges for testers. The most important challenges – namely browser and platform compatibility tests, availability tests, security tests, usability tests, performance tests, and finally the overall hardware and software compatibility tests – were briefly described. For each type of test, the main approaches taken from successful projects were sketched. Finally, the use of test tools to support the test tasks was described.

For the future, the authors hope that the idea of standardisation will lead to a more homogenous web infrastructure. This would mean that developing web browsers, web servers, and web infrastructure in general would become much easier. It would also mean that the number of tests dealing with the vast number of different combinations of hardware and software components of the web could be reduced. Testing would also become much easier. The testers would be allowed to focus on the main aspects of web applications, namely their functionality.

4 References

[1] Anderson M (1999) The top 13 mistakes in Load Testing Applications. Software Testing and Quality Engineering Magazine, Volume 1, Issue 5, S. 30–41

[2] Bazzana G, Fagnoni E (2000) Testing Web Applications, ICSTEST – International Conference on Software Testing, April 2000, Bonn

[3] Beizer B (1990) Software Testing Techniques, Second ed., Van Nostrand Reinhold, New York

[4] www.compuware.com

[5] Dustin E, Rashka J, Paul J (1999) Automated Software Testing, Addison Wesley, Reading

[6] Fewster M, Graham D (1999) Software Test Automation, Addison Wesley, New York

[7] HBCI – Homebanking – Computer – Interface Schnittstellenspezifikation, Bundesverband deutscher Banken e.V., Köln, Deutscher Sparkassen- und Giroverband e.V., Bonn, Bundesverband der Deutschen Volksbanken und Raiffeisenbanken e.V., Bonn, Bundesverband Öffentlicher Banken Deutschlands e.V., Bonn Version: 2.0.1, 1998

[8] HBCI-Testsuite, http://www.sqs.de

[9] Meyerhoff D, Berlejung H (2000) Guidelines for Performance Testing in Commercial Client/Server Software Projects, Conquest 2000, ASQF – Arbeitskreis Software-Qualität Franken

[10] Meyerhoff D, Huberty D (2000) Testing Internet Based Home Banking Software, ICSTEST – International Conference on Software Testing, April 2000, Bonn

[11] Meyerhoff D, Huberty D (2000) Practical Reuse of a Test Infrastructure for E-Banking, TEST Congress 2000, SQE Europe, London

[12] www.merc-int.com

[13] www.cup.hp.com/netperf

[14] www.radview.com

[15] www.rational.com

[16] www.segue.com

[17] www.sqs.de

[18] Windows NT Workstation, Microsoft Press, 1998

European Standards in the Field of Railway Signalling and their Influence on Software Testing Methods

HELMUT UEBEL, ANDRÉ FITZKE AND JOACHIM WARLITZ
Alcatel SEL AG (Germany)

Abstract: The once very simple mechanical signalling equipment of Railways has evolved into a complex layer of systems, all together forming the overall rail traffic management system. Most of the layers of this system nowadays consist of computer systems containing software .

In the past, every country had its proprietary standards, operating rules and technical solutions for signalling systems. This resulted in a multitude of systems in Europe, which were not compatible and had different requirements on safety, different rules for development and tests of hardware and software. The European Commission initiated a Directive on the Interoperability on the European High-Speed Network. The unified solution for interoperability in the signalling field is the European Rail Traffic Management System (ERTMS).

The requirements on modern railway signalling software are similar to other safety critical software as used in nuclear power plants or air navigation systems. A new strategy of validation and re-validation allows validation to become an ongoing process. Software validation is performed by an authority independent from the development project. So the validation takes up the role of approving the fulfilment of the quality objectives . The validation becomes more efficient and the effort for validation becomes more predictable.

Keywords: Railway Signalling, European Standards, Interoperability, Software-Testing, Validation

1 Structure of Rail Traffic Management

Railways already realised last century that it was necessary to introduce means of telling a steam locomotive driver if he can go or he has to stop. In the very early days of railways this was not really necessary, as trains were going only 30 km per hour and the driver could stop when he saw another train approaching. But with increasing speed, the braking distance was longer than the viewing distance of the driver and signalling movement authority was absolutely necessary.

From then on the once very simple mechanical signalling equipment has evolved into a complex layer of systems, all together forming the overall rail traffic management system as shown in figure 1. Most of the layers of this system nowadays consist of computer systems containing software .

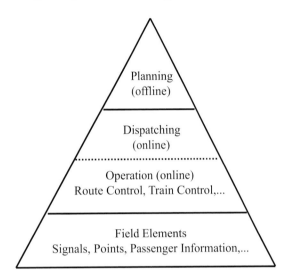

Figure 1: Layers of Rail Traffic Management Systems

The top layer is the planning, which is an offline task, mostly not safety relevant. In this layer, one could find for example:

- Investment planning
- Personnel planning
- Planning of cost structure for fares
- Timetable planning

These are activities, which could cause financial damage or disruption of service and delays if not performed correctly, but not a railway accident. Therefore they are considered as being not safety relevant or not vital (in the language of signal engineers).

The second layer is the real-time dispatching. This layer includes amongst other:

- Dispatching of train movements
- Dispatching of rolling stock
- Dispatching of personnel

- Passenger information
- Tracking and tracing of cargo

The core task is certainly the dispatching of train movements, which has to organise the traffic in an area of several hundred kilometres in such a way that the timetable is kept as well as possible, delays have to be minimised. Another task is to enable passengers to catch connecting trains in the case of delays.

There are plans in German Railways to supervise and control the whole network from seven dispatch centres, which widens the area of responsibility and allows for a better overview. The workload, however, on the dispatcher will increase and therefore software has to help the personnel in performing their tasks. Manufactures are presently developing algorithms for conflict detection and conflict resolution. Such a conflict can generally mean a conflict in track occupancy which means that two trains want to use the same stretch of line at the same time or a connection conflict. The algorithms would make a projection from the present status of the process into the future and detect these conflicts described at an early stage, where they could be solved without causing major disturbance in the overall traffic flow.

In future, this sector will become more important with European Directive 91/440, which imposes the separation of organisations for infrastructure and operation of trains on the railways and enforces the opening of the infrastructure to private operators and foreign railways. It is expected that a slot management system similar to air traffic will be introduced.

Another function is the automatic setting of routes depending on existing timetables from the planning layer. This task is generally not safety relevant, as the safety layer below is filtering all commands. Anything not in accordance with the safety rules is not executed and rejected by the lower layer safety system. There are, however, certain combinations of trains and parts of the network, which can cause hazards, for example dangerous freight or wagons exceeding the gauge width.

The most important and safety relevant layer is the operations layer. There are two main tasks to be performed, which are route control and train control. The route control is responsible for setting the path for the train and protecting it from other railway vehicles. This means that a route has to be searched which can be used by the train to get from a given start signal to given destination signal, all elements of the route have to be checked for availability and occupation by other vehicles, the points on this route have to be set, the flank protection points have to be set, all points have to be locked and only then the start signal will be set to the "go" aspect. When the train moves along the set route, the start signal is automatically reset to its "stop" position and the elements of the route are released from their locked status when the train has passed, they can then be used for other train routes.

Train control and train protection systems in its simplest form automatically brake a train when passing a stop signal. More advanced systems enforce train movements in a restrictive way, which means they supervise the speed and position of trains according to permitted line and train speeds, taking the signal aspects into account and brake them automatically in case of violation of the rules.

The high sophisticated end of these systems is the fully automatic, driverless operation of trains. Between these extremes there is a whole spectrum of system capabilities depending on the application.

The lowest layer of the pyramid is the equipment in the field, that means on the track and on board the rolling stock. It can be distinguished between actuators, such as points or more precisely point machines, signals and passenger information systems, and sensors which detect where trains are positioned. On-board equipment is mostly related to train control systems. Most of these systems are safety relevant with the exception of some, such as passenger information systems and tracing equipment for freight.

2 Challenges of Rail Traffic Management

The most important requirement in the appropriate levels is safety, which means that accidents caused by failure of these systems have to be extremely seldom. In the past, there was no clear definition of the level of safety to be achieved, national regulations mostly requested that new systems had to guarantee a level of safety higher than or at least equal to existing systems already in use.

A new aspect, which comes into the game with privatisation of railways, is security. In the past, railways always had their own private communication networks. There, it was physically not possible for external persons to access the railways' data transmission systems without breaking into railway property. Nowadays, the telecom departments of railways are frequently privatised and operate in the public domain, where it is not possible to exclude any intrusion. This is especially true when radio systems are used for transmission of safety relevant data. There is, however, no need to keep any data secret, which is a problem in military or even banking applications. Defences have to be taken against injection and corruption of information.

Infrastructure investment generally has a long lifetime, especially in railways. In most of the countries world-wide, a large number of interlocking systems are still mechanical, installed in the twenties and thirties. This means on the other hand that a system lifetime of some 20 to 30 years for modern equipment require that the manufacturers are able to maintain, repair, produce and engineer the equipment and also the software for a very long time, which by far exceeds the lifetime of the technology.

3 European Standards

As mentioned before, every country up to recent days had its proprietary standards, operating rules and technical solutions for signalling systems. This resulted in a multitude of systems in the European states, which were not compatible and had different requirements on safety, different rules for development test and assessment of hardware and software. To overcome this, the idea of European Standards was brought up in two fields, safety and functionality.

Safety standards do not refer to the functionality of equipment in the various countries, they only focus on safety. The aim is to achieve safety cross-acceptance of equipment within Europe, independent of specific applications. This can be achieved for systems, which are fairly independent of their application, such as a safe computer system, or a track monitoring system, which detects trains. The cross-acceptance avoids individual national assessment processes and opens the market for manufacturers and railways.

Product standards, in contrary to above described safety standards, specify the functionality of systems or equipment. In Europe, one of the problems of international railway journeys is the non-compatibility of national systems, such as electrical energy supply for locomotives, mechanical properties of rolling stock and last not least rail traffic management systems. The European Commission initiated a Directive on the Interoperability on the European High-Speed Network [4], which is the legal frame for the Technical Specifications for Interoperability (TSI) and product standards. With the application of this directive, future travel times of international trains will be cut and there will be an open market for railways and suppliers, which will generate more competition in technical solutions and price.

The unified solution for interoperability in the signalling field is the European Rail Traffic Management System (ERTMS), their first components being the European Train Control System (ETCS) and the European radio system GSM-R, based on the world-wide GSM standard for cellular digital radio. These two systems will eventually replace a multitude of nationals systems.

The bodies for standards were in the past based on the railways, the most important being International Union of Railways (UIC), which has its headquarters in Paris. For many years, this institution elaborated recommendations for their member railways. These were not mandatory, but many railways applied the rules and facilitated cross-border traffic.

In the meantime, new bodies were created which are composed of representatives from the member states of the European Union. Their standards are mandatory and override national standards. These bodies are not limited to railway tasks as UIC, but they have a wider scope of work. In respect to railways, CEN is responsible for mechanical tasks and CENELEC (European Committee for Electrotechnical Standardisation) for electrical tasks, including software. Within CENELEC, the Technical

Committee 9X (TC9X) is responsible for railway application and the Subcommittee 9XA (SC9XA) for signalling.

It is the task of this subcommittee to establish standards on safety and also on products. These standards have paramount importance on the sector of industry, as the European sector procurement directives mandate the application of these standards.

The establishment process is rather time consuming, the administrative work contributes a high portion to the time span needed for the overall process. This is based on the rules, that the member states play the dominant role in the decision process. Experts working on a voluntary basis, normally being paid by their respective organisations, however, perform the real technical work. The representative body of the member states nominates them and they are not representing any state or organisation. All standards are clearly based on compromises between the member states; a major disagreement will lead to a failure of the process in the voting procedures.

4 European Safety Standards

A number of standards have been created under the CENELEC technical committee, such as standards on railway environment, electromagnetic interference, energy and other fields. The main focus in this respect is signalling, where standards on the safety of the overall railway system [1], on signalling systems [2] and software for signalling systems [3] were created.

The overall (provisional) standard pr EN 50126 gives general guidance how to address safety and to allocate safety targets to certain functions in railways. The safety targets depend on probability of dangerous events and the consequences expressed in fatalities or effect on the environment in case of an accident. In this standard, however, no target numbers of risk rates are given, but the systematic process of risk allocation to the various functions and subsystems of a railway system is described.

The standard ENV 50129 is specific for signalling equipment and it is the first standard that assigns tolerable hazard rates or risk rates to subsystems or functions within systems. Further, it describes the whole life cycle process of safety relevant equipment from specification to implementation, validation, assessment and maintenance. As there has to be a certain classification to avoid individual processes for every product, classes of safety integrity have been defined, called Safety Integrity Levels. The lowest SIL is zero, it is applied for commercial equipment such as a ticket vending machine, which can cause financial damage when malfunctioning, but certainly not a train collision.

The safety relevant systems are in one of the classes SIL 1 to SIL 4, depending on the hazard they can create. An interlocking system for a shunting yard or an industrial railway operating at a maximum speed of 20 km per hour would be found in SIL 2, whereas an interlocking system for a high speed line would be found in SIL 4. The danger caused by the malfunction of a technical system also largely also depends on the fact if it is the only system to determine an action or if other systems are also involved.

One example is the German automatic train protection system INDUSI, which supervises the train driver's speed and alertness. It does not indicate anything to the driver; he has to follow the aspects of wayside signals and the set of written instructions. Only in case of over-speed the system reacts by automatically applying the emergency brake. To create a dangerous situation, both the driver and the INDUSI have to react wrongly. Such systems would be categorised as SIL 2. If a similar system would indicate the commanded speed as the new European Train Control System does, the driver is expected to follow the indication. This would result in a higher SIL category, as an error of the technical system would directly cause an operational hazard.

5 Examples of SIL 4 Systems

Electronic Interlocking Systems are the latest technology in interlocking, being functionally compatible with the older technology based on safety relays. Nowadays, electronic interlocking systems for main line railways have to be compliant with the safety requirements of SIL 4 and at the same time with high availability requirements. This can be met by computer systems based on a "2 out of 3" principle. Two computers are necessary to achieve the safety goals, their outputs are compared and data are only forwarded to the field elements if they match. If any of the two computers fails, the process would be stopped. To avoid this to happen, a third computer is working in parallel with the two others. By comparing the output of all three computers, which is done by the computers themselves, comparison information is generated by the three computers. A majority decision logic can clearly identify a faulty computer and isolate it, even if it delivers wrong comparison information.

Interlocking system developed and manufactured by Alcatel are in use in many countries in Europe and control mainly large station areas or complete lines from one central station.

A second example of a SIL 4 installation is the automatic train control system in combination with the above described electronic interlocking system on the high speed line between Madrid and Seville, which was taken into operation in 1992 (see figure 3).

The whole line has a length of 471 km and it is centrally controlled from Madrid. High-speed trains are circulating on this line with a speed of 300 km/hr, guided by the train control system LZB, which is also in use on German high-speed lines. The control centres of this system were first installed in 1972 on the line between Hamburg and Bremen and were the first commercial application of computers for safety related tasks in the industry – an example for a long system lifetime. Already in 1972, the 2 out of 3 principle was applied.

Figure 2: Electronic Interlocking in Germany

Figure 3: High speed line Madrid - Seville

A third system, shown in figure 4, that falls into the SIL 4 category and is software based is the fully automatic driverless operation of urban transit systems. One of these systems is installed in Vancouver, Canada where 150 vehicles operate and form the backbone of transport in the town. There is no technical personnel in the stations either; four to five people in the operations centre operate the whole system. Also the yard operation with composition and splitting up of trains is done by the system. 13 years of successful operation have proven that such systems are safe and reliable. Presently, the network is extended to another suburb of Vancouver, adding another 21 km to the network.

Figure 4: Urban transit system in Vancouver

6 Nature of Failures and Protection against Failures

The nature of failures can be random or systematic. Random errors are in their majority caused by failure of components. These component failures, for example the failure of a resistor, will occur with a certain probability expressed by the Mean Time Between Failures (MTBF) of the component in its given environment, but the time of the event cannot be predicted.

The other type is the systematic failure, which in reality is an error. The software would react in the same erroneous way again if the input data for the programme and the data environment would be identical. Another systematic failure could be caused by a design error of a CPU or another part of the computer, or wrong wiring.

The consequence of a failure can be non-hazardous, only affecting the system's availability. In computer systems, unlike previous systems based on safety relay technology, the nature of random failures and their effect on the system are hard to predict. Therefore, all possible failures are assumed to be hazardous in nature and the system architecture must prevent a safety critical effect of a failure on the system behaviour.

One of the basic requirements of the safety analysis is therefor that a single random failure must not result in a system hazard. The second basic requirement is that a second or multiple failures have to be assumed if the first failure is not disclosed in a short time. These requirements can be fulfilled by multiple processor systems, where a faulty processor is automatically detected and consequently isolated. The sufficiently low probability of multiple failures has to be proven by using probability calculations based on Mean Time Between Failures (MTBF) of the equipment.

Systematic failures are in practise mainly caused by software. With identical software running in parallel processors, the cross-comparison of outputs would certainly not protect against software errors, as the output data would be equal, but wrong. One method that makes the errors recognisable is to run diverse programmes in parallel computers, but this method is expensive and frequently leads to unexpected system halts, caused by slightly different, but correct interpretation of the specification. With identical programmes, the quality of the programmes has to be such that the probability of errors is tolerable for the safety application. This has to be ensured by a quality system and quality oriented processes in the development phase. For an overview of the different failures types see figure 5.

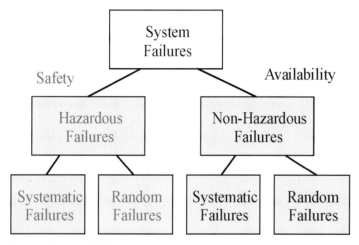

Figure 5: Types of failures

7 Software in modern railway signalling systems

The requirements on modern railway signalling software are similar to other safety critical software used in nuclear power plants, air navigation systems and military weapons. In particular these requirements comprise:

- detecting hardware faults
- avoidance of and protection against systematic faults
- performing the required more and more complex functionality in a way which guarantees the safe system behaviour even under "unusual conditions".

This article deals with the last two issues. Approaches to detect hardware faults on modern hardware architectures are not the scope there.

There are actually two different methods to develop complex software. The first method aims at avoidance of systematic faults in the early project phases by ensuring the consistency of the requirements. Later on the second method implements protection mechanisms in the software during architecture and design phase.

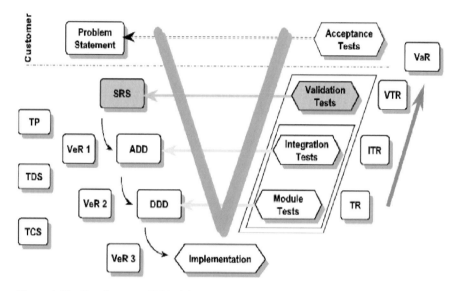

Figure 6: The Development V-Model

If we consider the V-model (figure 6) as the valid model for software development the process starts with the system requirement definition phase. In this phase a very close contact and partnership between the customer and the system engineering team is compelling for a comprehensive system requirements specification. It shall cover all functionality comprising normal operation and exceptional conditions (worst case scenarios). For example formal methods (B-Method, Petri Net, ...) are used to check the consistency of requirements. On the other hand requirements are often incomplete and the usage of formal methods does not guarantee a complete specification. An additional approach is the use of two different specifications established by independent specification teams. Despite of independence this approach has lead to similar results in the past. Therefore additional activities are required in the later phases of the development life cycle.

The main consequence based on those facts is that the Signal Engineer has to design a system which is able to ensure the safe system behaviour under all circumstances based on probably incomplete requirements. Safe system behaviour under all circumstances means that the system performs the normal operation and behaves in a deterministic way in case of a failure. Failures can be caused by:

- hardware random or systematic faults
- undefined operational conditions
- lack of system performance
- inherent systematic software failures
- or a mixture of the items above

A FMEA (Failure Mode and Effect Analysis) or Hazard Risk Analysis are appropriate measures to assess possible failures and their severity. The results of these analysis's lead to design constraints and additional assertions in the software during the architectural (ADD) and detailed design phase (DDD). The new CENELEC Railway Signalling standards (prEN50126, prEN50128, prEN50129, prEN50159-1/2) require these methods to introduce technical measures against systematic faults in the system design. All applicable measures which can be used during the different design phases of software needs redundancy. For the design of safety critical software the signalling engineers use information-(code), time- (same functionality at different times) and data (multiple storing and execution of same data) redundancy.

However small railway systems like level crossings, axle counters or track circuits embodies a complexity which prevents from simulating all possible failure conditions concerning all operational and environmental conditions in interaction with related signalling or other control systems.

The combination of avoidance of system faults in the requirements definition and design phase <u>and</u> protection against systematic faults in each development phase makes it possible to design safe systems knowing that failures are still remaining in software.

The following steps of the development life cycle deal with testing and validation. Testing can be decomposed into components testing, integration testing and validation- or system testing. Validation deals with establishing test cases, checking documentation and assessing the design of the product.

8 Validation of a safety critical system

Nowadays the functionality of railway signalling systems becomes more and more complex. One safe computer has to perform an increasing number of internal functionality. On the other hand safe computers operates a large number of communication interfaces with different protocols fulfilling different safety and security requirements.

Thus testing becomes more complex too. Components tests are derived from the design documents. Integration testing places emphasis on testing modules and subsystems and is derived from the architecture design. The validation and system testing has the following input documents:

- System Requirements Specification
- Failure Mode and Effect Analysis document
- Design documents (for increasing the knowledge in system design)

From these documents the Test Design Specification (TDS) is derived. The TDS arranges all inputs in test classes. Test classes comprise at least one test case and enable traceability of SRS, FMEA and Design items. Figure 7 depicts these relations.

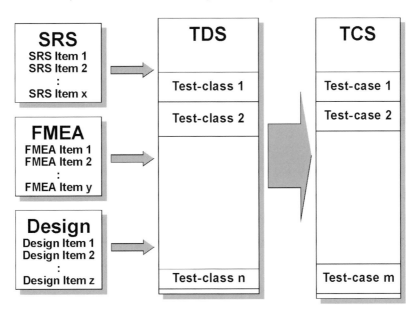

Figure 7: Structured approach to develop test cases

The completeness of test classes and test cases is assessed by the validation. Furthermore the validation checks that the tests are adequate.

A System Requirements Specification and Design Specifications are well known elements of each development life cycle. Development of safety critical systems requires additional effort to establish a Failure Mode and Effect Analysis (FMEA). The FMEA method had been developed by the NASA during the Apollo project. FMEA aims at detection of possible failures in the safety critical system. Therefore a analysis of critical components or functions is performed. At first all functions and components are identified. A second step deals with gathering of possible failures. These failures are assigned to components or functions.

Each possible failures leads to a effect. The next investigation tries to find system inherent counter measures to avoid this effect. The last section assesses the counter measures. In case the counter measures are sufficient, the failure analysis can be closed. Otherwise additional measures has to be defined. These additional measures can comprise:

- software or hardware functions
- test cases
- safety user instructions

Except of performing a FMEA the main activity of validation is testing. The testing process can be divided in static testing and dynamic testing. Static testing procedures deals with quantitative software analysis. Complexity metrics are an example for static software analysis and are used to identify critical parts of the software. High complexity of software often causes failures. A second method is the assessment of critical software paths. Critical paths are those parts of the software that perform the main functionality or parts that are essential to ensure a determined behaviour in case of an detected failure. In the latter case the exception handling procedures are checked whether they provide the functionality under all circumstances.

Figure 8 summarise all activities of validation which were described above. The documentation checking relates to the activities of the SRS. Validation has to approve that all requirements of the SRS are fulfilled by the system. This work includes traceability analysis and documentation checking.

This last part places emphasis on traceability of all items. The input documents are decomposed into small bricks. These small bricks are linked to test-classes. Test classes facilitates the grouping of test cases and convert the input items to testable items. From each test class at least one test cases is derived. The test cases are linked back to the input documents to keep the entire traceability information. Otherwise information would be lost by grouping the test cases in classes.

Each test case triggers one or more functions. A code coverage analysis is performed to evaluate the tested functions. If one function remains uncovered an additional test case has to be developed. This new test cases has to be involved in the traceability structure. Therefore all the links backwards has to be added (green parts of figure 9).

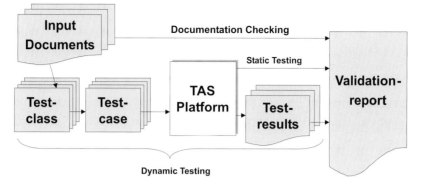

Figure 8: Summarisation of all validation activities

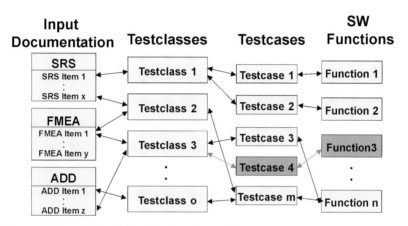

Figure 9: Traceability of all validation relevant items

If it is impossible to find a traceability structure for a new test case, it shall be assessed whether the affected function is necessary at all. Often the function is necessary but one of the input documents in incomplete. In this case the input documents has to be complemented.

9 Summary

Validation is performed by an authority independent from the development project. So the validation takes up the role of approving the fulfilment of the project objectives. Inputs for the validation are SRS, FMEA and design documents (mostly ADD). The validation carries out static and dynamic tests. Dynamic tests are regression tests. Test results gathered from different test runs are compared. This becomes important if several releases of software comprising different functionality's have to be validated.

Therefore the strategy of validation and re-validation was established. New components are validated. That means the entire validation is applied. Previous developed components that were not touched during the last development step are subject of re-validation. Re-validation means that all dynamic regression test cases have to result in the same values. Static analysis is not performed twice because the code has kept unchanged. The number of regression tests increase by each new release and validation.

The strategy above allows validation to become an ongoing process. Each new version of software has to be validated or re-validated depending on the number of changed items. So validation becomes more efficient and the effort for validation becomes more predictable.

10   References

[1] prEN 50126, Railway Applications: The Specification and Demonstration of Reliability, Availability, Maintainability and Safety (RAMS) CENELEC, rue de Strassart 35, Brussels

[2] ENV 50129, Railway Applications: Safety Related Electronic Systems for Signalling CENELEC, rue de Strassart 35, Brussels

[3] prEN 50128, final draft March 1999, Railway Applications: Software for Railway Control and Protection Systems CENELEC, rue de Strassart 35, Brussels

[4] Directive 96/48 EC, Interoperability of the Trans-European High Speed Rail System

Requirements for the Certification of Safety Critical Railway Systems

TOMISLAV LOVRIĆ
TÜV InterTraffic,
Institute for Software, Electronics, Railway Technology (Germany)

Abstract: In most application fields certification is required directly or indirectly by law for systems which potentially cause safety related risks to its users, its operators or to the public. This is also applies for railway systems, which are typically complex systems, consisting of multiple computer-based sub-systems. Other reasons for certification are competitiveness. A certificate issued by a trusted certification authority adds value to the product by attesting good development practice and high quality. It also provides confidence to customers and users of the system. Certification is therefore performed by independent, accredited experts and based on applicable standards and generally accepted rules of technology.

This paper will discuss the need for a certification process and explains the different development standards, roles, and activities involved. Each of the various phases of a system development life cycle is explained. While certification requires to apply and control qualitative and quantitative safety aspects, this contribution focuses on qualitative aspects, especially those related to software development and testing. An example on software module testing illustrates the process.

Concerning the documentation of safety evidence, the various standards require that the system is not only safe, but that the safety is also well documented. This paper gives hints how to tackle the complex and challenging certification process, and how to structure the complete safety evidence in an comprehensive and complete safety case. This enables a third party to understand all applied safety principles and to verify and consolidate the principles by following references pointing to the detailed safety evidence, if desired. The safety case is the final formal basis for the certification. Hints are given on how to address the needs of certification in advance, in order to collect all necessary information during the design process.

Keywords: Safety Certification, Assessment, Software Development, Testing, Railway

1 Introduction and Background

1.1 Safety Certification Based on Law in Germany

Since 1994 the authority to provide safety approvals in the railway sector is located within the Eisenbahn-Bundesamt (EBA). Every approval decision of the EBA is based on several inspection activities. Such activities can be performed either directly by the

EBA or by other accredited organisations that perform parts of the assessment or the whole assessment. The responsibility to provide the safety evidence is assigned the supplier of the system. The technical basis for the national approval are laws, directives, guidelines and norms, that build the generally accepted rules of technology (GART) in the railway sector.

A further example of the certification situation in Germany is the Notified Body for Interoperability of high speed rail systems, the EBC, as shown in figure 1. Again, independent assessors will assess the railway sub-systems or constituents and provide reports based on which the Notified Body will provide certificates of conformity or examination certificates. The figure also shows how European norms are considered by national law.

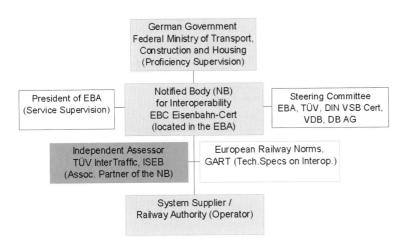

Figure 1: German Notified Body for Interoperability: (Decree of May 20, 1999)

1.2 Normative Basis

In the light of European harmonisation European norms receive increasing importance. For the railway sector the Eisenbahn-Bundesamt has already approved the usage of the European norms. Where ever there is an overlap, the European norms will replace the previously valid national norms. After finalisation of the European norms the related national technical safety standards will be withdrawn. One goal of the European norms is to provide common technical conditions in Europe and to reach cross-acceptance of safety approvals between European countries, provided that the approvals have been granted according to the European norms.

For the railway sector the three most important norms are prEN 50126 [2], which contains requirements for the complete railway system, prEN 50129 [3] with requirements for the complete signalling system and prEN 50128 [4] specifically for software in signalling systems. The norms describe the requirements that are the basis to reach approval of a system. They do not prescribe a specific technical solution. The three mentioned European railway norms are based on the more generic internal safety norm IEC 61508 [1] for Safety in electric, electronic and programmable systems, but they are specifically adapted to the needs and the history within the European railway sector. However, the basic concept behind the norms is very similar.

1.3 Roles and Responsibilities

Within complex safety approval processes many partners are involved. Figure 2 shows an example of the different partners and roles involved in the Copenhagen Metro mass transit system certification project. In this figure the Danish Railway Inspectorate Jernbanetilsynet takes a similar role as in Germany the Eisenbahn-Bundesamt.

Within the supplier (contractor) the safety manager is responsible for interfacing to the independent safety assessor and for managing safety related activities. It is worth noting that the Safety Assessor is not responsible for performing the complete verification of each design step. Instead, assessment is defined as the process of analysis to determine whether the design authority and the Validator have achieved a product that meets the specified requirements and to form a judgement as to whether the product is fit for its intended purpose.

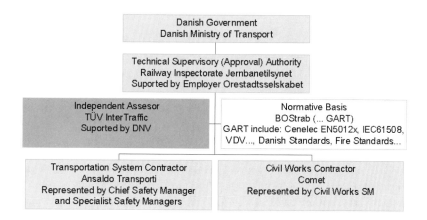

Figure 2: Safety Management Organisation for Copenhagen Metro, Public Mass Transit System

To reach his judgement the assessor relies on the suppliers V&V organisation, which consists of the Validator(s) and Verifier(s). The Validator is responsible for overseeing all verification activities and validating that the system meets its requirements. The verifier in turn is responsible for checking that each design step is a correct and complete refinement of the requirements from the previous phase. Depending on the required level of safety integrity for the system under design, different arrangements for independence are foreseen between the different roles. The higher the safety requirements are, the more independence must exist. One requirement is, for example, that the Assessor must belong to a different organisation than the design authority (with rare exceptions). Also, depending on the required safety integrity level, the Validator may not report to the same project management which is responsible for the design, and the Validator must have the authority to prevent the release of the system. Figure 3 summarises the layer of responsibilities where the final safety approval will be given by the authority, based on the Assessment Report of the Assessor.

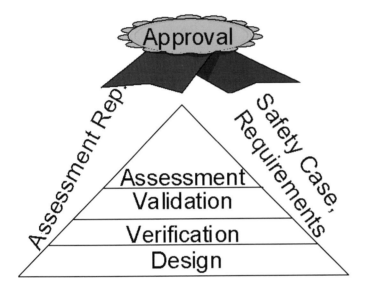

Figure 3: Layered Responsibilities

2   Requirements Derivation Process

2.1 Introduction

The level of rigor during the certification process and the required measures and techniques to be applied in the design will always depend on the level of safety responsibility that the system under design must cover. It would not be economic to build a system based on the highest possible safety requirements, even though it is not responsible for safety. It is therefore of utmost importance to know the safety responsibility that a sub-system has within the complete railway system. Lower safety requirements will result in less strict requirements for safety evidence. The safety requirements for sub-systems are derived within the railway system life-cycle.

2.2 The System Lifecycle and Apportionment of Requirements

Figure 4 shows the main phases within a railway systems life cycle. First, an understanding for the system and its requirements is developed, then the system definition phase defines the requirements for the system, its profile, and its interface to the environment. In close co-operation an in agreement with the approval authority, the risk tolerability criteria are defined.

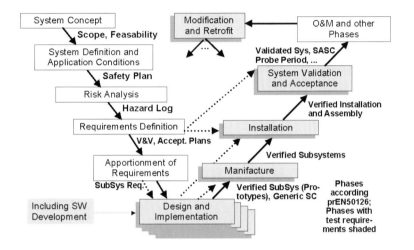

Figure 4: Railway System Lifecycle

The final level of risk is not defined in the standards, instead it is in the responsibility of national legislation. These criteria define what risk is considered tolerable to the society, or to the individual user of a railway system. The next phase mainly deals with the analysis of possible system risks. On a functional level, hazards are identified and analysed. In this context, hazards are system states that could under specific conditions lead to an accident. A first version of a safety plan will be compiled, explaining how to manage the risks involved in the system. This includes the definition of the planned safety activities and the roles and responsibilities involved in the safety management process.

During the risk analysis, the quantitative safety requirements for the system functions are derived. Based on the risk analyses, the requirements definition phase defines the reliability, availability, maintainability and safety requirements for the system. Also the safety functional requirements and necessary independence requirements between the functions are fixed. Unacceptable risks must be mitigated in this phase by adding respective safety requirements. These could be technical or non-technical safety measures. At the same time a validation plan is compiled, which defines how to validate these requirements in the later validation phase. It is important to note that the safety related functions include *quantitative* safety targets, which will enable the system to meet its risk tolerability criteria, as defined by the safety approval authority.

Before starting the design and implementation phase of the different sub-systems that constitute the complete railway-system, the system functional requirements must be apportioned to these sub-systems. Especially for the safety related functions, it is analysed, which sub-system(s) will realise them. Consequently, the sub-systems will inherit the safety responsibility of the system functions that they are in charge to implement. Examples and experiences with the allocation of safety integrity requirements in railway applications are given in [8].

In the design and implementation phase verified prototypes of sub-systems are produced, which fulfil their individual requirements. The following life-cycle phases deal with series manufacturing, installation and finally the railway system's validation and acceptance. After successful acceptance of the system and a trial-period, the operation and maintenance and other phases follow. In the following we will focus on the design phase, which is most important for hard- and software development.

3 Requirements for the Software Development

3.1 Introduction and Overview

The previous chapter described how the requirements for the individual sub-systems (as sub-systems of a complete railway system) are derived. Based on the functional requirements and the overall national risk tolerability criteria, the requirements are apportioned to the sub-system under design. Such requirements include non-safety requirements, i.e. the application function that the sub-system is in charge to perform, as well as safety requirements. The safety requirements can be separated into safety *functional* requirements, i.e. functional requirements with direct safety responsibility, and safety *integrity* requirements. An example for safety functional requirements is over-speed protection, i.e. to determine the actual speed, to compare it with the allowed speed, and to request an emergency brake in case of too high speed.

The safety integrity requirements can be split into *systematic* failure integrity requirements and *random* failure integrity requirements. The systematic failure integrity requirements define the necessary level for avoiding systematic faults in the design. They have direct impact on the organisational structure of the supplier's design team, quality assurance, and on the safety management. The European standards for railway safety distinguish 5 safety integrity levels, ranging from SIL 0 to SIL 4. Of those the level Zero (SIL 0) is the level for non-safety related functions, and the level 4 (SIL 4) is the highest safety integrity level for those functions with highest safety responsibility.

In contrast to systematic failure requirements, random failure integrity requirements can be associated with the ability of the system to handle random faults that occur during operation, for example due to ageing or environmental influences (EMC). Random failure integrity requirements are given by a number, defining the maximum tolerable hazardous failure rate that the system is allowed to show.

Whereas the systematic failure integrity requirements are regarded as qualitative requirements (i.e. non-quantifiable), the random failure integrity requirements are quantitative requirements. During the safety demonstration, evidence needs to be provided to show, that every random failure can be handled by the system, and that the failure effect remains contained within the system borders. Random failures can be handled by choosing appropriate architectures. These are either inherent fail safe components (e.g. based on inherent physical properties like gravitation), composite fail safe components (e.g. 2-out-of-2-systems) or reactive fail safe single items with checking. The prEN 50129 defines in Appendix C which failure modes need to be considered in the safety demonstration. The systematic and random failure integrity requirements are linked by a table within prEN 50129, Appendix A. The goal is to reach a balance between the measures against systematic failures and the measures against random failures. Since this paper mainly deals with the development of software, it focuses on the handling of systematic failures within the software design. However, the approach can be applied similarly to the hardware design. See also reference [7] and [9] for specific problems concerning safety evidence of random failure integrity.

If all sub-systems of a railway system are able to fulfil their individual safety requirements, then the overall railway system safety requirements will, in consequence, also be fulfilled. Concerning the software design process, the safety integrity level, as apportioned from the railway system safety requirements apportionment process, and assigned to the sub-system under design, will determine which measures and techniques need to be applied during the software development process. It also defines the amount of safety evidence that needs to be collected during the process, and the degree of independence between the different roles involved in the design.

3.2 The Software Lifecycle

The general design principles required for the software design process for all safety integrity levels (except SIL 0) are a hierarchical top down approach with stepwise refinement of the design, and with clear, consistent, and auditable documentation. For the sub-system under design, the system requirements (including safety and non-safety requirements) and the system architecture description build the basis to identify all (safety) functions that are allocated to the software. From this information, the Software Requirements Specification and the Software Architecture Specification are developed. The Software Quality Assurance Plan defines the software life-cycle and all design and verification steps required to comply with the required safety integrity level according to the standards. It is important to consider compliance with the standards based on the required safety integrity level in advance to the design, in order to be able to plan in the necessary activities and documents early in the life-cycle. The Software Quality Assurance Plan can already demonstrate how the supplier plans to comply with the safety standards. This can be a basis for agreements with the Safety Assessor in an early stage, and will avoid conflicts in later stages.

Figure 5 demonstrates the different phases of the software development process in form of a V life-cycle. The left branch of the V is related to the stepwise refinement of the design, down to the coding of software, whereas the right branch of the V is related to testing that the design achieves its requirements as defined in the previous phases (at the left side of the V). Figure 5 also indicates the requirement to define overall plans, that are not directly related to a single phase.

The philosophy for software certification in general is based on a phased development process with well defined entry and exit criteria for the different phases. Continued refinement steps lead from high level functional software requirements down to the development of the lowest level software design (module design specification), from which coding can be easily performed.

Each development phase is strictly documented. Test cases are set up to enable testing of the required properties. The quality of all activities and products/documents is controlled by verification and validation activities. This ensures that, at any phase, the design is a complete and correct refinement of the previous phase, and that design decisions are in line with the overall requirements. Testing and analysis is performed to verify the previously established acceptance criteria.

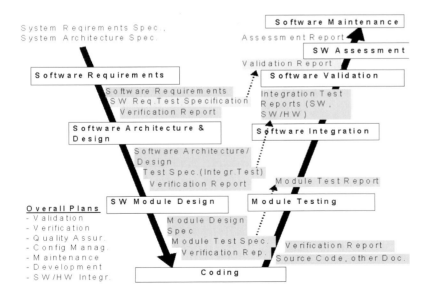

Figure 5: Software Lifecycle

In contrast to the top-down design steps, testing is performed in bottom-up steps from the lowest software level to testing of the functional requirements on the completely integrated system. In specific cases, deviations from this philosophy may also be acceptable (see e.g. [10]). This should be agreed with the Safety Assessor in charge for the certification.

Inherent to this process are the basic software design principles of top down design refinement, modularization, verification of each phase, documentation of each phase, and continued validation against system requirements.

For each of the phases shown in figure 5 prEN 50128 [4] defines requirements. For example, the goal of the software requirements specification phase is to develop a complete description of all requirements for the software under development. Note, that formal or semi-formal methods should be used to define the requirements unambiguously and completely, to allow any software engineer to develop the software without screening for requirements in other documents. The Software Requirements Test Specification already in this phase defines, how fulfilment of these requirements can later be tested. The Software Requirements Verification Report documents the quality assurance process applied to ensure, that the software requirements are complete, comprehensive and not in conflict with the overall requirements and the system plans. Possible deviations from the requirements or interfaces, or other quality criteria, are documented in the Software Requirements Verification Report. The next phase of the design should not be started unless a positive verification report on the phase is achieved.

The same philosophy applies to the other development phases. For example the software module design phase defines the detailed interfaces, data structures and algorithms that directly allow coding of the software module by software engineers. Also, the derivation of test cases by the software module design specification is possible. After coding of the software and verification of adequate coding by the Software Coding Verification activities, testable software is available. The Module Test Reports show that the modules behave as expected and documented in the Module Test Specification. The results of module testing are documented in the Module Test Reports, including non-conforming results and corrective actions. The degree of required structural coverage depends on the safety integrity level. For low safety integrity levels a purely functional testing (black box testing) is acceptable. The software integration phase combines the previously tested modules and allows testing of the interactions between the modules. Finally, the hard- and software integration phase covers the integration of the software on the target hardware (if necessary) and allows testing of the integrated system.

The final validation testing of all software requirements is done during system testing according to the Software Requirements Tests Specification. In order to validate all requirements it might be necessary to support the testing by additional analysis and simulations. The validation includes judgement on the appropriateness and compleness of all verification activities and results. All results of the validation activities and results are reported in the Software Validation Report.

According to the standards the assessment phase is performed after the validation. However, it is required to agree several activities with the assessor in advance. We always recommend to involve the Assessor very early in the life-cycle. The Assessor will assess whether the chosen safety integrity level is appropriate for the planned application of the software, and whether the development process and the resulting product is fit for the intended purpose. For this activity the Assessor has to have the ability to inspect all documents and information available on the product and the process. The Assessor will compile an Assessment Report on his activities. If his assessment judges suitability, then the approval authority will allow the software to be used for the intended purpose. During the operational and maintenance phase the software will be maintained according to the software maintenance plan. For each software change a change record is compiled containing the requirements affected by the change, an analysis of the possible impact of the change, and the specification of the change and a revalidation of the affected parts of the system.

3.3 Example of Software Module Testing

As an example, a tool for software module testing developed by TÜV InterTraffic shall be discussed. The tool has been used in projects where TÜV InterTraffic was not playing the role of the Assessor, but the role of an independent external verifier. Thus, the supplier was supported by us in providing the required safety evidence (e.g. the independence of the verifier from the designer). The example will illustrate some of the previous verification concepts. Figure 6 shows the general process. From the software module design specification (Detailed Design Doc.) developed by the design team the verifier generates the module test specification. The module test specification will contain the complete description of the test cases, containing – among others – a description of the tested scenario, the test inputs and the expected outputs, as derived from the documentation. From this, a tool will generate test drivers that allow automated processing of the test cases (e.g. drivers to provide the test input data to the module, stubs to replace called subroutines, collection and logging of the observed outputs and interactions). After the testing is complete, the test specification with the expected behaviour can be compared with the observed behaviour. A deviation can hint to a design error in the software (it could also be an error in the documentation or a fault made by the verifier in the test specification). In addition, the test coverage can be measured, i.e. which amount of code or branches has been executed by the tests. If the achieved coverage in not sufficient, the test cases need to be improved, or it must be analysed why the code cannot be reached. The tool that we use is a proprietary one, since we have to deal with different development environments of our various customers.

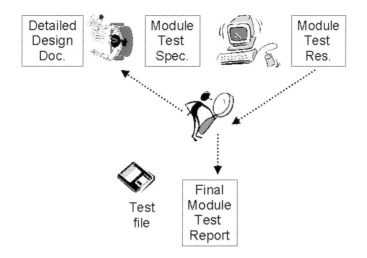

Figure 6: Software Module Testing

The following features of our equipment should be mentioned: The test specification contains for each test case the test case number, a description, the input data (including global variables), the expected output data (including global data), the expected called subroutines with the number of expected calls to it. In addition, for each called subroutine we can specify for each test case number the expected inputs that shall be provided by the module under test (for each call), and the output values that the stubroutines should provide when called (can be different for each call).

The test results log the following information: The occurred inputs, the occurred outputs, the real subroutine calls (including the number of occurred calls). For each subroutine it is logged for each test case number: The number of calls, the occurred inputs for each call, the provided outputs for each call. In addition, the code and/or branch coverage can be calculated.

The tests are generally set up for low intrusion, as far as possible, and high observeability / adaptability. This is reached by use of original hardware environment, and use of original development tools. Also, the test results are derived from the original (non instrumented) source code. High observability is reached using an in-circuit emulator (ICE) for monitoring and mapping the data to be observed and logged.

The formalised test specification that we can provide with our tool support a fully documented / logged, repeatable test process (auditable). The test cases and results are completely unambiguous (completely machine readable). Additional comments can be given for better traceability / readability. Intelligent data specification is supported (e.g. also structured data, and different number bases (binary, decimal, ...). The environment supports easy incremental test improvement and reuse (regression tests). So the tester can concentrate on the creative part of developing test cases. Also, automated consistency and correctness checks support the test management. This includes the automated test frame generation that makes testing easily repeatable.

The described environment has proven its effectiveness in supporting successful certification of safety critical railway software with requirements ranging from SIL 2 to SIL 4. Due to its flexibility is can be adopted for different environments and programming languages without major difficulties.

4 The Certification Process

Concerning certification, in general, it is one task to perform all the necessary activities in a professional manner, like the detailed software testing described before. But it can be another challenge to collect a sufficient amount of evidence during this process. It is the suppliers responsibility to provide *evidence* that a sufficient safety, verification and validation management has been established, and that the product complies to all requirements. This evidence is collected in the safety case document. Even though the safety case is only required (and of course can only be completed) at the end of the development, it is one of the main "inputs" to certification.

The structure of the safety case for safety related electronic systems in railway applications is defined in [3]. After the system validation phase the safety case is completed and builds the basis for certification. The safety case summarises all safety arguments and refers to all relevant safety evidence documents, that have been compiled during the whole design process (safety plan, verification reports, analysis, test results, …). The safety case is structured in six parts which allow easily to identify specific information. The degree of detail of the description of the safety evidence depends on the required safety integrity level.

The first two parts define the system and the quality management. The latter contains the documented evidence that the quality of the system is guaranteed by an appropriate quality management process during the whole life-cycle. The safety management report is the third part of the safety case. Similar to the quality management the safety management minimises the risk of safety related systematic faults in the design. The safety management report describes the safety management organisation and all activities performed during the safety life-cycle (those activities for the management of safety goals, especially hazard identification and analysis, verification and validation activities and safety audits). Main parts of the safety management report are the safety management organisation and the Safety Plan.

The fourth part, the Technical Safety Report, provides evidence on functional and technical safety of the system. It again contains six sub-parts. These include the safety evidence for the fault free operation, based on the description of the system, the interfaces, the requirements, and the verification and validation results. Another part of the technical safety report deals with the effects of faults on the system's behaviour. In this part it is shown that the safety is kept under all credible single failures (fail-safe principle). Structured analysis like the top-down fault tree analysis and the bottom-up Failure Mode Effect and Criticality Analysis can be used to prove sufficiency of the quantitative safety requirements of the system. The analysis must include an analysis of common mode and multiple failures. For those properties that depend on multiple units, the independence between the units needs to be analysed. In addition, environmental influences are considered in this part of the safety case.

It is also worth noting that part five deals with safety related application conditions. All conditions and assumptions are described that need to be considered for a safe operation of the system. This can be seen as an interface to allow modularity between safety cases. It allows re-use of safety cases which can lead to cost improvements. Safety related application conditions can be related to installation and configuration conditions, allowable modes of operation, necessary verification procedures, or specific calibration needs. A system that is using a sub-system safety case needs to consider its safety related application conditions. It must show that all sub-system safety conditions are either fulfilled or carried forward in further application conditions for the complete system. In order to easily identify all relations to other safety cases there is a separate part, part six of the safety case, dealing with all such relations. This part must identify related safety cases of sub-systems and show, that all application conditions from these safety cases are either fulfilled, or carried on in part 5 "Safety related application conditions". Finally, the last part of the safety case is the summary.

A challenge during compilation of the safety case is, that it should provide a complete and comprehensive collection of safety arguments. On the other side, it should be simple enough for an independent party, to objectively check the evidence of safety. All decisions and assumptions need to be made visible and consistent and traceable to the underlying detailed documents. Experience shows that this is not an easy task, especially due to the complexity of the complete safety evidence. One approach could be to have a structured approach, starting from the safety goals and all assumptions. In the next step, the goals and the assumptions are made evident by arguments and analysis. The final layer is formed by references to the detailed safety evidence that has been collected during the different phases of the life-cycle, like testing results, detailed analysis, simulation results, etc.

From our experience as a Safety Assessor, who performs assessment of the overall activities and judges whether or not the activities (and the outcome, of course) are sufficient to grant the required/desired certificate, it must be highly recommended to plan the activities right from the beginning. A project accompanying safety certification process is based on intermediate milestones. It does not start at the end of the development process. This allows an easy detection of deviations or risks and their proper correction early in the life-cycle. This increases the chance of a smooth and unconditioned certification. Usually, the need for major change requests can be avoided.

To establish Quality, Safety and Verification/Validation plans and to agree them with the Assessor in an early phase is a solid foundation for a smooth assessment process. This not only increases mutual confidence. It also allows to realistically plan the activities and to put the effort into the right direction from the beginning.

If the need for safety certification is not planned in from the beginning, the safety claim could be higher than the available safety evidence. This requires additional effort after completion of the design phase. But then the information is much more difficult to retrieve. It is a general experience that, unless the requirements for certification are planned in from the start, it is unlikely that all of the required evidence has been collected during the development. Therefore, to avoid costly subsequent efforts, we recommend a project accompanying assessment. Refer to [5] for our project accompanying safety assessment approach.

An other advantage of the early involvement of the Assessor is not only to avoid to underestimate requirements, it could also help not to overestimate them. Sometimes existing internal quality assurance procedures are already suitable for the project, even though there are differences to the European norms. An early involvement of the Assessor clarifies whether the procedures are suitable, or where additional measures need to be installed for the intended project. It should be noted that the European norms contain a lot of requirements and recommendations, that always need to be tailored to the specific project. The final processes and documents of the different suppliers will never exactly match all the recommendations of the norms. Here, the experience of the Assessor is important to judge the suitability for the intended safety related project.

In projects where we do not hold the role of the Independent Assessor, we offer to support a supplier in his task to provide the safety evidence for his product. Often, the focus of our consultancy activities is in the areas of requirements engineering, hazard and risk analysis, safety case preparation, and other tasks that support the safety management. In addition our independent and accredited institute performs detailed analyses that will improve the confidence of the Assessor in the safety of a product. It should also be noted, that we offer various verification activities to support the supplier in his time critical undertakings. The supplier could also use our verification know-how to build his own verification group for future projects, without risky complications due to the new experience with the certification.

5 Summary and Conclusion

This paper has presented an overview of the main requirements during the certification of safety critical systems. It has been shown why the requirements depend on the overall safety goals and are layered depending on the safety requirements derived from the complete system. Depending on this safety requirements allocation, the standards define appropriate measures and techniques and the level of rigor to be applied during design and certification.

The safety case, as the final collection of the complete safety evidence, must cover all measures to avoid systematic faults and to handle all random or remaining systematic faults. It concentrates in a balanced manner to the safety of the product and the quality aspects of the underlying process. All partners involved in the certification project will play predefined roles and need to fulfil the respective competence and independence requirements. The early involvement of an accredited Safety Assessor is not only increasing confidence to potential customers (e.g. for acquisition activities), it also helps to determine possible risks and estimate efforts early in the life-cycle, and to reduce the overall costs of the certification process.

Acknowledgements: Many thanks go to Petra Hörnig, Stephan Jubin, Rüdiger vom Hövel and the other members of the ISEB for their help, fruitful comments and the untiring discussions on the topic, and to my wife for an other weekend of patience.

6 References

[1] IEC (1997) IEC 61508 Functional safety of electrical/electronic/programmable electronic safety-related systems, Version 4.0 05/12/1997. International Elektrotechnical Commission

[2] CENELEC (1997) Final Draft prEN 50126; Railway Applications, The Specification and Demonstration of Dependability, Reliability, Availability, Maintainability and Safety (RAMS), Issue: June 1997. European Commitee for Electrotechnical Standardization

[3] CENELEC (2000) prEN 50129; Railway Applications, Safety Related Electronic Systems for Signalling, Issue: April 2000. European Commitee for Electrotechnical Standardization

[4] CENELEC (2000) Final Draft prEN 50128; Railway Applications, Software for Railway Control and Protection Systems, Issue: May 2000. European Commitee for Electrotechnical Standardization

[5] Wigger P, Haspel U (1998) Safety Assessment of Copenhagen Driverless Automatic Mass Transit System. World Conference of Railway Research, WCRR, Lissabon, 1998

[6] Lovric T (1999) Zertifizierung Sicherheitskritischer Softwarebasierter Systeme, 15. GI/ITG-Fachtagung Architektur von Rechensystemen ARCS '99, Jena, Oct. 4–7 1999.

[7] Lovric T (2000) Fault injection for quantitative safety validation of software based reactive systems, In: Computer Aided Design, Manufacture and Operation in the Railway and other Mass Transit Systems, Proceedings of Comprail 2000, Bologna, WIT Press, p 135 ff

[8] Schäbe H, Wigger P (2000) Experience with SIL Allocation in Railway Applications, 4th International Symposium "Programmable Electronic Systems in Safety Related Applications", TÜV Rheinland / Berlin Brandenburg, 3.–4. May 2000/Cologne, Conference Proceedings

[9] Gall H, Kemp K, Schäbe H (2000) Betriebsbewährung von Hard- und Software beim Einsatz von Rechnern und ähnlichen Systemen für Sicherheitsaufgaben – Grundlagen der Rechnersicherheit – Betriebsbewährung – Forschung – F 1570, Bundesanstalt für Arbeitsschutz und Arbeitsmedizin, Dortmund

[10] Boulanger J L, Gallardo M, Validation and verification of METEOR safety software, In: Computer Aided Design, Manufacture and Operation in the Railway and other Mass Transit Systems, Proceedings of Comprail 2000, Bologna, WIT Press, p 189 ff

Test Environment for Terminal Certification

CRISTIAN RADU
Integri n.v. (Belgium)

Abstract: This paper describes a suitable test environment for terminal testing. The types of terminals considered are the card acceptor devices used in electronic banking, but the methodology presented can be easily extended to other types of terminals, for example the GSM handset. The proposed test environment is constructed with a dedicated test tool named TERTIO developed by Integri. The complexity of the test agents involved in the test environment depends on the desired level of automation of the tests and on the overall cost accepted for the testing activity. TERTIO improves terminal testing through the use of the *State Transition Tree*, which models the expected behaviour of the terminal under test as a finite state machine.

Keywords: electronic banking, terminal testing, test agent, card emulator.

1 Introduction

Nowadays, more and more devices accepting payment cards appear. On the one hand there are the classical terminals used in payment systems, e.g., Point-of-Sale (POS) terminals and Automated Teller Machines (ATM). However since the introduction of smart card technology, a number of new applications have emerged. Electronic purse based payment schemes make it economically possible to have cheap terminals, integrated in vending machines, parking meters, or electronic fee collection gates. To a large extent, the GSM handset can also be considered a terminal accepting cards, certainly considering the dual card handsets, which will combine the internal GSM SIM card with a user card.

Payment system operators do no longer develop these terminals themselves, but rely on external suppliers. Therefore, operators issue functional specifications for the terminals, which form the basis for the development by the supplier. To assure that the resulting terminal complies with these functional specifications, the terminals must undergo a certification process. This certification process is either executed by the payment system operator itself or by an independent testing company.

The testing of a terminal is a quite complex task, considering its interaction with external devices, such as smart cards, authorisation hosts, or clearing systems. This paper presents a methodology and a test environment for terminal certification. The tool forming the hart of this environment is referred to in the remainder of the paper under the acronym TERTIO (**TER**minal **T**est **E**nv**I**r**O**nment).

TERTIO controls the interaction of the terminal under test with various Test Agents and can configure them to answer various testing purposes. A Test Agent can simulate the behaviour of an entity interfaced with the terminal, is able to detect erroneous formatted data coming from and to introduce errors in the data forwarded to the terminal under test. An emulator of a smart card, a clearing host application running in a test session, or a test operator performing a number of tasks on the terminal are typical examples of Test Agents.

The certification process starts with an analysis of the functional specifications of a terminal in order to define the representative test cases. TERTIO allows defining the test cases in a hierarchical way in a *Test List*. Once the Test List is established, the test programmer can write the actual test scripts, contained in a *Test Library*. The tool allows establishing links between the description of tests contained in the Test List and the scripts that actually run the tests in the Test Library. During the execution of tests, all actions are logged. At the end of a test, each of the Test Agents is checked to find out if any errors are detected. TERTIO improves terminal testing through the use of the *State Transition Tree*, which models the expected behaviour of the terminal under test as a finite state machine. The State Transition Tree facilitates the definition and programming of the test scripts. TERTIO stores the test information in a repository and defines a number of standard test reports and statistics.

2 Terminal environment

The set of entities that interact with the terminal during various transactions forms the *terminal environment*. Identifying the terminal environment is the first stage towards defining the test environment. In order to simplify the paper, the terminal environment refers to a Point-of-Sale (POS) terminal, which is used to perform a payment transaction in a debit or credit electronic payment system. However, the same methodology can be easily adapted for other types of terminals.

In a payment transaction, the *smart card of the user* is inserted in the POS terminal. Through the user interfaces of the terminal, e.g., specialised keyboard and display, both the *Merchant* and the *Cardholder* interact with the terminal. After the amount to be paid is inserted by the Merchant, the Cardholder accepts or rejects the conditions of payment. In case the Cardholder accepts the conditions, the terminal sends to the card each command indicated in the protocol of the payment transaction and receives the corresponding response. The terminal verifies the completion code returned by the card and processes the information contained in the response. To verify the correctness of some responses involving cryptographic computations, the terminal can ask security services to its *Security Application Module (SAM)*. This is a tamper-resistant integrated circuit card incorporated in the terminal, which is able to perform cryptographic computations like encryption/decryption using symmetric-key or asymmetric-key techniques, MAC generation/verification, and signature generation/verification.

A payment transaction involving a debit card containing a local account can be completed off-line, without the intervention of a third party. After the completion of each payment transaction, the balance of the local account of the card is decreased with the amount to be paid and a record is written in the *Transactions Journal* kept in the non-volatile memory of the terminal. Periodically, the terminal communicates with the *Clearing Host*, representing the bank of the Merchant or the payment system operator, to send the content of the Transactions Journal. After assessing the correctness of each transaction recorded in this journal, the Clearing Host refunds the Merchant for the cumulated amount obtained from all the cleared records. The Clearing Host, which is responsible for the management of the POS terminals, can update the parameters of the POS terminal, including a fresh red-list containing all the cards that misbehave in the system. This transaction between the POS and the Clearing Host is referred to as a *collection transaction*. During a payment transaction involving a debit or a credit card that is linked to a central account, the terminal requires the authorisation of this transaction by an *Authorisation Host*, representing the bank of the Cardholder or the payment system operator. The payment transaction is completed only after the acknowledgement of the Authorisation Host. An overview of the terminal environment, showing the POS in interaction with all the parties mentioned in the above scenario, is presented in Figure 1.

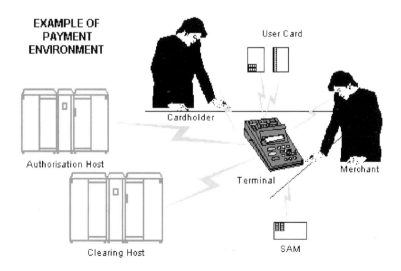

Figure 1: POS Terminal in an electronic payment system environment

It can be noticed that a number of interfaces can be defined between the terminal and each party that interacts with the terminal:

- *User card interface* – it consists of the set of all the command/response pairs exchanged between the terminal and the card.
- *SAM interface* – it is the set of all the command/response pairs exchanged between the terminal and the SAM.
- *Man-machine interface* – it consists of the specialised display, keyboard, and printer that allow the interaction of the POS terminal with the Cardholder and/or the Merchant.
- *Authorisation Host interface* – it represents the set of all messages exchanged between the Authorisation Host and the terminal for authorising debit and credit transactions.
- *Clearing Host interface* – it represents the set of all messages exchanged between the Clearing Host and the terminal during a collection transaction.

The processing of the terminal is described in its *functional specifications*, which typically cover:

- the interface with each entity, specifying the format of the command/response pairs or the format of the messages exchanged with the host computers;
- the data structures managed by the terminal, like the Transactions Journal, Terminal Parameters, and Red Lists;
- the protocol of each transaction supported by the terminal;
- the messages displayed for the Merchant and the Cardholder;
- the sequence of keys that is needed to trigger a certain function provided by the terminal;
- the initialisation and error recovery procedures.

The behaviour of the terminal is completely determined through its interfaces with the entities composing the terminal environment.

3 Test management

The certification process starts with an analysis of the functional specifications of the terminal to define all the *representative* test cases. Representative tests should fulfil the following requirements (Beizer 1990):

- *effective*: the main purpose is that tests should find errors;

- *exemplary*: the tests should be representative for as many cases as possible;
- *maintainable*: the effort to adapt tests, if the functional specifications of the terminal change should be minimal;
- *economical*: the tests should be written and executed with as little effort as possible, such that the time needed to execute tests should be minimal.
- *robust*: the tests should not be sensitive to the state of the unit under test. If the state does not correspond to the pre-requisite of the test, the test is able to recover from this situation and bring the unit into this desired state.
- *repeatable*: it must be possible to repeat the test. Note however that this does not imply that exactly the same input/output will occur because this is not always possible, e.g., due to random numbers generated by the unit under test, or due to counters maintained by the unit under test. However it is important that the same test case can be repeated.

TERTIO allows defining all the representative test cases in a hierarchical way. It can add for each test or group of tests the reference to the specifications, a short description, and a version number. At the end of this phase, the *Test List* is available in a file.

Once the Test List is established, the test programmer can write the actual *test scripts*, contained in the *Test Library*. The programmer can easily link the tests from the Test List with the scripts in the Test Library.

During the actual execution of a test one can distinguish three stages:

- Firstly, all the entities and the terminal itself have to be set in a known state. For example, if the purpose of the test is to check that the terminal rejects a payment transaction with a red-listed card, then before performing the payment transaction itself a collection transaction has to be carried out. During this transaction the Clearing Host sends to the terminal a fresh red-list including the user card that is used to execute the test. This is named the *pre-requisite stage*.
- Secondly, the action of the test is performed. This action depends on each type of interface. For example, when the current entity interacting with the terminal is the user card, an action can be modifying the completion code returned by the card to an error code unexpected by the terminal in that status. This is named the *action stage*.
- Lastly, the *post-requisite stage* is performed. In this step, some processing must be performed to guarantee that all the entities are in a consistent state at the end of testing, or some supplementary transactions must be fulfilled in order to access the results of the tests. For example, when a test is performed to check that the terminal refuses a payment transaction with a red-listed user card, the first reaction of the terminal is to abort the payment transaction, fact that is accessible to the test operator through the man-machine interface of the POS terminal. However, a collection transaction has to be carried out with the Clearing Host in order to allow the testing tool to access the content of the Transactions Journal,

where an incident has to be recorded regarding the attempt of a certain red-listed user card to perform a payment transaction.

The reporting after the test completion can be obtained based on the test scripts. The test operator has the possibility to interpret errors in the functionality of the terminal, which are revealed during testing, and to define the so-called *defects*. A defect is an unexpected behaviour that has been detected during the test execution. It can be a bug, a functionality that is not implemented, or any other issue requiring a corrective action. TERTIO allows the test operator to define and track defects.

In order to be able to control the interfaces of the terminal during testing, an appropriate test environment has to be defined, which can be co-ordinated by TERTIO.

4 TERTIO – Terminal test environment tool

The *test environment* is defined like a set of Test Agents interacting with the terminal to be tested under the control of a specialised program referred to as the *Terminal Test Environment Tool,* or shortly TERTIO. A *Test Agent* in the test environment plays the role of an entity in the terminal environment (Fewster and Graham 1999). A Test Agent is featured by the following four characteristics:

- A Test Agent emulates the external behaviour of the corresponding entity from the terminal environment by the point of view of the interface with the terminal. Thus, the terminal under test does not sense the difference between interacting with the Test Agent or with the corresponding entity.

- If the data coming from the terminal is erroneous, the Test Agent will detect the anomaly.

- A Test Agent is able to induce errors in the data forwarded to the terminal. Examples of errors are format errors in the response of the user card, a time-out in operating a sequence of keys expected in a certain status of the terminal, or a wrong MAC verification value returned by the SAM.

- A Test Agent can be controlled by TERTIO during all of the three stages of execution of a test.

In principle, any Test Agent in the test environment can be implemented through an emulator of the corresponding entity from the terminal environment. An emulator is a software tool that models the functional specifications of a given entity and completely simulates the behaviour of that entity. Considering that TERTIO has the possibility to control an emulator, then the flexibility of the test environment increases, the efficiency of testing activity is improved, and there exists the possibility to automate the majority of the tests. However, this solution increases the overall cost of the testing project, considering the fact that the emulator is a complex and expensive software tool. Therefore, it is worth evaluating in which conditions a Test Agent should be implemented as an emulator, when it can be implemented as a "pass-through" testing tool, or when it can be represented directly by the real entity from the terminal environment.

A Test Agent can be implemented through an emulator of the corresponding entity from the terminal environment if the following conditions are fulfilled:

- the pre-requisite stage of the test involves complex operations in order to establish the correct internal sate of the Test Agent and it demands the direct intervention of TERTIO in the data structures of the Test Agent;
- the action of the test consists in instructing the emulator to produce a wrong response, which should be detectable by the terminal following correctly the functional specifications;
- TERTIO must have full access to the internal state of the emulator in order to evaluate the result of the test.

Implementing the Test Agent as an emulator offers the best flexibility for testing but increases the cost of the testing environment. Nevertheless, if the target is to automate and optimise testing to a maximum, this solution is the only one acceptable.

A Test Agent can be implemented with a "pass-through" tool, which captures the output of the entity in the terminal environment and modifies it according to the action to be performed by the test, if the following conditions are fulfilled:

- the Test Agent can be brought to an initial state suitable for the test without the intervention of TERTIO, which does not need to intervene directly in the data structures of the Test Agent;
- the action of the test consists in inducing a malicious error that should be detected by the terminal following correctly the functional specifications;
- the test operator can obtain the result of the test without the need to access the internal state of the entity in the terminal environment.

Implementing the Test Agent as a "pass-through" tool is a trade-off between the degree of flexibility and the cost of the testing environment.

A Test Agent in the test environment can be represented by the corresponding real entity in the terminal environment if the following three conditions are fulfilled:

- the Test Agent can be brought to an initial state suitable for the test without the automate intervention of TERTIO, which does not need to intervene directly in the data structures of the Test Agent;
- there is no action controlled directly by TERTIO to be performed on the corresponding interface of the Test Agent with the terminal;

- the result of the test does not depend of the Test Agent or the test operator can obtain the result of the test without the need to access the internal state of the Test Agent.

Allowing the real entity in the terminal environment to play the role of the Test Agent in the testing environment does not involve supplementary costs but reduces the flexibility of testing with respect to the corresponding interface.

In order to exemplify the way of choosing the Test Agents depending on the kind of test executed such that the overall cost of the test environment to be kept to a minimum, the payment scenario at a POS terminal presented in Section 2 is revisited. Let us assume that the behaviour of the terminal is tested for the case of a payment transaction using a debit card linked to a personal account in the bank, for which the Authorisation Host is required on-line to accept or reject the payment. In this case the test environment involves the following Test Agents:

- Test Agent 1 is the *User Card Emulator*, which replaces the real user card. This choice allows TERTIO to set up the initial internal state of the card in a convenient way for many different test situations without the need to use a large set of testing cards, since the payment transaction depends to a large extent on the parameters stored in each card. This also allows the testing tool to easily modify the responses of the card in order to verify that the terminal starts the correct error recovery procedure in case of a protocol failure.

- Test Agent 2 is the *SAM Pass-Through*, which is a tool that captures the command/response pairs exchanged between the real SAM of the terminal and the terminal under test. This conversation is forwarded to a test SAM, where the responses of the real SAM still can be conveniently modified to answer the purpose of the test. In this case TERTIO has no direct access to the internal state of the SAM. However, the tests performed in connection with the payment transaction do not involve frequent changes of the parameters of the SAM.

- Test Agent 3 is the *Test Operator* who performs the actions of both the Cardholder and the Merchant from the terminal environment. In this case, the Test Operator is guided through the graphic user interface of TERTIO.

- Test Agent 4 is the *Authorisation Host Emulator*. The need of using an emulator as a Test Agent instead of using directly the Authorisation Host is determined by the fact that the terminal is going to be tested with respect to various errors that can appear in the authorisation response obtained from this host. Therefore, it is convenient to have an emulator, the parameters of which can be easily modified according to the needs of the tests.

- Test Agent 5 is the Clearing Host itself running in a test session. This choice is mainly determined by the fact that this interface will not be directly involved in the execution of tests.

An overview of the test environment in this case is presented in Figure 2.

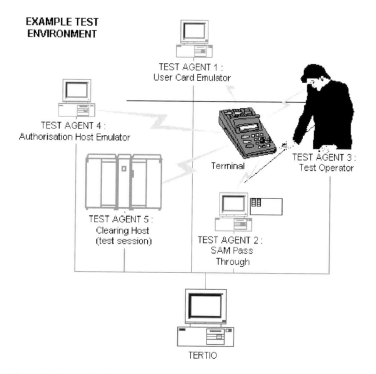

Figure 2: Example of test environment for POS terminal

The test environment can be adapted depending on the type of terminal, and the set of testing tools that are available for the corresponding terminal environment, e.g., emulators and "pass-through" tools.

TERTIO can control a Test Agent in three different ways:

- *TERTIO User Interface*: for the most primitive Test Agents, interfacing can be done via the graphic user interface of TERTIO. When TERTIO wants to have a certain behaviour of the Test Agent, it will display the action to be undertaken by the test operator, e.g., "Enter test card n°3", or "Instruct Authorisation Host Emulator to return response code '00'", or "Interrupt Power".

- *User Defined DLL*: this is interesting when a proprietary Test Agent provided by the terminal manufacturer is used for controlling the interface. In this case the test programmer can extend the test script with a number of functions, which reside outside the TERTIO tool.

- *RTC*: RTC stands for Remote Test agent Call. RTC allows a full control of TERTIO on an emulator or a pass-through test tool, including changing of parameters and data, starting event scripts, and checking log files.

When the RTC facility is used, TERTIO allows preparing a script that will be executed on a remote Test Agent when a certain event occurs. The so-called *event script* can modify the behaviour of a Test Agent that runs it.

5 Graphical User Interface

This section focuses on the Graphical User Interface of TERTIO. The data tree structures which are used by the test programmer are introduced and illustrated: the Project Tree, the Terminal Data Tree, the State Transition Tree, the Test List Tree, the Test Script Library Tree, and the Test Grid Modal Window.

5.1 Project Tree

In Figure 3 is displayed the *Project Tree* that controls the execution of a test session for a POS terminal.

Figure 3: Project Tree for POS testing

The Project Tree is used to define various test sessions. In the example displayed in Figure 3, there are two different folders containing test sessions for ATM terminals and POS terminals. The "POS Terminal Testing" folder includes two distinct sessions, one "Demo Session" and the other a session for testing "POS Type AX".

Each test session contains the references to the objects that are loaded when a test session is opened, e.g., terminal data tree, state transition tree, test list, test script library, log, and links to the Test Agents.

A standard Project Tree contains one template. The user may derive new test sessions from this template, in order to separate different terminals or different test environments.

5.2 Terminal Data Tree

The *Terminal Data Tree*, shown in Figure 4, contains information that can be used for the programming of the State Transition Tree (STT) and during the execution of the test scripts. Typical data residing in the Terminal Data Tree are terminal parameters, red lists of user cards that were misbehaving in the system, screen messages to be displayed by the terminal, and records of the Transactions Journal. The programmer of the test scripts decides which data to keep in the Terminal Data Tree. The script language can access and manipulate all data contained in this tree.

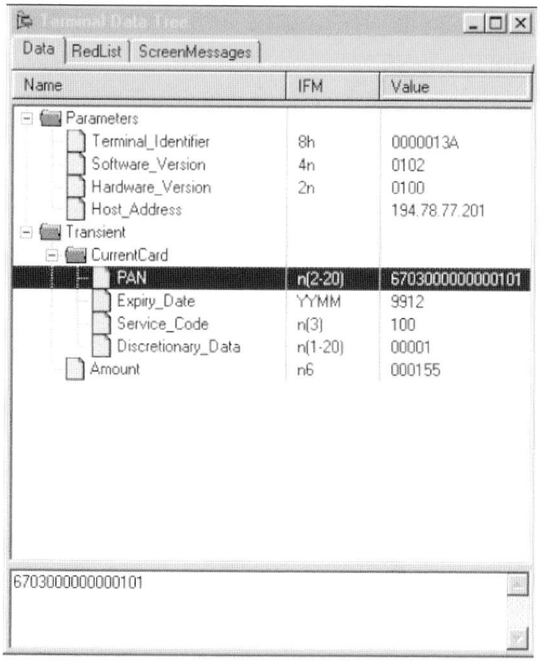

Figure 4: Terminal Data Tree

The structure of the Terminal Data Tree also reflects the organisation of the internal memory of the terminal. In the example presented in Figure 4, the data which is grouped in the folder "Parameters" represents data that is kept in the non-volatile memory of the terminal under test. The data that is grouped in the folder "Transient" represents data that is kept in the RAM memory of the terminal.

5.3 State Transition Tree

To facilitate testing, TERTIO offers the possibility to simulate the behaviour of the terminal under test. Because the processing of a terminal can normally be considered as a finite state machine, it is quite straightforward to represent this processing in a finite state graph. TERTIO allows programming this finite state graph in a so-called *State Transition Tree* (STT), as shown in Figure 5 below for an over-simplified terminal.

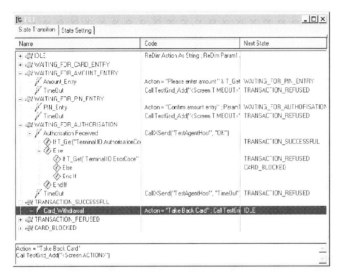

Figure 5: The State Transition Tree, an advanced feature for writing terminal test scripts

The script in the STT contains the necessary code to control the test environment. For example, the code executed on the PIN_Entry event commands the appropriate Test Agent to enter a PIN. Making use of the STT facilitates the writing of test scripts, since the script only needs to indicate in which state the terminal has to be set before the action specific to the given test is performed.

5.4 Test List Tree

The *Test List Tree* describes the tests that are necessary to be executed on the terminal under test in order to certify it according to its functional specifications. Each item of this list contains all the relevant information relative to a test, such as the reference to the specifications, a short description of the action performed by the test, a version number, as well as other information needed to describe a test. The test programmer can add any kind of property at a certain level of the Test List Tree, which will refer to either a single test or to a group of tests. The Test List Tree is linked to the Test Script Library Tree, which contains the scripts of all the individual tests. The use of a Test List is optional but improves reporting considerably. A snapshot of the Test List Tree can be seen in Figure 6.

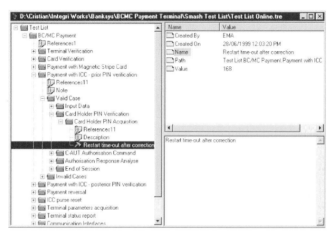

Figure 6: Test List Tree

5.5 Test Script Library Tree

The *Test Script Library Tree* is the data structure that contains the actual test scripts to be executed. The TERTIO tool is provided with an extended set of software libraries offering the most common cryptographic, numeric, bit-wise, and string operations, including support for accessing and manipulating the data trees.

The number of tests that is needed in order to certify a terminal can be quite high. However, the test programmer can identify classes of tests that are similarly organised. Therefore, in order to facilitate the programming of the test scripts and to reduce the maintenance cost of the test scripts, the tests in the same class can be written applying object oriented principles. Thus, the test programmer can write an abstract frame of the test scripts in the same class and then obtain each test script in the class by deriving the abstract frame or over-writing some of its member functions. Using this facility in an appropriate way can considerably reduce the number of code lines that must be written for each test script in the class. The Graphic User Interface of TERTIO displays the Test Script Library Tree as shown in Figure 7.

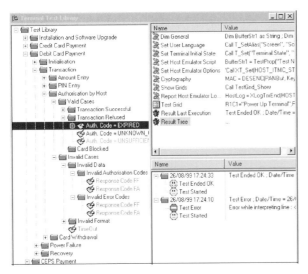

Figure 7: Test Script Library Tree

5.6 Test Grid Modal Window

Using the Remote Test agent Call (RTC) facility or a user defined DLL, TERTIO can control an automated Test Agent implemented through an emulator or as a "pass-through" tool. In this way, TERTIO allows a high degree of test automation.

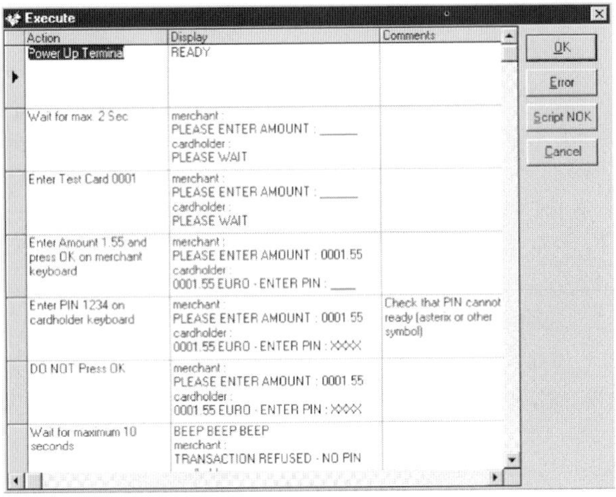

Figure 8: Example of Test Grid Modal Window

However, in case the Test Agent cannot be automated, *test grids* are displayed for the test operator in order to assist him managing the Test Agent. When executing a test, a modal form appears that is referred to as the *Test Grid Modal Window*. One column indicates the action to be undertaken by the test operator, e.g., enter user card, or type in a PIN. Another column indicates the expected reaction of the terminal to be certified, e.g., display message, pickup card, and so on. The test operator must follow the guidelines given in this test grid and if needed, enter a description of any error detected. Figure 8 shows an example of a Test Grid Modal Window.

When the manufacturer of the terminal provides the test programmer with a dedicated DLL for directly accessing the keyboard and display during the testing, a test script can be entirely automated. In this case, the execution of tests can be performed unattended and no test grid windows are needed.

6 Implementation aspects

While TERTIO can support interfacing to any correctly written emulator, the presentation in this section assumes that the types of emulators and pass-trough tools used in the testing environment are those produced by Integri. They are referred to as the *THALES Emulator, CERTO,* and *THALES Pass-Through* tools. The THALES Emulator is used to implement the User Card Emulator (Test Agent 1), CERTO implements the Authorisation Host Emulator (Test Agent 4), while THALES Pass-Through implements the SAM pass-through tool (Test Agent 2).

A typical configuration of a THALES Emulator, used for the emulation of a user card, is presented in Figure 9.

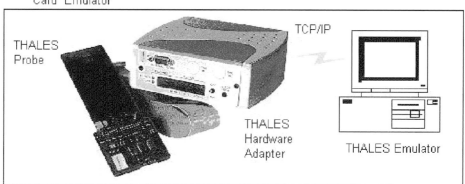

Figure 9: Typical configuration of the THALES Emulator

The software and hardware components of the user card emulator implemented with THALES are listed below:

- THALES software package – this component co-ordinates the activities in the THALES Emulator mode. This component is fixed indifferent which type of card is emulated.

- *Definitions Tree* data structure contains the syntax of the command/response pairs and the completion codes (the status words SW1, SW2) of the commands supported by the emulated card. This data structure represents the basic information for parsing the command/response messages exchanged between the emulated card and the terminal. The Definitions Tree also contains the message identification patterns of the commands accepted by the emulated card and, optionally, the templates of the file headers in the emulated card (MF, DF, EF) as well as the templates of its elementary files.

- *Card Tree* data structure contains the main resources of the emulated card. The resources consist of the file structure of the emulated card, a set of temporary variables used during the processing carried out by the emulated card, and the I/O buffer, storing the command received from the terminal and the response computed by the emulated card.

- A DLL library that implements the behaviour of the card – a separate function implements each command accepted by the card. The execution of the function is triggered by the corresponding command received from the terminal, while the function computes the emulated response to be returned to the terminal and updates correspondingly the status of the emulated card in the Card Tree data structure.

- PC running the THALES software package configured in the THALES Emulator mode, storing the Definitions Tree and the Card Tree data structures, and emulating the behaviour of the card through the execution of the functions in the DLL library.

- THALES hardware adapter (HWA) of type STAR 1150 provided together with a probe connected to it through a multiple-wire cable. One side of the probe is going to be inserted into the terminal under test, which is the POS terminal in our case study. The contacts of this side of the probe can be seen as the contacts of the emulated card. The other side of the probe, which is equipped with a smart card slot, is not used in this mode. The main role of the hardware adapter is to implement the transmission protocol (T=0, T=1) between the emulated card and the terminal under test, which both comply with the ISO 7816, regarding the physical and electrical characteristics. The hardware adapter is connected to the PC through a TCP/IP connection. The THALES hardware adapter can also capture and log the whole sequence of command/response pairs exchanged between the emulated card and the terminal.

The test environment contains a number of Test Agents that are either emulators (Test Agent 1 and Test Agent 4) or pass-through tools (Test Agent 3), all controlled by the terminal test tool environment TERTIO. From an economical point of view, it is important to realise a mapping of the Test Agents and TERTIO itself on computers such that a trade-off can be reached between the overall cost of the test environment and its performance. In Figure 10 is presented a possible solution of mapping.

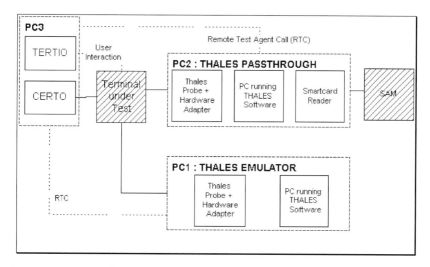

Figure 10: Mapping Test Agents on computers

In order to reduce the complexity of the test environment, it is possible to run the CERTO module within TERTIO, on the same PC. However, two separate PCs are needed to run the SAM Pass-Through tool (PC2) and the User Card Emulator (PC1). Both PC1 and PC2 communicate with the PC running TERTIO via the Remote Test Agent Call (RTC) facility, implemented with a TCP/IP connection.

7 Summary

Certifying terminals is a complex task. The construction of the test environment from the corresponding terminal environment is a transformation that allows a correct identification of various Test Agents and their possible implementations. The terminal test tool TERTIO is the heart of the testing environment. It co-ordinates the actions of all the Test Agents towards a high degree of test automation and efficiency. A terminal test environment can be completely built using other testing tools provided by Integri, like the THALES Emulator, CERTO, and THALES Pass-Through, which can communicate with TERTIO via the Remote Test Agent Call (RTC) facility.

8 References

Beizer 1990 Beizer B (1990) Software Testing Techniques, Second Edition. Van Nostrand Reinhold, New York.

Fewster and Graham 1999 Fewster M, Graham D (1999) Software Test Automation. Addison-Wesley, New York.

Myers 1979 Myers GJ (1979) The Art of Software Testing. John Wiley & Sons, New York.

Remote Testing of Embedded Software

JAVIER FERNÁNDEZ PERPIÑÁN
DTK GmbH (Germany)

Abstract: This article is based on the experience of DTK in testing of software and especially describes the test of an embedded system for the railway area. In this specific project we had to create a test environment fulfilling at least the following major requirements:

- Supporting a methodical determination of the test cases in order to achieve a high functional coverage of the requirements.

- Providing a high degree of test automation.

- Managing all parts of the test information, such as test cases, test data and test results.

- Allowing a tester to perform all test activities from a remote network, i.e. the system under test can be accessed and controlled from a remote place.

- Flexibility to increase easily the number of workplaces.

The result was a general environment which can be used to test any kind of system or software.

Keywords: remote testing, embedded systems, test automation, testing tools, test environment

1 Introduction

If we take the terms *remote* and *embedded* away from the title of this article, what remains is just *Testing Software*. Well, this is exactly what this article is about. It describes a test environment perfectly adequate to test any kind of software but with special features which allow remote controlled testing. This capability is attractive when the test team has no possibility to perform the test activities locally and the system under test cannot be moved or reproduced somewhere else.

The need of an integrated test environment becomes obvious to each test team which has to deal daily with the following difficulties:

- *Measurement and achievement of the desired coverage of requirements:*
  Any test is based on a specification which describes what the object under test should do. The more complex the specification is, the more difficult it is to determine the test cases and to achieve the desired test coverage. A methodical

procedure for the determination of the test cases is therefore essential for this purpose.

- *Insufficient homogeneity due to the individual methods of the team members:*
  Each system is unique and testing is never an easy issue. Therefore the creativity of the testers is an important factor which should be encouraged. But not less important is the homogeneity of the process, including reporting of results. Each test person should share the same terminology, tools, templates, aims, etc. This is the only way transparency, clarity and completeness can be achieved. This makes it possible for a test person to understand the work of another one and is a decisive factor for good team work.

- *Bottle necks due to insufficient resources:*
  Important tools, archives, documents, etc. should not be fixed in specific work-stations and only be accessible there. It is desirable to have access to all relevant resources of the test environment from each workstation. Moreover, a good organisation provides a low rate of collisions for resources of limited access.

- *Manual realisation and repetition of test procedures costs time:*
  Test procedures should be automated as far as possible. This means a higher initial effort but it pays off in the end.

- *Loss of information due to bad archive organisation:*
  All documents, test data and test results should be stored in a well organised manner. All that can become a huge amount of data and to lose control over it can have dramatic consequences.

The test environment described here was created as a specific solution to remotely perform unit and integration test of an embedded system, namely an interlocking system for railways. However it was developed with the aim to create a general product resolving the difficulties listed above and which is applicable to any kind of software or system.

To make the subject matter more comprehensible, I will refer to the concrete tool constellation and topology used for the mentioned system and specify which parts would have to be adapted to apply the solution to other systems.

2 Testing Process

Identifying and defining the different phases of the testing process is an important step which must precede the planning of the test environment. Figure 1 shows a possible testing process.

In the following we will take a look at the phases of the process.

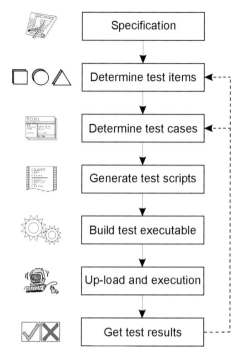

Figure 1: Testing Process

2.1 Studying the specification

Each test should be based on a specification which provides a detailed functional and technical description of the subject under test. Important qualities of a specification are correctness, clarity, unambiguity and completeness.

The test team must be well familiar with the structure and contents of the specification to be able to achieve a good functional coverage.

2.2 Determining the test items

Independent items suitable to be tested are extracted from the specification. The selection criteria for these items varies depending on the focus and kind of test. The determination of the test items is not easy because the limit between different functions, modules or other entities can be difficult to determine. In these cases it is recommendable to spend some effort analysing more deeply the specification and refining the selection criteria. Well selected test items can considerably reduce the test effort. Static metrics, such as complexity metrics, can help to determine the test items.

As an example, if the subject under test is the timing module of an operating system and the focus is on unit testing, a possible test item could be a timer queue.

2.3 Determining the test cases

For each test item one or more test cases must be determined. A test case describes a specific situation to check the behaviour and output of the test item for a possible input. Since checking all possible inputs is generally not feasible, test cases for a representative group of inputs are created. For example, if we are testing a function which accept values from -99999 to 99999, we could take a couple of negative and positive inputs outside the range, the boundary values and some negative and positive values within the range. The input 0 could be also interesting. If other specific values cause a special behaviour of the function, they must obviously be included in the set of inputs. This information must also be extracted from the specification.

It is advisable to keep the test cases abstract, i.e. the critical values define the test cases. If the function of our example had a different behaviour for negative and positive numbers, we could define the following input set:

1. Input < -99999
2. Input = -99999
3. -99999 < Input < 0
4. Input = 0
5. 0 < Input < 99999
6. Input = 99999
7. Input > 99999

We have defined the relevant intervals, but we should not yet think about which representative values we will choose for our concrete tests.

An important question is when to stop with the determination of the test cases. How can we be sure that we have enough cases to cover the whole functionality of the test item? On the one hand, a good way to achieve a good functional coverage is to follow a systematic procedure. Tool support for this purpose is favourable and in the case of complex test items highly recommended. Who can keep all details of a complex piece of software in mind and think about all possible logical combinations and dependencies? On the other hand, coverage of the code can be dynamically measured with the help of test tools. In this way the scope of test cases can be amplified until the desired code coverage has been achieved. It is important to consider and combine both strategies because the code coverage alone does not assure the functional coverage and vice versa.

2.4 Generating the test scripts

For each logical test case one or more specific data combinations must be generated. These concrete instances of the test cases define specific values for the inputs and expect specific values for the outputs. In the case of unit and integration test they can be implemented in the form of test scripts able to be compiled and executed. The code under test, of course, must be included. If dynamic measurement of code coverage is required, the code under test must be instrumented. Since the instrumentation changes the code, it is advisable to also perform a black-box test with the same test cases in the original code. There are several test tools supporting both black-box and white-box testing.

The structure of the test scripts is quite regular:

- *Environment set up:*
  Necessary global and background elements are created and initialised.
- *For each test case:*
  - Initialisation of input data for the test case instance
  - Execute element(s) under test
  - Check output data and report results
- *Clean environment:*
  Free memory, clean database, etc.

This regular structure allows a certain degree of automation of the script generation. For this purpose it is important to minimise the user intervention in the input of test data. This is especially difficult in the case of system or GUI tests, where the user usually plays an important role, however it is not impossible. Capture-replay tools, for example, can help to increase automation.

2.5 Building the test executable

The code under test (instrumented in the case of white-box testing) and the test scripts are compiled and linked in a test executable, which should be able to run in the target system. Usually the output of the test executable is a test report containing the results of the executed test cases and the measured coverage.

2.6 Up-loading and executing the test

It is important that the test executable runs in the target system. This is highly recommended for safety critical systems and convenient in any case. The reason is that the behaviour of the code depends on the hardware platform. Tests which run successfully on the host system could fail on the target system. Sometimes the resources of the target system are insufficient to support the instrumented version of the test executable. In this case the white-box test can be performed on the host system and the black-box test on the target.

2.7 Evaluating the test results

The test results are evaluated in order to decide whether the test was successful or not. This depends on the direct results of the checks, which returns normally a passed/failed statement, and the achieved coverage.

If a check has failed, the first thing to do is to check the test script. If there is no error in the test script, then a deviation or error has been found in the software.

If the required coverage has not been achieved, the error is analysed in order to determine whether new test cases must be added or dead code has been found.

The errors are treated according to the defined process, which is individual depending on the project or company.

3 Testing tools

Selecting the right tools for the right tasks is as important as it is difficult. It is not possible to evaluate all existing tools to decide which one is the most appropriate for our needs. However, it is possible to define *a priori* which qualities and features we are looking for. This can considerably reduce the scope of candidates and make the search easier. The tools presented here were selected following this strategy.

It follows an overview of the selected tools.

- SQS-TEST®
- Input-oriented Test Case Specification: supports the methodical specification of input-based test cases.
- Test Data Definition and Management: supports the generation and management of specific test data for the specified test cases.
- Test Process Specification and Management: supports the generation of test procedures and test automation.
- Distributed Test Environment: allows the remote execution of tasks.
- CANTATA®: Supports black-box and white-box unit and integration testing.

3.1 SQS-TEST® / Input-oriented Test Case Specification

This component of the test suite SQS-TEST® (see also www.sqs.de) allows the methodical specification and management of input-based test cases. The task is organised in well defined steps which can be summarised as follows:

- Create a new project or open an existing one: A project is the highest item in the organisation of the tool.

- Create and/or import all necessary data structures: Each project has a pool where input and output data structures can be created or imported and maintained.
- Create a new test item: For each test project one or more test items must be created.
- Assign the related data structures from the pool to the test item.
- Define all relevant equivalence classes for the elements of the data structures. The tool allows a formal definition of the equivalence classes which is very useful for the automatic definition of test data (see next section).
- Define all known effects and, if possible, assign effects to the single equivalence classes.
- Identify and define dependencies between elements: Some effects are produced by the combination of elements or equivalence classes. The tool will automatically generate all possible combinations for the equivalence classes of the dependencies.
- Analyse each combination, summarise combinations which cause the same effects and assign effects to the combinations.
- Let the tool generate positive and negative test cases. The tool will show equivalence classes or combinations which are not yet included in at least one test case. The test cases can be completed manually to achieve completeness.

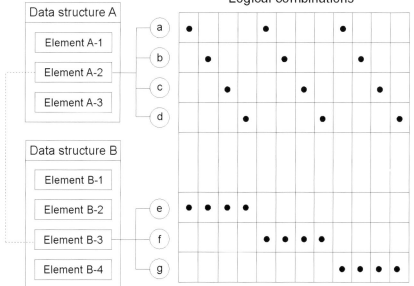

Figure 2: Test Case Determination

Figure 2 shows how the combinations for a dependency are created.

A very interesting feature is the automatic generation of a document with the detailed description of each test case. Moreover data export to standard tools, as for example MS-Excel®, is also possible.

An interesting indirect feature which we have determined in different projects when applying the methodical specification of the test cases is the detection of any defect or weakness in the specification. If some information is missing or contradictory, you will find it out.

3.2 SQS-TEST® / Test Data Definition and Management

The test cases are intentionally kept on an abstract level, without defining specific values for the elements. When we have specified all test cases as described in the previous section, one or more instances with specific data must be created for each one.

This component of the test suite supports the definition and management of test data. An interface to the test cases specification is available and allows the automatic definition of test data for elements which were formally described. For other elements the definition of test data must be manually assisted.

The test data is organised in combinations which can be reused when needed.

3.3 SQS-TEST® / Test Process Specification and Management

Once we have specified the test cases and the test data, we have to create scripts or procedures to execute the tests. Test cases define *what* we want to test and test procedures *how* to translate the tests into action.

This component of the test suite is a programmable environment based on Unix programming which allows the creation, control and automation of test procedures. An interface to the component described in the previous section (test data) is of course available. This allows among other things the automatic generation of test scripts.

3.4 SQS-TEST® / Distributed Test Environment

This component allows the remote execution of programs within the environment or network, and therefore is the heart of remote testing.

The Distributed Test Environment tool considerably increases the flexibility of the environment. For example the compilation of a piece of code on a specific machine could be started and monitored from any workstation.

Combining the Test Process Specification and Management tool with the Distributed Test Environment tool gives us everything we need to achieve a high degree of automation in our test process.

3.5 CANTATA®

This testing tool supports unit and integration testing. Cantata's main features are (see also www.iplbath.com):

- Automatic instrumentation of the code for testing purposes.
- Black-box as well as white-box testing.
- Generation of templates for the test scripts.
- Aid to program test cases (libraries, macros).
- Measurement of different levels of code coverage.
- Automatic generation of test reports.

The SQS-TEST® suite does not overlap with CANTATA®. The first tool supports the *determination* of the test cases and the *definition* of test data and test procedures. The second tool supports in the *programming* of the test cases and *measurement* of the code coverage. Beyond it we can integrate the instrumentation and script generation procedures in SQS-TEST® and in this way avoid a big part of the manual operation of CANTATA®.

The achievement of a high functional coverage based on the specification assures a good code coverage, as long as the quality of the specification is high enough. Our experience has shown that following a methodical specification of the test cases it is possible to achieve at least 80% decision coverage in the code. In the case that a higher degree of code coverage is required, we add new test cases with the help of CANTATA®.

4 The Test Environment

4.1 Elements of the Test Environment

We can distinguish four main physical elements playing an essential role in the test environment:

4.1.1 Host System

The host system is the interface to the target system, which is the system under test. Usually we do not have direct access to the target system, but we perform all operations through the host system. It is convenient for the automation that both host and target systems are physically connected, for example by means of a serial link. Important operations are for example uploading and downloading of software and data. The test ex-

ecutable must be uploaded and after the test has run the test results must be downloaded. Other functions include setting up, resetting, debugging, etc.

4.1.2 Target System

This is the system under test. Some requisites are necessary to achieve test automation.
The test executable should be able to run on this system. If enough resources are available we will be able to upload and run both the instrumented and the original version
of the test executable. The target system should also be able to return data to the host
system in order to download the test results.

It can be necessary to perform some modifications to the system for testing purposes,
for example to avoid manual operations which could hinder automation.

4.1.3 Server

One or more servers provide the typical server functionality, including among other
things floating license management, database functionality (archive), process management, distributed environment management, etc.

The SQS-TEST® suite has a client-server architecture and both SQS-TEST® and
CANTATA® allows floating license management.

The whole test data, documents, etc. are stored and managed in and by the server in a
well organised manner. In this way it is possible to keep control on the test projects and
easily back up and restore all data if necessary.

4.1.4 Workstation

The intention of the distributed test environment is to allow control of the whole environment from each work station. In this way each member of the test team can perform all test activities and access all data without leaving his or her workplace. Test
cases specification, test data definition, script generation, test process execution and
test result evaluation are possible from each workstation.

Moreover the environment is quite flexible since workplaces are interchangeable.
Further if a new tester joins the team, the only thing to do when preparing a workplace
is to install the client software in a new workstation.

4.2 Topology of the environment

How can we connect the four elements explained to create an environment adequate
for our purpose? This depends of course on the purpose. There are numerous possible
topologies and we should choose in each case the cheapest one which will work, since it
can easily be extended as the need arises. Each system is unique and needs a specific
solution.

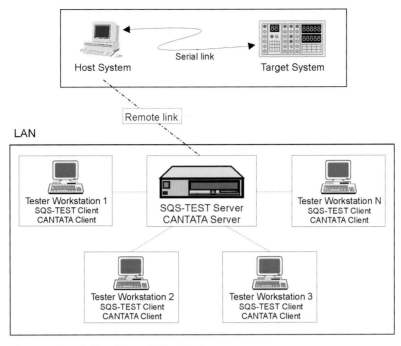

Figure 3: Sample Topology of a Test Environment

Figure 3 shows the topology we used for our test environment. The squares represent physically separated rooms or places. On the one side we can see the LAN with the server and the workstations, where the test teams work. On the other side we observe the host and target systems. The protocol we used to connect the host system to our LAN was TCP/IP. The target system had to be adapted for testability. As an example, the reset function of the target system could only be performed manually. This hindered of course the automation. Therefore we had to build a hardware device in order to perform a reset of the system from the host.

The connection between host and target system was a serial link. The resources were enough to allow white-box testing on the target system. The test results were sent back to the host system through the serial link.

Important characteristics of the environment and its topology are:

- *Extendibility:* it should be possible to extend the environment easily if necessary. The described environment allows this since the whole process can be managed via the client software from each workstation.

- *Availability:* bottle necks must be avoided. In the case of the tools, this can be achieved increasing the number of floating licenses. Since this can mean a considerable investment, the optimal number of licenses must be determined. To avoid a bottle neck at the target system, the accesses must be as short as possible. The whole execution process of a test session should not take more than a few minutes, including up-load of the test executable and down-load of the test results.

- *Performance:* the whole concept will not work on a slow system. The work and money invested in the initial phase cannot be recoup later if the testers have to wait for the system after each minor operation. Moreover this has fatal effects on the morale of the team. It would not be a good idea to try to save money by acquiring low quality equipment.
- *Stability:* obviously the crashes within the environment must be rare. The effects of an unstable system are known to all of us. Again, beware of low quality equipment and software.

5 Summary

We will now reconsider the problems and aims listed in the introduction and the solutions proposed:

- *Measurement and achievement of the desired coverage of the requirements:*
  The methodical specification of test cases combined with the measurement of code coverage assure a good functional and technical coverage.
- *Homogeneity:*
  The well defined process with tool support achieves homogeneity without hindering the creativity of the testers.
- *Bottle necks due to insufficient resources:*
  The distributed environment allows each tester to access the whole resources of the system from each workstation. Parallel work is possible due to the client-server nature of the tools. Performance and stability allow efficient work.
- *Automation:*
  Test procedures can be automated in a high degree and in many cases totally. Regression test is not a problem since all tests can be run automatically at any time.
- *Archive organisation:*
  All documents, test data and test results are stored and managed by the tools, so that control over them can be kept easily.
- *Remote testing:*
  The distributed test environment allows testing from the distance, which can be another room in the same building as well as another company in a different city.

The point of this is to find the right combination of tools and equipment and the right topology and set up an ideal environment for each company or project. Decisive factors are the scope, the focus and the criticality of the project, the complexity of the system and the required coverage.

Last but not least, I would like to point out that the environment has to be accompanied by a well defined test process containing the concepts, aims and defining the procedures to follow for the different test steps.

6 References

Balzert 1998 H. Balzert (1998) Lehrbuch der Software-Technik, Software Management, Software Qualitätsicherung, Unternehmensmodellierung, Spektrum Akademischer Verlag

prEN 50128 – 1998 European Standard, CENELEC, prEN 50128 (July 1998), Railway applications – Software for railway control and protection systems

Watson and McCabe 1996 Watson and McCabe (1996) Structured Testing: A Testing Methodology using Cyclomatic Complexity, NIST Special Publication 500–2535

Myers 1979 G. J. Myers (1979) The Art of Software-Testing, New York, 1979

Part III

Tools

Testing Tools, Trends and Perspectives

MIRIAM BROMNICK
Ovum Ltd (United Kingdom)

Abstract: Testing is the defence against business damage resulting from software errors. This chapter looks at the challenges of testing e-commerce applications. In this dynamic environment what is needed to find and fix errors, at the point where they are cheapest to fix? What are the different testing needs and how is the balance between non-functional testing and functional testing different? The chapter explores why, for e-commerce, the cost/benefit balance between automated testing and manual testing is shifted towards automated testing.

The current support for automated testing of e-commerce applications is examined and a summary of the testing tools market is given, with predictions of how the automated testing tool are likely to develop. Methods for selecting testing tools are outlined. The chapter concludes with guidance for testing managers and practitioners.

Keywords: E-commerce application testing, Automated testing tools, Testing terminology, Non-functional testing, Developments in automated testing tools, Selecting automated testing tools

1   Trends: e-commerce applications and testing

Testing is the defence against business damage resulting from software errors. Testing is an opportunity to see if an application meets the needs of the customer. Accurate and reliable services are required, the customer does not care what is going on below the surface of an application. Testing can prevent badly performing web sites, lost business, bad publicity and even legal action resulting from software failure. Within e-commerce the risks of software failure increase and so the need to test increases. Lack of testing becomes immediately visible, however by tradition software testing has been:

- badly understood
- badly done
- demoted to something done at the end of development
- often delegated to end users
- denied investment in automated tools.

1.1 Trends: the challenges of e-commerce

The objective of testing e-commerce applications is to find and fix errors in the software at the point where they are cheapest to fix. Therefore it is important to understand:

- the challenges to testing in building e-commerce applications
- the technology required for the testing of e-commerce applications
- how far the current testing tools go towards supporting e-commerce
- the future of the tools
- how to approach your testing of e-commerce applications.

For e-commerce applications the cost/benefit balance between automated testing and manual testing is shifted greatly towards automated testing. This is due to the amount of repeated testing that is needed. In addition the complexity of e-commerce application testing eliminates the possibility of building bespoke testing tools for a particular project or organisation.

1.2 Trends: developments in 'Internet time'

E-commerce applications are usually developed with demanding deadlines. They require extensive testing, and testing is a large scale activity with many parts. Therefore good management of the testing process is essential. Due to the complexity of e-commerce applications it is unlikely that an e-commerce project will have the resources to conduct all conceivable tests. The order of testing the components of an e-commerce application will also require careful planning and management. Consequently the activity needs to be well planned to get maximum assurance from the tests that are carried out.

1.3 Trends: changing definitions

Software testing is about demonstrating that a piece of software is fit for its intended purpose and can be split into two main categories; functional testing and non-functional testing.

Functional testing – Does it work?

Functional testing will prove that an application works and that it conforms to laid down criteria. Those criteria may be laid down by:

- the organisation developing the software
- an external organisation such as a regulatory body
- a customer of the organisation that is using the software
- a trading partner.

Functional testing of a traditional application is used to prove that an applications delivers the correct results, using enough inputs to give an adequate level of confidence that it will work correctly for all sets of inputs. However within e-commerce applications functional testing needs to go further. It needs to prove that an application with deliver the correct results, using adequate input, for all types of data that may be *accessed*, *exchanged* or *processed* within the application.

Some functional testing will be required in isolation, before all components within the application are ready to be integrated. Under some circumstances testers will need to simulate components, even when the real versions are available, in order to get more control and repeatability over the tests.

In addition functional testing must take account of the complexity of the multiple technologies that are integrated in e-commerce (for example an e-commerce application may use data from the back offices of an organisation, using a relational database or an ERP package). Within this environment the software will need to maintain applications states and sessions for each client. These will need to be tested to make sure these are maintained correctly, both for successful and failed transactions.

Functional testing will need to prove that the application works for each client type and that personalisation functions work correctly. In addition e-commerce applications are likely to use advanced presentation techniques, such as dynamic contents (for example video clips) and these require a special approach to testing.

Non-functional testing

Non-functional testing is used to check that an application will work in the operational environment. Non-functional testing requires an environment that simulates, or is as near as possible to the final infrastructure. For e-commerce applications the challenges increase, as the number of potential hits to a web site at any one time is complex to predict.

Non-functional testing includes:

- load testing
- performance testing
- usability testing
- reliability testing
- security testing.

Load testing

For e-commerce applications it is necessary to test scalability with functionality. It is necessary to ascertain that the application behaves correctly under loads when 'server busy' responses are received. Load tests require the simulation of users of the application under test. Some of these will be simulated at the presentation level, some at the interface between the client processors and application servers, and some at the interface between servers.

Performance testing

This is required to assure that an e-commerce application performs adequately, having the capability to handle any foreseeable workload and delivering its results within an acceptable time, whilst using an acceptable level of resources. Performance testing provides input to capacity planning.

Performance testing is an aspect of operational management. Contractual service relationships between trading partners and operational management are an important factor of e-commerce. Therefore performance testing becomes vital as it provides baseline facts for creating of contractual service agreements.

Usability testing

This is necessary to prove that the application is usable in its intended role, considering human/ergonomic and environmental factors. Usability testing will include checking the content of web pages and that they are personalised in an acceptable way.

Reliability testing

This is to check that the application is rugged and reliable, and can handle the failure of any of the components involved in providing the application.

Security testing

This is necessary to check that the application's data is secure. It involves checking that the user's identification is authenticated, that the user is authorised to do what they are doing, and that all messages retain their integrity.

1.4   A development cycle with testing

Testing needs to be built into the development cycle of any piece of software within an e-commerce application. The requirements of the testing activity need to be determined, because testing without an objective wastes time and resources. The requirement has to be translated into a set of specific objectives, listing exactly what you need to see from the test results. These will be refined from general, high-level objectives into test cases. Each test case needs to have a scenario that describes what will be put into it, and what the result should be. These scenarios should be re-used from the analysis and design processes. All this requires the support of planning, managing and monitoring in the same way as any other development activity.

1.5 Regression testing – what is it?

E-commerce applications are likely to experience frequent changes, for example because of:

- changes to upgrade the application (the presentation layer is likely to experience frequent change)
- changes to the environment (for example changes to a browser, or a URL moving)
- introduction of a new client type
- changes to content
- rework to correct previous errors
- moving from one 'build' of the applications to the next 'build', for example a new build may represent a level of development that is necessary to maintain the applications' integrity with a partners application. Not all the changes are visible to the customer
- new versions of the infrastructure.

After each change it is necessary to check that the enhancement has been successful. Additional testing should be performed to check that unintended changes (which are likely to be errors) have not been introduced. This kind of testing is known as 'regression testing'.

Regression testing is usually associated with functional testing, but the concept is valid with other testing objectives (for example, to check that the latest round of 'enhancements' have not impaired performance).

1.6 Trends: testing jargon

The testing industry applies various labels to levels of testing, for example:

- unit testing
- module testing
- link testing
- system testing
- user testing
- acceptance testing.

These labels have been used to describe the purpose of the test at the time it was done, reflecting the relative position of the person carrying out the test in the overall hierarchy, rather than the test itself. The build of e-commerce applications is unlikely to follow a traditional, 'waterfall', systems development lifecycle. Cycles of releases are likely to be weeks and days, rather than years and months. Therefore these testing labels no longer carry much relevance.

2   Testing Tools: current support for testing e-commerce applications

2.1   Market summary

Over the last 3 to 4 years there has been amalgamations and mergers within the test tools vendors. All the major players have revised their products to address the needs of testing web applications (Mercury Interactive, Rational Software and Compuware), and particularly load and performance testing. These mainstream tools all saw a rapid growth with client-server technology and their vendors have used this as a platform to develop capture playback tools for the web. Some of the major toolsets now include facilities specifically designed for the web.

A second division of web specific testing tools now complete with the major players. Segue, RSW, RadView and Cyrano have all developed tools for functional and load testing of e-commerce applications.

A number of smaller, specialist vendors still exist. Some of these are addressing tools for web testing, however other remain in niche markets, for example addressing the needs of safety critical and telecommunications application development.

A recent development in the testing tools market is where vendors are 'renting' test tools. Mercury Interactive (and some smaller vendors) are now providing a service where they will construct tests for you and run those tests across the web for you on their servers. Therefore you do not need to have the expertise to develop the tests or the resources available to run those tests. These hosted testing services provide an entry point to automated testing for those without the resources to execute automated testing. The attraction is speed and availability, rather than cost savings.

2.2   What do the tools currently support?

Functional testing

The current generation of automated test tool include adapted GUI-based tools for use on web browsers. In addition some tools have been developed specifically to emulate web clients. These web testing tools simulate load on a variety of servers, and can recognise the inter-relationships between load testing and functional testing.

The available tools will support regression test, but they rely on good design to ensure that the tests are designed in a way to require minimal updates.

The next-generation of e-commerce applications, with the possibility of automated testing of back office functionality across enterprises, offers a new challenge to testing tools vendors. The mainstream testing tool vendors are still developing tools to meet the current generation of e-commerce applications.

Direct testing of processing on servers is poor in the current generation of web test tools. Their focus is on the browser, with most tools supporting functions such as web integrity of web pages. The web application test tools are limited to specific back office servers and in the types of middleware that they support. It is however possible to use results from some of the current web testing tools to deduce what logic the server has executed.

Security is another area where only limited support is offered from the mainstream testing tools. Specialist tools in this area have focussed on frontier checks and firewalls. Only one of the main players, Cyrano, has integrated some support for testing security of e-commerce applications. Otherwise automated security testing can only currently be achieved by specialist security testing tools.

Scalability and load testing with functionality

Load testing is essential for e-commerce applications. However load testing of the type used for traditional architectures is not adequate for e-commerce applications. These applications rely on web servers to handle their requests. When an application uses the output from a web server it is essential to check that the application responds to any denial of service in a constructive way. This can only be achieved either by including a background load element within the functional testing phase, or by specifically simulating all possible component failures.

A limited amount of functional testing needs to be included in every load test to determine that transactions are being completed. The distinction between load testing and functional testing is not clearly defined for next generation e-commerce applications. Automating testing allows you to repeat your functional tests under different loads.

Some testing tools can now simulate the use of a range of IP addresses in a test session, a step towards making performance tests realistic but still a long way short of a simulation of the network.

Performance testing

Performance testing requires testing tools for full remote simulation of the network. Merely stress testing a web server or an application server will not in itself render useful information. Preliminary work needs to be done to identify key factors in the performance of the specific application so that they are simulated during the test.

Regression testing

Regression testing is the dominant form of testing within e-commerce and it requires automation as:

- automation gives the opportunity to perform large-scale regression testing economically, often running it overnight without human attendance
- regression testing is only cost effective if automated.

For functional testing the overhead incurred in recording and maintaining a script for automated tests will not be justified unless the script is to be run several times. The break-even point is likely to be approximately four runs of the script. Therefore it is economical to build functional tests with regression testing in mind and to use automated test tools to build tests that:

- can be repeated (different clients, different loads etc)
- are held in a repository
- are easy to use
- are easy to update and maintain.

Test management

Automated management of the testing process has limited support and has in the past not been an area of attention for the vendors, however this is changing. Some specialist tools can be used to interact with the mainstream testing tools to support test management. What automation is provided does not address the specific needs of managing cross enterprise testing, for example no automated workflow management is included in the current tool sets.

3   Testing tools: selection of automated testing tools

3.1   Costs and time

Automated testing tools can be expensive; both in the initial investment and in the time needed to deploy those tools, including training and other human costs. Therefore it is important that the right testing tools are selected.

3.2 Selection criteria

The requirements for testing tools can be grouped into a number of different areas, including:

- test planning and management
- requirements analysis and test case generation
- inspections and reviews
- code quality analysis
- functional testing
- load and performance testing
- web application testing.

For each of these groups of criteria you should first decide what your needs are and then work out the capabilities of the tools.

In addition you will need to be confident about the vendors background as well as considering the usability of the tool.

You are unlikely to get independent answers to all these questions from the testing tools vendors themselves and may need to consider other sources of independent information. An example the dimensions that Ovum's uses to evaluate testing tools is illustrated in figure 1. This diagram shows the scores of a popular web testing toolset.

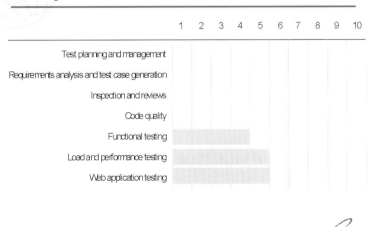

Figure 1: The dimensions Ovum uses for evaluating automated test tools

4 Perspectives: requirements for testing e-commerce applications

4.1 Predictions for the future

The changes we see on the horizon include:

- greater automated support for web application testing
- improved support of test management and planning activities
- automated integration of testing and quality assurance with design
- automation of inspections and reviews
- facilities to test components in isolation
- automated security testing within the mainstream testing tools.

Improved automated support for web application testing

The web application testing tools are likely to continue to be developed to support a wider range of architectures and protocols. For example some of the mainstream tool-sets have had recent releases to support load testing of wireless web applications.

In addition the toolsets are being upgraded to automate complex testing. Technically, web pages are complex entities and increased complexity increases the risk of failures. Next-generation e-commerce applications are likely to use many complex functions. Several mark-up languages are used to define the content of web pages. A single page can contain numerous different types of objects: text, links to other pages, interactive dialogs, images, audio or video clips and program components such as Java applets and ActiveX components. These exemplify three very different behaviours:

- fixed objects which do not change while they are being displayed
- interactive objects which send new output to the user interface in discrete blocks in response to user input or messages from the web server
- dynamic objects which continuously change their output without requiring any external stimulus.

Testing of dynamic content requires a new approach. Conventional testing, whether automated or manual, is based on the comparison of specific outputs. It is not useful to regard a dynamic output (visual, audio, or otherwise) as a sequence of millions of static outputs even if this is a correct physical interpretation. A more practical solution is to split the testing into a two-phase process:

- validate that a particular combination of programs, scripts and data can generate an acceptable output
- test that the application delivers this combination of programs, scripts and data to the client terminal.

The appearance of a web page is determined by the browser and modified by user options set on the particular browser. The behaviour of a browser can be modified using features such as cookies. It is therefore necessary to test the content at a logical level rather than at the level of comparing screen displays, and it may be useful to test the operation of an application on a range of browsers. To achieve this, tests need to be both automated and portable.

Support of Testing Management

Over the last 2 to 3 years the need for tools to support test management has been recognised by the mainstream testing tool vendors. Some test management functions are included in most of the major tool sets. However for large and complex application these facilities do not meet the need for automated management of all testing and quality assurance activities.

In addition testing of e-commerce applications involves inter-dependant activities with tasks that may be conducted by staff in different enterprises. This increases the need for good planning and management. Automation is required to support distributed test management and test planning. Tools are needed to support creating and monitoring the critical path through the testing activities. This is important to you if you are responsible for overall delivery to the market and where you own the primary customer relationship.

In circumstances with demanding deadlines it is vital that time spent on testing is directed towards the important tasks and not squandered (for example by duplicate testing or testing interesting, but unimportant, parts of the application). Testing of e-commerce applications requires intensive project planning and control, with the ability to process shared information about the status of distributed activities.

Test management is still mainly conducted in an unsophisticated way and therefore it is unlikely that the vendors will see the improvement of these facilities as a high priority. We expect incremental improvements in this area. It is likely to be 3 to 4 years before the tools reach the necessary level of sophistication for fully automated test management support.

Testing integrated with design

Tools are required to automatically build test cases that can test the functionality of distributed applications. These test cases must allow for a variety of clients, and the possibility of data being accessed, exchanged and processed from any location over the web.

In addition tools are required that can test parts of the application when other parts are not present. Any test that does not involve the entire application system will require a harness in which the components under test can function. The harness drives the components under test and simulates their interaction. Developers who needed to test parts of code in isolation have used this technique for along time. These principles now apply for isolating whole components of applications, and tools are required on a larger scale to simulate both clients and servers.

Tools should also facilitate the automated checking of the integration points in an application. Once the operation at these boundary points has been proven it is easier to diagnose software errors in the presentation or the process layers.

Inspections and reviews

Inspections and reviews are much neglected processes. They are techniques that can bring benefits early on in the lifecycle. Possibly one of the reasons they are neglected is due to the overheads in organising them. Therefore we look to see some tools that will automate the organisation and reduce the bureaucracy in setting up and completing reviews. We expect tools that will support distributed reviews across the web.

In addition we expect automatic static analysis of code to be included in the mainstream tools. That facility would gives you the ability to automate your desk checking and give you the ability to predict troublesome areas of applications.

Testing components in isolation

Tools to test beyond the presentation level will be difficult and expensive to develop. Although there is a need for automated support of sever side testing, both where one server is used and for applications integrating many servers, we expect that it will be some time before tools are fully developed in this area.

These tools would be harder to use than capture playback tools and so are likely to be less popular.

This is an area that will continue to evolve from the current e-commerce testing tools. Tools will develop to meet the needs of isolating components for testing. This isolation is likely to enable presentation and sever side testing to take place both individually, and then allow them to be integrated together. Tools will also emerge to check the integration of components in isolation from testing their functionality. The support of testing tools for different types of middleware is likely to grow and follow the products that become the dominant infrastructure products.

Tools that could verify the correct operation of application components would:

- simplify the task of test design as test cases could consider each logical unit separately and not be concerned with testing the interface points
- Reduce the overall number of tests as you would not need to test each combination of logical path through the application.

Security

We envisage that the main testing tool vendors will be forging partnerships with security tools vendors. This will be a fast moving area, driven by market awareness of security risks. Some security testing tools will be included in the main testing tool suites. This is likely to include facilities to look for vulnerabilities, by simulating certain categories of attack, such as attacks by overwhelming the site with a large numbers of hits.

4.2 What can test managers and practitioners do now

Develop a test strategy

To be efficient testing needs to be directed to meet the critical risks of e-commerce application. Test strategy needs to be developed to address the risks of specific applications. Then the testing process needs to be managed to adhere to that strategy. Managing the testing process provides a key to successful e-commerce applications.

Automated testing

Currently available testing tools will help you complete tasks quickly and efficiently, specifically in testing the presentation layer, regression testing and load and performance testing. Testing tools come in different shapes and sizes. You may decide to make a strategic decision to invest in tools to support your entire build processes. Or you may decide to make a tactical investment in a value for money test tool to assist you meet your immediate deadlines.

Investing in automated testing tools provides some insurance against the risks of e-commerce, however just selecting a testing tool is not the solution to the problem. None of these tools help you to determine what testing activities you need, and few give any significant help selecting what you should test. It is left to you to determine which risks you need to focus your testing on and whether the test tool is taking you where you want to go in building your e-commerce application.

Server side testing

You need to make sure that you plan enough time for testing of the business logic layer. It is likely that this will be mainly a manual activity.

Follow best practice

There is no alternative to automated testing for building successful e-commerce applications. However use of testing tools cannot build quality into your design and development. You need to ensure that testing is considered integral to the build of any component of your e-commerce application. The quality of your management of the build processes will determine the success or failure of your application.

Author's Index

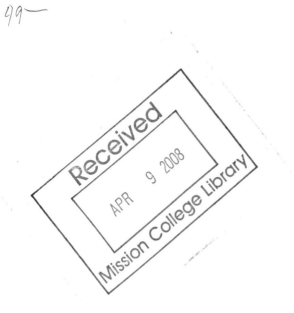
Production: Druckhaus Beltz, Hemsbach